01 14

BOB DYLAN

ALSO BY RON ROSENBAUM

In Defense of Love

Manhattan Passions

Travels with Dr. Death

Explaining Hitler

The Secret Parts of Fortune

The Shakespeare Wars

How the End Begins

A Sort of Biography

BOB THINGS DYLAN HAVE CHANGED

RON ROSENBAUM

MELVILLE HOUSE
BROOKLYN • LONDON

BOB DYLAN : THINGS HAVE CHANGED

First published in 2025 by Melville House
Copyright © 2025 by Ron Rosenbaum
All rights reserved
First Melville House Printing: August 2025

Distributed by Penguin Random House LLC,
1745 Broadway, New York, NY 10019 USA. www.penguinrandomhouse.com
Portions of Chapter 5 were originally published, in different form, in the *New York Observer.*

Melville House Publishing
46 John Street
Brooklyn, NY 11201
and
Melville House UK
Suite 2000
16/18 Woodford Road
London E7 0HA

mhpbooks.com
@melvillehouse

ISBN: 978-1-68589-225-8
ISBN: 978-1-68589-226-5 (eBook)

Library of Congress Control Number: 2025939402

Designed by Beste M. Doğan

Printed in the United States of America
1 3 5 7 9 10 8 6 4 2

A catalog record for this book is available from the Library of Congress

The authorized representative in the EU for product safety and compliance is Easy Access
System Europe, Mustamäe tee 50, 10621 Tallinn, Estonia. gpsr.requests@easproject.com

For Ms. X, once again, for her
insight, enthusiasm, encouragement. And love.
"We'll never be apart"

God said to Abraham, "Kill me a son"
Abe says, "Man, You must be puttin' me on"…
—BOB DYLAN, "HIGHWAY 61"

CONTENTS

PREFACE

I feel I've been writing this book all my life. In a sense I feel Dylan's been writing my life—unknowingly—all his.

Meanwhile, I expect many readers will come to this book only after or because of seeing the film *A Complete Unknown*, and I appreciate your continued interest in this great American artist and Nobel laureate songwriter. I welcome as well those with a lifetime familiarity with Bob who I believe will still find some important new ways to think about him and appreciate his work. Some of these may be controversial, but has he ever been noncontroversial?

You could think of this book as a kind of follow-up, a how "things have changed" for a still incompletely known Bob Dylan.

But don't expect a chronology of biographical facts. There are books by Michael Gray and Clinton Heylin, among others, who have done that worthy task with super-max diligence.

No, I wanted to do a book that focuses on him as a songwriter, and focuses closely on some aspects of his songwriting themes and memes that are likely to be little known yet highly relevant. Such as, for instance, the exploration of Dylan's theodicy—a word not synonymous with *theology*, but a subdiscipline that focuses on evil, on the attempt to reconcile the persistence, often prevalence, of "radical evil" (Hannah Arendt's initial term before she shifted to "banality") with a supposedly benevolent God.

A very serious side of Dylan, not his only preoccupation but an important one, implicitly or subtly evoked in more lyrics than you might think, and often key to understanding them more fully.

One of my chapter titles sums it up: "Dylan's Argument with God."

It may offend some, but I've long been an investigative type of writer who, when he discovers something unexamined or poorly examined, something not really given the attention it deserves, feels it would be in bad faith to conceal it for fear of controversy. Theodicy is something I've been studying with great Jewish and Christian theologians and philosophers ever since researching my book *Explaining Hitler*, a book that assesses the different reactions and rationales for that radical evil. If you doubt my belief that it was on Dylan's mind, consider a long-overlooked quote in Dylan's long-overlooked early attempt at a novel he called *Tarantula*. The Dylan quote in that book that struck me like a bolt from the blue was this: "Hitler didn't change history / Hitler WAS history." In other words, we live in a creation so pervaded by evil that its entire history is a reflection of Hitler more than a loving God.

All this may have had major consequences in his life. His naked *anger* at the Old Testament God for not lifting a finger to save "His" people from the death camps. A failure even, especially, proudly pious Jews fail to offer a convincing defense of—His inexplicable and to some of us unforgivable absence during the Holocaust, or certainly a failure to intervene with his alleged superpowers.

He was certainly aware of and has intervened (popular belief has it) in deciding Super Bowls. That anger at the Old Testament deity, I believe, is one of the sources of *Dylan's* vulnerability to a born-again New Testament sect that hijacked his soul for several years.

I say this as someone who spent a week talking with Dylan, often about God and evil, just a few months before this bar mitzvah boy's shocking conversion into a ranting Christian preacher became known. Yes, there were personal troubles and professional pressures. We talked on Warner Bros. Burbank back lot, where Dylan was attempting to cut and loop the many thousands of feet of film footage into the film he called *Renaldo and Clara*.

It was in part a *Children of Paradise*–like memoir/tribute to the world and the people of the *Complete Unknown* era that launched him into fame and glory, a film interspersed with sizzling, electrifying rock from the Rolling Thunder concert tour and a complex and confusing allegorical plotline that starred Bob, his soon-to-be-divorced "mystical wife," Sara, and his longtime, part-time love, Joan Baez. What could go wrong? Well, for one thing, he couldn't seem to cut it down further than four and a half hours, which eventually doomed it commercially. Warners hastily withdrew it from theaters after a few weeks, and Dylan, Inc. seemed to be doing everything to hide it ever after, although by now I believe it should be released at least for its curatorial value as a portrait of the artist as a tormented dreamer. And one mission I always had for this book was to arouse some enthusiasm to give *Renaldo* another life.

I'll mention one other discovery I've never seen dwelt upon before: a key aspect of Late Dylan songwriting, a metaphysical key I've found to unlock the often difficult-to-decipher Late Dylan lyrics. I began trying to understand why, when asked about his past performances, live or recorded, he seemed obsessed with the difference between *sincerity* and *authenticity*. And recurrently when asked about past performances or recordings, he insisted, "That wasn't me," "I'm not there," "It ain't me," and the like. Following that clue led me to what I believe is the skeleton key to understanding the often apparently unintelligible "discontinuity of selves" of the philosophers, physicists, and even, especially, litterateurs like the Argentine fabulist and metaphysical savant

Jorge Luis Borges. Call it a way of construing Late Dylan lyrics that opens the door to all of us getting more pleasure from them.

Ironically, at its heart is a metaphysical thought experiment about a single frame in a filmstrip. The way an actor in a single cell in a strip of film metaphorically can't know anything about the cell before them or the cell to come. They're part of a discontinuous series of selves only given animation and a kind of life when the projector is turned on. I won't try to explain the consequences of this here, but I connect it to the seemingly disconnected utterances of many Late Dylan songs in chapters to come.

Dylan a metaphysician? See for yourself.

There is much more that I'd have to write a book to contain. Oh look, I did. I've written a six-hundred-page book on Shakespeare (*The Shakespeare Wars: Clashing Scholars, Public Fiascos, Palace Coups*, Random House, 2006) that doesn't scratch the surface, though I think you're unlikely to find a better brief study of the variations in the early texts of his plays. And yes, Dylan is not Shakespeare, I feel the need to emphasize, he's a songwriter who sometimes can suggest Shakespearean depths, if not heights.

But I think I owe newcomers as well as old hands a brief introduction to your author.

My Dylan experience began with that Joan Baez LP of Dylan covers and was stirred by his appearance and performance at Martin Luther King Jr.'s DC March. I had my share of crazy *Highway 61*–type Dylan road trips, ended up teaching his lyrics as poetry in a seminar as part of my Yale Graduate School fellowship, soon fled academia and became default Dylan correspondent at *The Village Voice*, and I had my life changed by that 1965 Forest Hills concert where Dylan debuted "Desolation Row" and his electric guitar backup band for the first time since the Newport Folk Festival uproar. I covered the opening 1974 "return" concert in Chicago, and later wrote essays (which you can google) on his memoir, *Chronicles*, a book I loved and admired as writer and former Village resident. Including a long disquisition in praise of "Up to Me," the wonderful song dropped from the great

Blood on the Tracks album, with my speculative conclusion (you can judge for yourself).[1]

I guess I should mention my weeklong interview with Dylan is accorded the longest time he ever gave a journalist, a breed he often mocked ("You know something's happening, but you don't know what it is, do you, Mr. Jones?"). But I found him to be kind or at least tolerant as he chain-smoked his way through two or three hours a day answering my many questions nervously scrawled on yellow legal pads while I took occasional swallows from a pint of tequila I brought to steady my nerves. (These talks took place mostly in a tiny back-lot bungalow I thought of as a private barroom.)

Anyway, I've been working on this book for years, and though I could not presume to write something knowledgeable enough to be a full-bore biography, I thought I could give you a book focused on those songs and his songwriting—and the theodicy and metaphysics of the persona they reflected.

Thus, this.

And just as a kind of coded signal to the Dylanologists, Bobolators, Dylanists (my choice cognomen), I was the one who, in that epic interview, got Bob to describe the *sound* he'd been seeking, which he memorably described to me as "That thin, that wild mercury sound." What a wonderful phrase—"wild mercury"—soon stamped on bootlegs.

He found it, that sound, and eventually things changed. That's Dylan for you. Hard to pin down as a drop of mercury. Mercury, the fleet messenger god of Olympus; Shakespeare's fast-talking wit, Mercutio; Dylan, mercurial to the end.

May he stay forever young.

---

1 See "It's 30 Years Later! Bob Dylan's Tracks Gloriously Bloody," *The New York Observer*, July 12, 2004. Does the title derive from the title of the novel by Dylan friend and rival, Richard Fariña, who died in a motorcycle accident and whose first (and last) novel was called *Been Down So Long It Looks Like UP TO ME*? [capitalization mine]. Read David Hajdu's great book on the youth of Dylan and Fariña, *Positively 4th Street*.

BOB DYLAN THINGS HAVE CHANGED

CHAPTER 1 **BOTH SIDES NOW**

You don't have to be a Marxist to recognize that Marxist thought—and self-proclaimed Marxists—have had a profound impact on history.

Similarly, one doesn't have to be a Bob Dylan fan, one doesn't have to like Bob Dylan *at all*, one does not have to possess what I like to call the Dylan receptor—an inordinate predisposition to his work—to recognize that his work has become a remarkably influential and reverberant phenomenon in the history of American culture. I want this to be a book for all parties.

It is a landmark in the recent history of Jewish art, akin to the dark flowering of the Jewish American novel in the 1960s: Jewish art but—as the Swedish Academy recognized—with a wide multicultural reach.

One doesn't have to feel as Daniel Matt did. Matt is one of the foremost Jewish scholars of the twenty-first century; he is the dedicated translator of the *Zohar* from the medieval Aramaic and has published nine volumes so far of the fourteenth-century Kabbalist "book of illuminations."

3

I first discovered Matt's enthusiasm about Dylan when I was apprised of an exchange of letters with Gershom Scholem, his mentor and renowned scholar of the Kabbalah in the previous century. I was alerted to the letters by the editor of *The Jewish Review of Books*, Abraham Socher. As a (relative) youth, Matt had been on a Wanderjahr traveling in the Himalayas and had written Scholem in Jerusalem asking, among other things, if he had heard the works of Bob Dylan.

When I emailed Matt to ask him about the matter, I didn't expect him—now a professor at the University of California, Berkeley, while he pursues his *Zohar* project—to have recalled or retained his youthful enthusiasm for Dylan or to speak of it so eloquently. "I used to worship Dylan," he wrote back, and, though he no longer "worshipped" him, he did not disclaim his earlier enthusiasm. "I thought of him as Baba Di-lan, Aramaic for 'our gateway' to truth and wisdom. I always wanted Dylan to be very deeply Jewish whether or not he was," Matt wrote. "I felt that he saw things in their stark reality, that his prophetic vision penetrated to the core of everything and his poetic genius enabled him to share that with others."

Stunning. But this is precisely what makes Dylan different, exceptional, and strikes a chord in so many—non-Jews as well.

I suggest that this is perhaps an answer to the primal Passover question about Dylan: Why is this songwriter different from all other songwriters (if he is)—different enough to be awarded the Nobel Prize in Literature, for instance?

He is different, at least, for those who have the Dylan receptor. An element of what Matt felt is at the heart of those who have become Dylanists (a word I prefer to the irritating Dylanologist, with its scarcely concealed sneer embedded in it). So much so that it's almost genetic. Like mediums, or sensitives, as the Victorians called them, Dylanists sense something eerie, numinous, almost otherworldly, as if the voice actually comes from another realm.

And to some, it does come down to the voice. The sound of a particularly gifted cantor chanting soulfully, sonorously, underneath the lyrics, perhaps. We know that Dylan's father, Abraham, imported a Brooklyn rabbi halfway across the country to distant snowbound Hibbing, Minnesota, for a full year so that he might give young Bobby Zimmerman bar mitzvah lessons. I sometimes think that millennia of dark and celebratory tonal inflections distilled and imparted at a particularly vulnerable age when the voice changes may have bequeathed something to an unusually receptive soul such as Dylan's as much as early rock and roll and folk music.

Or was the special sound the distilled strangeness of the Holy Land in upper Minnesota's white-blanket apocalypse? In chapter two, I reprise Dylan telling me of the strangeness of looking out into the snow-blind whiteout winters and their mesmeric effect. Of the mystical "projections" he said he saw behind the snowy curtains.

Or was this specialness the subtle, invisible, spectacular effects of the magnetic fields emanating from the Mesabi Iron Range mountains on whose slopes his suburb was perched? The Mesabi Range is said to have the greatest concentration of iron ore on the continent, a magnetizable concentration that is responsible for the frequent nighttime light shows put on by the aurora borealis, or northern lights. As the earth's magnetosphere is sporadically drawn irresistibly, magnetically, down to the electrified particles in the stratosphere, a confluence creates a flashing, fluorescing, incandescent, old-fashioned jukebox effect that lights up the dome of the night sky with its glowing, pulsing colors. The night Dylan "went electric" is a phrase that would later have resonance in his career. The iron ore, as anyone who has seen the northern lights can tell you, was transmuted into awe. Dylan grew up with this thrilling phenomenon recurrently illuminating his nights.

All this is carried on that rusty ore-cart voice that still drives some people mad. I believe it is precisely this numinous sonority underlying the words and music—and especially that raspy, *nasty* voice—that draws so many so powerfully to Dylan, at least initially. It carves a jagged path across the cortex with a rusty scalpel and sets him apart from other folk singers, such as Phil Ochs, and other rock stars, such as Mick Jagger. One can love them but not feel anything comparable. This makes Dylan different from just about every singer except Leonard Cohen. Indeed, it was Cohen—who might well have been on the Swedish Academy's shortlist had it not been for Dylan's presence—who had the best take on the controversy over Dylan's Nobel Prize in Literature. Just a month before he died in November 2016, Cohen was recorded saying of the controversy, "Giving Dylan a Nobel Prize is like pinning a medal on Mount Everest that says 'Best Mountain.'" In other words, the prize is irrelevant in that it doesn't offer an explanation or an exegesis of his uniqueness.

"I don't know anyone like myself," Dylan said to me in my interview of him in 1977; "I've got something different in my soul."

There is a story I've heard, which may or may not be apocryphal but which if not literally may be at least metaphorically true. The gist was that only a few world-class violinists have possessed the talent to make their violin sound—*sing*—like the human voice. Jascha Heifetz was said to be one, and the others all supposedly came from a certain small region of Czarist Russia (and by implication a certain genetic configuration). If Dylan's voice singles him out, then those who are deeply affected by it, by more than just the lines of the lyrics, may be a larger but still select group.

Other songwriters and other musicians who recognize this quality of Dylan's voice are in utter awe of him. Some musicians tell about him introducing a song *as it's first played* and the kind of psychic alchemy—or perhaps magnetic field?—of their being able to follow along by watching his fingertips once under his spell. To hear them speak of this, it's almost as if Dylan is the musical equivalent of Isaac Bashevis Singer's wonder-working rabbis.

Of course, there are those, including many Jews, who lack the Dylan receptor—or, to abuse the biological model, who have a virtual immune response to Dylan, a wholesale allergic rejection. One can't find fault in a reaction so deeply seated as to be ineradicable. I am not making an invidious distinction based on taste. When

Scholem replied to Daniel Matt's inquiry, he was dismissive: "I have no desire to listen to *Desire* [Dylan's 1976 album]," he declared in a somewhat labored pun.

These are the two poles faced by anyone writing about Dylan: those who adore, and those who abhor. And for those who adore, there is the great schism over his post–Jesus Freak period. Some stopped listening, or listened only to those pre-Jesus period classics. Few are neutral on the issue. I believe it is possible to love Dylan too much or in the wrong way. Which is why I can't take the Dylanologist insistence that every word, every line, is perfect or an esoteric code we must crack. (I loathe the term Dylanologist, barely concealing as it does an ignorant sneer. Which is why I prefer the term Bobolators, after the "bardolators"—those who worship Shakespeare in a counterproductively indiscriminate way, a critique most cogently advanced in a *London Review of Books* essay by the great British critic Frank Kermode, who argued that we must be willing to say that Shakespeare on occasion wrote sloppily, even badly or incoherently, if we are to say he wrote with great sublimity for the most part with any credibility. The same with Dylan. I just have no patience for those who abuse close reading.)

In Dylan's polarizing period, one should be able to find *some* merit in the works. I have long realized that it is a waste of time to try to *persuade* someone to like Dylan's songs. It is almost an innate thing, which is why I make the metaphoric suggestion of a Dylan receptor present in some, not others.

Nevertheless, I want this to be a book that will be of interest not just to Dylanologists but also to those who wonder what the fuss is about.

Two sure tipoffs to the fact you're dealing with someone lacking a Dylan receptor: First, they're willing to concede they "sort of" like "Lay Lady Lay," Dylan's worst, or at least most embarrassingly schlocky, song. Second, they will demand querulously: "You're not saying he's a *poet*, are you?"—as if they were defending civilization itself. "He's NOT a poet!" No, he's a songwriter, and yes, Homer was sung and Sappho was sung and William Blake was sung, but I sometimes can't resist asking such agitated souls whether they're familiar with the seventeenth-century Metaphysical poets and works such as John Donne's "A Valediction: Forbidding Mourning" and Andrew Marvell's "To His Coy Mistress." (They almost never are, because they are almost always ignorant of poetry while feeling no compunction in declaring that Dylan is not a poet.)

I mention Donne's "Valediction" because it is a poem I found myself entranced by at about the same time—as a Yale undergraduate English literature student—that I came upon Dylan's three early love songs, "Don't Think Twice," "One Too Many Mornings," and "Boots of Spanish Leather." All, in their own deeply moving yet complex ways, "valedictions, forbidding, mourning."

I found myself excited by the synergistic combination of their verbal ingenuity and romantic urgency—all in the key of regret. Dylan owns regret; no songwriter has made it a focus of such powerful, intense—and nuanced—lovelorn lyrics. Literature, the Swedish Academy correctly called it. (I'm only slightly embarrassed by having taught his lyrics as literature when I was a graduate Fellow at Yale a long time ago. Ahead of the curve.) But let's face it, literature is both diverse and divisive; some favor Shelley, some Keats, and neither are wrong. (Well, in my mind there's no contest: the answer is Byron.)

My solution to the problem of two main audiences—one who will and one who won't abide Dylan, one who adores and one who abhors—has been not to go over the well-trodden ground of previous biographies more than necessary and unless I have a perspective to add. Instead, I feel there are things that haven't been said about Dylan's *impact* on American and world culture. A focus on the intersection of the Dylan phenomenon and some currents of cultural history should be of interest—as with Marxism—whether you are a devotee or not.

For instance, one question is how a Jewish artist of Dylan's generation reacts to the Holocaust as he comes of age just fifteen years after it, when the work of forgetting has not yet given birth to the work of remembering. In Dylan's early career, his repressed rage transmuted into a bleak, black, traumatized worldview, and the deep cynicism embedded in his ordinary language has outcroppings in his lyrics, such as the sudden naked emergence in a fragment of a poem he wrote that appears in his quasi-novel *Tarantula*: "Hitler didn't change history / Hitler WAS history."

As someone who has written a book about scholarly attempts to "explain" Hitler, particularly in the light of theodicy—the role of a God in the face of the death camps—I may have come upon a rather radical formulation regarding Dylan's impossibly dark view of the cosmos. When he was just twenty-five!

This is all the more remarkable because Dylan grew up like I did (he was five years older) in the 1950s, when there was almost a deliberate desire to repress the memory of the Holocaust. Or to hide and disguise its raw truth under the verbal sign "six million." (One of the unearned advantages I have in writing this book is that my life has been, for all practical purposes, coterminous with Dylan; my high school was a redbrick replica of his externally, and it was apparently a cultural simulacrum, like mine, of cheerleader/jock–Dobie Gillis, All-American High.)

But my repression lasted longer (probably until after the 1961 Eichmann trial, which was when many Jews of my generation began to wake up to the reality behind "six million"). And Dylan's awakening had greater consequences—one of them being, I believe, the root cause several decades later of his conversion to the God of the New Testament. In some distorted way it could be seen as an act of defiance against the Old Testament God, who was, as the great Jewish historian of the Holocaust Yehuda Bauer put it to me in Jerusalem, "conspicuous by His absence" from the death camps.

Indeed, a persistent subtext of Dylan can be somewhat crudely explained by the way his generation of Jews felt itself caught in the vise of *two* holocausts: Hitler's, just fifteen years in the past before the Eichmann trial began to open eyes in 1961, and the apparent onrushing nuclear holocaust that suddenly threatened in the 1962 Cuban Missile

Crisis. The entire Jewish-inflected, surreal, absurdist horror of the black humor movement, from Lenny Bruce to Joseph Heller (along with Dylan), can be seen as a product of the specter of these twin holocausts.

Nonetheless, I refuse to rationalize or insist there is a *continuum* that unites the pre- and post-Jesus Dylan—that is, the Dylan who came before Jesus supposedly visited him in a Tucson, Arizona, motel room and sealed the grip of a Christian mind-control virtual brainwashing sect, and the Dylan after. (Just look at the robotic preacher of dogma visible in the YouTube videos haranguing and preaching and scolding his audiences at the time. I've preserved some transcripts; they are horrifying.)

I believe the rock-critic sycophants seeking crumbs from the table of Dylan, Inc., such as liner-note commissions (and the glam Grammys-for-writers they portend), were disgracefully unwilling to come out and say what a terrible thing happened when this self-described Christian sect—the Vineyard Fellowship—got hold of a vulnerable Jewish soul. It reminded me of the ugly medieval "trials" that Jew-hating authorities would hold, pitting a "converted" Jew against his original religion represented by a poor scholar destined to lose not just the debate but often his life. In Dylan's case, the cultural crime was the brainwashing and negation of an important Jewish-inflected voice in the culture.

But instead, Dylan specialists offer various sophistry-filled attempts to claim Jewish Dylan and Christian Dylan was all a "continuum." This disgrace is now palpably visible in the YouTube videos of Dylan preaching grim New Testament (Book of Revelation, mainly) Hell and damnation to "concert audiences" for the three years he surrendered his mind and soul to the shackles of the sect. No wonder, after he somehow escaped this bondage, that he included no fewer than three versions of one of his post-Jesus songs—"Mississippi"—on his tellingly titled retrospective *Tell Tale Signs* compilation.

It is sad to hear him sing/confess in that song. "Only one thing I done wrong," he intones tragically to a sonorous blues line, "stayed in

Mississippi a day too long." Yes, Mississippi, that slave, lynching, and Jim Crow state, a place of shackles. In this song's allegory, they stand for the mental shackles Dylan wore too long. He also tells us that, despite his escape, there are lasting scars: "You can always come back, but you can't come back all the way."

We are fortunate; many converts of mind-control sect in the 1970s and 1980s that captured 1960s rebels never came back at all, and so the allegorical account Dylan gives of his struggle to embrace the world in the wake of his bondage is something that I pay close attention to in his autobiography, *Chronicles: Volume One*, especially the overlooked Sun Pie episode. He knows and wants us to know that this was a terrible period for the part of him that still heard the "chimes of freedom." I just can't abide those who defend the mental equivalent of slavery. It was the low point of his life.

And then there is an overlooked high point, if we're considering the intersection of Dylan with contemporaneous cultural currents: the women's liberation movement. Second-wave feminism, with its focus on consciousness raising in addition to equality issues ("the personal is political"), was born at about the same time that Dylan first became a cult figure. I think there was a connection; Dylan benefited from the women's movement. I was there, you might say; my colleagues at *The Village Voice* were several of the most influential writers of the early women's movement, such as Susan Brownmiller, Sally Kempton, and Vivian Gornick. Most notably, Ellen Willis, the brilliant cultural critic who was a cofounder of New York Radical Feminists, wrote eloquently about Dylan in her role as music writer for *The New Yorker* and other publications.

This has shaped my belief that the recognition of Dylan's distinctiveness was at least in part the product of the way intelligent women responded early on to Dylan's lyrics and the complexity and respect his portraits of women and love offered, a depth that went beyond the moon/June "American songbook" template. My belief was reinforced when I read Willis's persuasive Dylan essays—and, if I may add some personal testimony, when I met one of the original radical feminists, a founding member of the Redstocking Collective, over an exchange of Dylan lyrics ("love at first cite," I like to recall it), and we lived together for three years. Dylan was the soundtrack to our emotional lives.

In fact, I believe Dylan became the soundtrack to the emotional lives of many couples as his work grew deeper and more nuanced and powerful.

DYLAN AND THE HISTORY OF LOVE

I'm not sure Dylan has been given his due as a figure in the modern history of love. Perhaps the most persuasive evidence of this is the efflorescing number of babies first-named Dylan. It's a safe guess that many of these are children conceived during or because of Dylan love songs. (I had never met a person named Dylan before the early 1980s—twenty years or so after he started recording—when they suddenly began appearing all over the map.) There is probably no greater tribute to a songwriter's love songs.

But I believe there is something about Dylan's love songs that earn him a special place in the modern history of love. People I know have told me Dylan has taken them deeper, to more intimate entanglements. It may have something to do with the rhapsodic way his songs embody the *loss* of love, the regret, the remorse, the memory, and the pain rather than the skipping-through-rainbow-puddles stage of love or the rigid funeral march of the blues. It's his songs making the feelings of love and loss of love real and immediate again. It makes that which was lost painfully inescapable. A way of expressing—and evading—finality.

Tom Stoppard made playful fun of the idea of "the invention of love" in his comic drama of the same title, singling out the nineteenth-century poet pedant A. E. Housman for his insistence that one could trace the Western experience of love to the Roman poet Catullus. Having painfully and lovingly translated Catullus, and having been, despite the difficulty, held in awe by how powerful his transmittal of passion was (*Odi et amo!*), I can understand what Housman is saying, however ahistorical the claim is.

How wonderful it is for Catullan lyrics to have survived and sustained themselves over two millennia, an object lesson in the continuity of human nature. I am glad to see him so honored. Though, of course, Housman's rapture shockingly leaves in the shadows the greatness of Sappho, a thousand years earlier, evident in just a few fragments as old as Homer. Yet as young in spirit as Patti Smith.

Going forward, one must acknowledge the other chief contenders for the title of the invention of love: the Provençal troubadours of the twelfth and thirteenth centuries whose mystical adulterous passionate chastity was celebrated (celibated?) by C. S. Lewis (*The Allegory of Love*) and Denis de Rougemont (*Love in the Western World*) as the locus of the modern world's "invention." Perhaps Dylan's magnetic odes—sparked by the northern lights of his childhood—empowered his lyrics in a *Zohar*-like "book of illuminations" way. A light for lovers.

Although I would not go so far as to ascribe to Dylan the *reinvention* of love, I believe he took it both to a higher level and a full fathom five deeper than the slough of dullardism it had sunk to in the 1950s. For myself, I've found that the most resonant recent line that gestures toward what Dylan has been doing is the one that give an ambiguous close to Philip Larkin's remarkable poem "An Arundel Tomb."

For those unfamiliar with this long lyrical work, the poet stumbles upon the worn six-hundred-year-old stone-carved dual funeral casket of the fourteenth earl of Arundel and his wife. A stone casket whose lid features an armed knight (the earl) and his wife holding hands side by side, a worn and flat image on the top of the casket. One little detail arrests Larkin's poet "with a sharp tender shock."

The earl is depicted garbed head to toe in chainmail armor, including mailed gloves, but he seems to have removed one glove—the one closest to his wife's side—so that he can grasp his wife's hand flesh to flesh (albeit flesh rendered in stone, of course). Was that ungloving, loving impulse true to life, or was it some figment of the stone carver's imagination? The poet can't decide what to think about this apparent six-century-old gesture of love. Did the stonemason create the gesture out of whole cloth—was it *his* romantic imagination—or was it commissioned?

In other words, how authentic was it? Which brings us to another cultural preoccupation that has been an abiding, even obsessive, concern in Dylan's work. Authenticity versus sincerity.

It seems to me that, for Dylan himself, authenticity had to pass two tests: That a work of art acknowledged the death-camp world in which it was set—that it took into account an honest theodicy and awareness that any invocation of God was posed by theodicy, the question of the apparent absence of God in Auschwitz. And secondly, that it did not suffer from the disease of performance, or the necessity to create an illusion, to mime authentic feeling night after night after any and all authenticity had been wrung from it. He distinguished between authenticity and performative sincerity.

Dylan seems very serious about this, and he returns to it over and over in interviews. When one interviewer, Mikal Gilmore, asked him about an earlier performance of one of his songs, he insisted, "that person doesn't exist." Other formulations were "that's not me," "he's not there" (which is the title of Todd Haynes's film about various incarnations of Dylan), and, of course, "it ain't me." The cumulative impression is of someone *embarrassed* by essentially tricking emotion from his listeners with the falsification that is sincerity.

Indeed, the strict logic of this critique of performance made every iteration of the original songwriter's manuscript a betrayal of itself. Which is why I try to explain in a later chapter in this book the parallel between Dylan's spiky insistence that he never existed before and a metaphysical thought experiment proposed by Jorge Luis Borges, who liked to play with the idea of the discontinuity of the self. Borges's idea was that we are an infinite succession of discontinuous selves that exist like the still photos on a reel of film, and only when run at twenty-four frames per second does it give the illusion—but only the illusion—of continuous movement.

I believe Dylan was driven to declare the discontinuity of the self with a kind of metaphysical desperation. It makes it seem, in most cases, the person performing whatever song has been sung before—*that person* has never sung the song before, so as to give the impression (or give the convincing illusion) of the words leaping from him freshly minted. He hated (or so he said) miming sincerity as opposed to expressing authenticity. This was the kind of thing the great Shakespearean director Peter Brook demanded of his actors—as the purpose of rehearsal—that they would get to the point of giving the impression in performance (indeed, feel the reality) of Shakespeare's words being the *only and inevitable* ones they could utter—words coming to mind for the first time onstage because of what was happening onstage, not because of what happened in the play, script, or rehearsal.

Authenticity, like the Holocaust, like the mystery of love Dylan paid tribute to and investigated, was an abiding preoccupation for him. He was himself consciously inauthentic when he first began to perform, and not just regarding the change of name (which was chosen not in reference to Dylan Thomas, as he insisted to me in our interview, but, as he would later aver, to Marshall Dillon from the 1950s television Western *Gunsmoke*). However, creating a folkie, hobo, train-hopping Woody Guthrie–like persona was a work of genius only while it worked, before it was exposed. How long, one wonders, would he have sustained it?

It's worth recalling a couple of ways he presented himself, constructing his myth when he first came to New York:

> Yeah, well, I was with a carnival when I was about
> thirteen and I used to travel with a carnival—all
> kinds of shows.

[Where?] All around the Midwest. Uh, Gallup,
New Mexico, then to Texas, and then . . . Lived in
Gallup, New Mexico, and . . .
—Billy James interview, October 1961

I traveled with the carnival when I was about
thirteen years old. All the way up to [when] I was
nineteen. Every year, off and on, I joined different
carnivals.
—*Oscar Brand Radio Show*, October 29, 1961 (aired
November 4)

All untrue, of course; he had an all-American suburban high school career. But there was nothing dishonest about his love of what has famously been called "the carnivalesque" in literature (by Mikhail Bakhtin) and in America. Although sometimes I wonder if his circus/carnival imagery may in some way echo the fact that the horrifying Duluth lynching his father told him about involved traveling circus workers, their marginality making them even more vulnerable to ill winds of murderous racial malevolence.

But then came the first price of fame: a splashy article in *Newsweek* (about a year after those first "carnival" interviews) exposed the mostly suburban banality of Dylan's youth. I think the shock of this exposure is underestimated. Biographers tend to treat it as something Dylan shrugged off, but it could just as well have been mortifying to him in the close-knit folk community so devoted to authenticity.

Perhaps it was precisely this exposure of his inauthenticity that was at the root of his later fanaticism, to the deepest metaphysical core of his being, about authenticity. He was preoccupied with being "genuinely" authentic, not merely folk-sincere.

And authenticity *was* the watchword of the folk-music world, a profession of authenticity he eventually violently rejected. He was irritated enough to tell Nat Hentoff in 1966, "Folk music is a bunch of fat people."

To return to the fourteenth earl of Arundel and Larkin's poem. An abyss of doubt about the authenticity of love and its representation and expression opens up for the poet when he sees the stone-carved hands clasp. He closes provisionally on a semifamous final line in "An Arundel Tomb": "What will survive of us is love."

For those who know Larkin's work, even the provisional affirmation is almost shocking. He's already skeptical in the poem (just the stonemason's fantasy?), and in his letters he goes further, seeming to shy away in something like embarrassment, even mortification, from this unaccustomed moment of affirmation. In his letters, Larkin doubts the wisdom of the apparent oversentimentality of the final lines but stops just short of the way W. H. Auden retracted his affirmation when he banned any publication of his poem "September 1, 1939" if it contained *its* original final line—"We must love one another or die"—Auden having become so mortified by the greeting-card sentiment it suggested.

But Larkin, like Dylan, seems more divided, or he has a different question: "What will survive of us is love" doesn't necessarily mean what will survive our death, though that's perplexing in itself. Rather, what will survive our parting, our loss of one another, our connection during life? Where did what was love go? Is it like an indestructible energy field, a magnetic field, an invisible matrix of entanglement of two particles (lovers) that remains radiant? Or is its radiance a flaring across the night sky, like the northern lights—momentary incandescence that disappears into the dome of the night? Is love a structure of energy, a disturbance in the Force that persists even after separation, even if the particles are no longer entwined, their spin no longer aligned? Larkin's phrase says, "What will survive of us is love"; Dylan's love songs ask, What is the "what"?

And does love survive in Dylan's songs only in an anguished afterlife, only when it is "authentic," not performative or staged? Or is all love performative, staged according to cultural templates from the Catullan to the Provençal to the ecstatic, Dylanesque, rhapsodic Large Hadron Colliders of emotion?

This leads us to another example of the intersectional questions raised by Dylan's work: his abiding, career-long preoccupation with the question of authenticity and appropriation on many levels in a culture now presided over—and divided by—a "reality show" host. This makes the question of how one defines the authenticity of "reality" of even greater moment and urgency. Is realness defined by the triumph of the will (of the interpreter-performer) that makes it so?

Dylan has always exhibited a peculiar kind of performance anxiety—the reluctance to mime authentic emotion when performing an "emotional" song, for instance, usually a love song. But can the anger in "The Lonesome Death of Hattie Carroll" be sustained with authentic fidelity to the original impulse, done dozens and dozens of times? Few other singers seem as preoccupied with this problem.

Is the feeling that Dylan seems to summon up so powerfully for listeners "real," is it "sincere," is there an unbridgeable gulfs between sincerity and authenticity? We see it first—the joy in perceived authenticity—in his claimed elation at the discovery of the authenticity of Woody Guthrie's songs. But at the end of his career, in a communiqué to the Nobel Prize Committee, Dylan has a surprise about the reality of that relationship to Guthrie. The question persists through songs like "Is Your Love in Vain?"—always demanding to know whether what's lost was real. We also see it in his initial attraction to the folk-music scene, with its concern for a definition of authenticity that boils down to precise *replication* of once-authentic original versions of Scottish and English Child Ballads (a collection of largely pre-Renaissance works published by Victorian curator Francis James Child).

Dylan's shift to rock and roll of the sort he heard on post-midnight radio as a preteen was more authentic, closer to the American musical roots represented by Buddy Holly's fusion/collage of hillbilly country and Black R&B. Was anything truly authentic, or was it "roots" all the way down, or was Lead Belly, whose back-country Black blues Dylan discovered as a youth, the only one who could claim to be truly authentic? Perhaps listening only to Lead Belly and imitating him was a dead end for a white boy in search of authenticity. But with that fantastic fusion represented by "Like a Rolling Stone," at last he'd found a way to attain his own signature authentic self.

Listen to the literally visceral way Dylan describes the breakthrough to his own authenticity in writing "Like a Rolling Stone":

> I found myself writing this song, this story, this
> long piece of vomit about twenty pages long, and
> out of it I took "Like a Rolling Stone" and made it
> as a single. And I'd never written anything like that
> before and it suddenly came to me that that was
> what I should do, you know. I mean, nobody had
> ever done that before.
> —Martin Bronstein interview, CBC Radio,
> February 20, 1966

That was the goal: to astonish himself with something "nobody had ever done . . . before." This was true authenticity (as opposed to sincerity).

And what was his ultimate resolution of the conflict between authentic affirmation and the defiant accusation of theodicy? Affirmation of love's authentic survival. Accusation of God's authentic failure. A conflict only rarely resolved. His anthemic works, such as "Every Grain of Sand," contain *both* affirmation and accusation. The phrase "every grain of sand" can be found in the Bible, in Blake, and in I. B. Singer's astonishing *Magician of Lublin* (another work I believe Dylan must have come across in his first years in New York City when he was couch surfing in the apartments of Village autodidacts) with its persistent subtext of anguished theodicy. Indeed, Dylan is as much like the shape-shifting escape artist Yasha in Singer's *Magician* as he is the conflict-torn prince in Shakespeare's *Hamlet*.

Which brings me to another example of a cultural preoccupation: Dylan was obsessed with being torn between affirmation and accusation. He resolves this conflict without really resolving it by allowing the two to coexist and conflict within each song. His best songs offer a quasi-spiritual life, an affirmation that is undermined by an accusation. Dylan's pervasive dark theodicy subverts the ecstatic mode so many find appealing. The accusation is one that Jewish theologians have wrestled with for centuries: that a just and loving God cannot be reconciled with the pervasiveness of evil and suffering in the world.

The affirmation, the ecstatic side of him, can be found in some of his love songs but even more so in a few anthems like "Forever Young" and "Wedding Song" and in some masterpieces that—as I ultimately conclude—don't so much resolve but contain the contradiction. An anthem such as "Every Grain of Sand," in which God is responsible for good and evil, makes it a song of both affirmation and accusation.

How does Dylan's Jesus period fit in? Was it an aspect of his search for authenticity? I was there—face-to-face with him at the peak of his anguish, there on the Warner Bros. Burbank back lot—to see the vicious crosscurrents, personal and professional, that set him up for some kind of breakdown. I could sense his desperation for some source (even an arbitrary source) of authenticity. No, I don't forgive the evangelical group that took advantage of a man in pain by seducing him into their mind-control community. They were not offering comfort to him, not even submission to Christ so much as submission to them, their narrow harrowing hellfire preaching against almost all of humanity but themselves. No one else's but theirs was the way to be authentically "saved." They turned him into an automaton. And few spoke out against this scandal.

I should probably briefly discuss the authenticity of my own Dylan affiliation, if that's what you want to call it (anything but Dylanologist)—my "conversion," as I clumsily called it when Dylan himself asked me why I liked his music or what I liked about it. It was one of the few times during our week of interviews in 1977 that he expressed an interest in his interlocutor. Not that he had been cold, or the cruel trickster famous for mocking interviewers. In fact, I think there are so many good moments in the interviews (such as his description of the sound he'd been seeking— "that thin, that wild mercury sound"—which is ensconced in Dylan lore, the title of bootlegs, and quoted unattributed by Dylanologists forever) because he eventually took pity on the poor fellow with the yellow legal pads covered with scrawled questions, doggedly, anxiously changing the tapes. He was, in a word—when people ask—*kind*. Until I made the mistake of using the word "conversion." I began humorously telling him, "Well, my conversion was . . ."

"Conversion?" he interrupted me, quizzically.

I couldn't know at the time what a loaded question that was. Up to then, Dylan had been unexpectedly patient with me in my nervousness. I think he sensed my intense exegetical preparation and desire to learn—not to catch him out. But then . . .

Conversion. It was late 1977. He was on the brink, the cracks were beginning to show and to widen painfully for what was to be a major Fitzgeraldian crack-up. The divorce from his "mystical wife," Sara. The bitter child custody battle that had reached the stage where "private investigators" were serving documents to administrators at their children's schools on behest of one or both parents. (Could anything be more painful?)

And then there was the film, *Renaldo and Clara*, his bid to become a major figure in cinematic circles and to bring to life the magical, romantic, yet fractious spirit of the Eminent Bohemians of the Village folk scene that had given him his start. It was to be an American *Children of Paradise*. But the editing was torturing him. Moreover, he had made one easily foreseeable mistake: casting his estranged wife, Sara, opposite his longtime love, Joan Baez, as female leads.

The result—in addition to some exquisite music from what is known as the Rolling Thunder tour—was that he was now virtually strangled by the miles of unspooled film, like the serpents of Laocoön binding him. Thousands of hours of film had to be cut down to what was eventually a "slim" four-hour-plus version. When released commercially, it was sneered at by reviewers and avoided by all but the most fervid

Dylanologists. (I knew a French girl in SoHo who watched every single one of the twenty-six showings at the famous Bleecker Street Cinema—the one showing *The Sorrow and the Pity* in *Annie Hall*—when it opened in January 1978. She would have seen twenty-six more if it hadn't stopped playing, by which time she was usually the only one in the theater. The gold standard of Dylanology.)

This failure was a tragedy, really, because, in addition to breathtaking musical performances, the film now has curatorial cultural/ historical value both for the original *Children of Paradise* ambitions and for what became of them. It's an essential document of the way America changed in the 1960s. ("I own the sixties," Dylan once said to an interviewer, "do you want them?") One of my ambitions in this book is to convince Dylan and Dylan, Inc., which has withdrawn the film entirely from circulation (you can't even see it in bootlegs), to rerelease a version. Perhaps it could be available in the new Bob Dylan Archive at the University of Tulsa's Woody Guthrie Center.

So, in 1977, I was seeing Dylan at the worst possible time. Of course, I sometimes take my own share of blame, my besieging him with reams of questions handwritten on yellow legal pads, and my interest in his Jewishness just at the time he was exploring Christianity. He was getting tired of those like the brilliant Jonathan Cott, who in a recent interview had bombarded Dylan with less than stellar—okay, frankly tedious—Hasidic tales and demanded that he say they explained his songs. Not another one, Dylan might have thought. Could I have been the straw that broke the camel's back and drove Dylan to Christianity to escape questions about his Jewishness?

In fact, I rather think it was theodicy: his rage at the Old Testament God for His apparent indifference in the face of evil led Dylan to the ultimate reproof of that deity, a dramatic abandonment for the God of the New Testament.

So "conversion" was not exactly the right thing to say, it appeared.

Let me explain now what I mean. He had long been "in dialogue" with his Jewishness: the name change, the embarrassing exposure of his Zimmermanness, the berating assault by Jewish zealots the likes of "One-Legged Terry," a bombastic Israeli (I met him) whom Dylan tried to co-opt by playing Jewish for a while, taking his firstborn son to the Western Wall for a bar mitzvah in 1970.

But to return to "Like a Rolling Stone" and why it was a conversion experience for me and so many others. It's often forgotten what the circumstances were, just how *new* Dylan's masterpiece sounded when it came out in 1965. I heard it first on a ferry ride from my hometown on the South Shore of Long Island to the beautiful beaches of Fire Island with some high school pals, celebrating the first anniversary of our graduation.

It came over the roar of the ferry engines from a tinny transistor radio.

There was nothing like it. It was Dylan's "wall of sound," resembling in some way the last great Phil Spector masterpiece, Ike and Tina Turner's "River Deep, Mountain High."

But it was not a love song. Not a conventional love song, anyway, like everything else on the radio, where music lived those days. It was a song that ostensibly mocked and ridiculed a once-privileged and entitled debutante type who "used to ride on a chrome horse with your diplomat, who carried on his shoulder a Siamese cat." Verse after verse rehearses her once-proud state and her now-desperate humiliation, then asks her sneeringly, "How does it *feel* / To be on your own . . . / a complete unknown / like a rolling stone?"

And yet one's sympathy inevitably shifts from the mocker and his mockery to the outcast, the one on her own with "no direction home" (the line Martin Scorsese took as the title for his brilliant three-hour Dylan documentary). No direction home because no definition of home. No longer able to embrace a land built on slavery and genocide (of the native population), now murdering brown people halfway around the world by the hundreds of thousands and sucking up its own into the killing machine.

BARD OF ALIENATION

Maybe it was the fact of being on a ferry adrift between two realms (like Charon's ferry?)—between adolescence and adulthood, between fantasy and reality, when the self is defined against the backdrop of a fearsome unfeeling world. There was definitely something generational about my "conversion." I was caught up in a nationwide generational emotional break with the past—the explosive force of the baby boom. Maybe it was the fact that this was the summer of my first (academic) failure, when I had flunked out of a designedly unflunkable course for freshmen known as "Physics for Poets." I could attribute failure to my astonishment at and inner rejection of the Copenhagen model of quantum physics taught then—that all reality was or might as well be a matter of statistics and probability. I think it was about that time I found myself enwrapped in the circularity of the quintessentially Zen-like double helix Dylan enigma: "She knows there's no success like failure and that failure's no success at all." Was I—staring failure in the face—attaining success at failure, in my failure at success? I still don't know.

But it was really that I spurned tutoring and classes and the final because I didn't want to stop reading this amazing nine-hundred-page baggy monster of a novel, John Barth's blasphemous satire of America's colonial origins, *The Sot-Weed Factor.* Looking back, that book was Dylanesque in its blasphemous ridicule of American icons such as Captain John Smith. It was a key document in the black humor moment that I still reread and recommend to anyone who hasn't read it yet. In my case, it was a fortunate failure that landed me in Greenwich Village (to take a makeup course at NYU) the summer when Dylan was in the air in the city. "Mr. Tambourine Man" in the Byrds' electric version floated out of every cab and café, calling us to follow him on some fuzzy quest.

The more I think about it, though, that sense of a quest was not delimited to the feeling of suddenly being "on your own." That feeling of being an outcast aligned with Dylan's consistent sympathy for losers. Not sympathy for the Devil of that contemporaneous Rolling Stones song represented life's winners. I will always remember the great writer Murray Kempton telling me that he always learned something more from "the loser's locker rooms" of life, a phrase he applied not solely to sports but also to history and prose writers. In fact, he confided that his favorite prose stylist of the seventeenth century was the earl of Clarendon, whose multivolume *History of the Rebellion and Civil Wars of England* was written from the losing Royalist Cavalier side—those who had fought Cromwell's Puritan armies, who had once had thrones and power and now found themselves out on their own, no place to call home. The Cavaliers produced the best lyric poets, even if not the best warriors.

All of which was an undercurrent of some kind of American musical magnificence—more than a wall of sound, "Like a Rolling Stone" was a wall of astound. Punctuated by the increasingly haunting question "How does it feel?" Leaving the moon/June template behind like a shuttered and disintegrating Disneyland.

The song spoke to a generation whose sensibility was formed by the story of an outcast, on his own, no direction home. A fellow named Holden. One of the discoveries I made in reading through an old Dylan anthology is a vignette of him in the year after he arrived in New York City in 1961. It appeared in what was clumsily called *The Mammoth Book of Bob Dylan* in a story reprinted from the old *Saturday Evening Post* (which went through a period of competing with *Esquire* for New Journalism cred) and was written by Jules Siegel, one of a mostly forgotten New Journalism epigones.

Siegel describes a Village party where people are gossiping about this chubby-cheeked adolescent lying lazily on the floor telling people he has been cast as or is going to play that archetypical outsider, outcast Holden Caulfield, in a film. And indeed this is something Dylan told me—that he had been influenced by *The Catcher in the Rye*. All this before we learned (in 2014) about the ur-source of J. D. Salinger's disillusioned sensibility that Holden partook of. Salinger was one of the GIs who liberated the Dachau concentration camp outside Munich after fighting his way with his unit from Normandy and finding, in Dachau, that the crematoria were still smoking. He later told his daughter Margaret that one can "never really get the smell of burning flesh out of your nose entirely." So one can trace a nested series of subtexts of disaffection, disillusion, disenchantment, and the deadpan rejection of the false face of piety and propriety from Dachau to Salinger to Holden to Dylan, if one so chooses. I choose to, and I discuss the connection further chapter four.

I could have told Dylan more about my "conversion" if I hadn't sensed a "don't go there" signal from him. I could have told him about the true capstone of my conversion and the song that, for me and many others, reframed the zeitgeist and drew us into Dylan's world: his August 1965 Forest Hills concert, the one in which he debuted "Desolation Row." It has been called "the greatest Dylan concert ever."

It's gone now, the old Forest Hills tennis stadium with the grass courts and the ivy-covered walls, turned into that figment of English major scholars imagining the lost paradise of the great English poets, "The Green World." I can't help thinking of the line from Andrew Marvell's great poem "Bermudas" (oranges hung like "golden Lamps in the green Night") or, from his "The Garden" and its evocation of apocalyptic pastoral, "annihilating all . . . to a green thought in a green shade." Cumulatively, the venue created an extraordinary spell that dreamy August night.

I had been there the year before to hear a Joan Baez concert and was elated when—after intermission—she brought on a raggedy-looking Dylan to sing a couple of duets with her that thrilled me. But this time it was to be all Dylan, and, though I didn't know it at the time, it was to be highly controversial: the first half acoustic Dylan alone, the second half the Satanic (as some thought) electric Dylan with a backup electric-guitar-based sound.

There is one thing I think is particularly important to say, one myth I am able to dispel about that concert: the legend of the booing.

Just a month before, Dylan had introduced his electric guitar and his electrified, amplified backup band at the Newport Folk Festival. And he had been booed by the largely folkie audience. Although it's still argued whether the booing had to do with overamplification or with electrification per se, entire books are now devoted to this issue, including one entitled *Dylan Goes Electric!*, which seems to recapitulate his role as villain opposed to the far less talented, self-proclaimed political folk purists who attacked him. This has been a pattern in some recent Dylan books that indulge in tedious nitpicking of his character and behavior: they miss the forest for the trees, the forest being he's a genius and his detractors could not get over themselves enough to recognize that—or that geniuses are not often celebrated with medals for good behavior.

So there was some suspense about what Dylan would do a month later at Forest Hills, and the first half of the concert (the part, as we'll see, that changed my life) was acoustic and went smoothly. Nonetheless, it is still widely reported that, after intermission, when he came onstage and set up an electric backup, the very notion of it was booed. And was booed continually throughout.

I'm here to say that's not true. There *was* some initial booing, but it focused on some witless, obsessed fan who ran out onto the stadium turf, making for the band shell with who-knows-what in mind, until security people intercepted him and hustled him off the scene. Yet the myth has grown that Dylan was booed at Forest Hills, and I'm glad to set the record straight. As is said at the close of *The Man Who Shot Liberty Valance*, a contemporaneous classic Western film, "if you have to choose between printing the truth and printing the legend, print the legend."

However, it's possible I was still in a trance from hearing the debut of "Desolation Row" in the first half of the concert.

All you need to know of this carnivalesque pageant, this mad New Orleans funeral for the West, this mad dance of the death of civilization, can be found in the first two lines. In the velvety hush of that green night, it begins: "They're selling postcards of the hanging / They're painting the passports brown."

This was a different America than the one most of us in Dylan's generational cohort grew up with. And though I didn't know why at the time, I could feel the hush come over the stadium at those first words, "They're selling postcards of the hanging." Not that he gave it melodramatic emphasis. Probably *because* he did not. He just murmured the awful words softly.

And the next line, "They're painting the passports brown." It would be a while before a full understanding of the implications came home to me. During the years I was researching my book on scholarly attempts to "explain" Hitler, I came across, in the basement archive of Munich's Monacensia library, a cache of crumbling, yellowing newspapers. These were the last remnants of the heroic efforts of the premier anti-Hitler newspaper in Hitler's hometown during his rise to power, *The Münchener Post*.

Paging carefully through years of archive papers, I found myself struck by the drumbeat of oncoming doom, especially the reports of the murder of Hitler opponents all over Germany by Nazi death squads. This was a factor overlooked in explanations of Hitler's rise, which often depended too much on his supposed charisma and ignored the effect documented by the *Post* in daily headlines such as "Brown Murder in Thuringia," "Brown Murder in Posen," "Brown Murder in Franconia," and "Brown Murder in Nuremberg." (Brown, of course, because that was Hitler's chosen color for his movement. His headquarters in Munich was known as "the Brown House.") These murders went unsolved and unpunished, though everyone knew who was guilty; the entire judicial system had been infiltrated by Nazis and Nazi sympathizers in the decade of Hitler's rise.

The association of brown with murderous fascism is not as well remembered as it once was. But Dylan did remember: "They're painting the passports brown." The imagined nightmare nation he was conjuring up was transitioning, you might say. Turning brown. Reminding us what kind of world we Americans lived in and might be living in again.

What seems most salient to me, looking back, is that this was my Daniel Matt moment. This was when I realized or felt something akin to what Matt would later say of Dylan: "I felt that he saw things in their stark reality, that his prophetic vision penetrated to the core of everything."

It was a moment that reframed my coalescing dark vision of the world. It was the moment I became a Bobolator—or, more specifically, began to think of myself as a Dylan exceptionalist. I thought of him as not just another singer/songwriter whose work I admired, played, and replayed; rather, I incorporated him into my consciousness. His work became a kind of dark kaleidoscopic lens through which I viewed the world and related to people—those who got it and those who did not.

Exceptionalism is tricky, and I devote some attention to it in my books on Hitler and Shakespeare. Was Hitler on the continuum of other murderous evildoers in history, or was he off the grid in a rare exceptional realm of "radical evil" (to go back to Hannah Arendt's pre-"banality" phrase) of his own? Was Shakespeare on the continuum of other great writers, like Goethe and Tolstoy, or was he off the grid in a realm of verbal magic all his own? I find these questions fascinating, though unresolvable.

Being a Bobolator means taking Dylan's exceptionalism for granted. A mere starting point! A place to begin marveling—and conveting.

I like to find others who started from a place of Bobolatry. I'm thinking of F., a Harvard summa cum laude who, after graduating, went off—like Matt—to travel in the Himalayas and ended up being caught in a war, the Indo-Pakistani war, turned herself into a war correspondent, and got a newsmagazine cover. She was brilliant—and a Bobolator. There was also my friend Tom F., who initiated me into the cult of the never-released Dylan love song "I'll Keep It with Mine."

Of course, not all Bobolators were the kind of savants I loved to find. There were a distressing number of cultlike devotees who found every song of Dylan's, no matter how mediocre, to be secretly brilliant, you just had to find the key. They wouldn't even acknowledge the idea of mediocrity in Dylan's corpus.

It was almost as foolish to argue with them as it was with those who lacked the Dylan receptor. They could often be intelligent and possessing of good taste (except in one respect). But the Dylanologist goons sometimes made me doubt Dylan.

As one of the first adherents of the loosely allied close-reading "Empsonian" school of literary criticism, with its exaltation of "seven types of ambiguity," I could find meaning or ambiguity in every word and gesture. Take, for example, the cover of Dylan's *Nashville Skyline* album: Was he tipping his hat hello or goodbye? Frank Kermode's *LRB* essay on Shakespearean ambiguity sealed the deal for me: we must be able to say that something Shakespeare wrote was sloppy or incoherent, less than exalted, if we wish to be able to express in all honesty our awe at that which deserves exaltation.

The real break, the disintegration of my Dylanist leanings, came, of course, with his conversion to born-again evangelism, the low point of his life, just a few months after I'd met with him and found him a genuinely thoughtful, skeptical, questing soul. Obviously I was not a good judge—or else he was a good concealer—of something going on underneath. That something that emerged after he claimed Jesus visited him in the Tucson motel room, the emergence of this Cotton Mather–like fire and brimstone *scold*, was deeply dismaying. "Fearing not," as he once warned, "I'd become my enemy in the instant that I preached," I just couldn't make excuses for this. Although much of my anger was directed at those who stole his soul and turned him into a robotic preaching automaton, a simulacrum of himself, I couldn't help feeling resentment toward him for a kind of betrayal. Yes, "Judas" (as some folkie shouted at him for "going electric" a long time ago at a 1966 concert in the U.K.). He was always betraying someone. And so, for years even after Dylan reemerged in the 1980s from these shackles and started to become himself again, I wouldn't listen or pay attention.

Then I heard him do a duet with Patti Smith on his late ballad "Dark Eyes," and I realized he'd written a perfect Chekhovian song. And I even found myself enraptured by Lou Reed's cover version of one of Dylan's incomprehensible biblical songs, "Foot of Pride," with which Reed electrified the crowd at the 1992 Madison Square Garden concert tribute to Dylan. I began to reevaluate.

When Yale University Press came to me and asked me if I wanted to write a short biographical meditation on Dylan—not just another conventional biography to add to the glut—I said I hadn't been paying attention to him for years, deliberately, because of the "conversion." But then I started listening again and found, among the dross of Late Dylan, some songs that absolutely, stunningly, *repaid* attention. (Christopher Ricks's definition of a work of art was "anything that repays attention.") I was shocked at how good some were, at how Dylan had reinvented songwriting—certainly his own—and I was able to see how mediocre other songs were and the way critics failed to distinguish the few pearls of great value from those of mere paste.

I still get into arguments with those who love "Lay Lady Lay"— that schlock country music song, with its implicit assumption of male sexual privilege and entitlement over women. It was a low, low point in Dylan's career, even though I love country music. Indeed, one of my favorites of his songs is "I Threw It All Away."

Being with fellow Bobolators can be an exciting intellectual communion, but being a Bobolator is a lesson. It brings to mind one of William Blake's aphorisms, "The road of excess leads to the palace of wisdom." This has wrongly been described as praise of excess. No! It is praise for the journey's end, its telos. "The palace of wisdom"—the ability to *judge*—is only arrived at through excess recognizing itself.

In conclusion, I don't regret having become a Bobolator; I would have never come close to understanding Dylan without understanding—experiencing—that which gives rise to Bobolatry. But I would have never been able to write about him without discarding Bob-olatry for something more, something that incorporates the ability to make distinctions, which is the essence of "the palace of wisdom."

I come to you with humility and dawning wisdom as a *recovering* Bobolator.

CHAPTER 2

IN WHICH THE AUTHOR EATS A GRILLED CHEESE SANDWICH WITH BOB DYLAN AND ASKS HIM ABOUT GOD

Bob Dylan was telling me about the prophetic-seeming "projections" he saw as a young boy. Looking out the window of his snowbound house in Hibbing, Minnesota, in the heart of the Mesabi Iron Range. Looking into the whiteout depths of the perpetual snowstorm the winter months brought and seeing things. Having visions.

"I had some amazing projections when I was a kid," he said. "And those visions have been strong enough to keep me going through today."

"Today" was the very fulcrum of his career, a moment when he was finishing a cinematic summation of his remarkable rise and the culture that helped create him—his own version of *Children of Paradise*—and also a day when he was teetering on the edge of a profound spiritual crack-up that would take him down within a few months. Before the long climb to reach the Nobel heights.

It was November 1977, he was thirty-six years old, and we were talking at a greasy-spoon lunch counter on the back lot of the Warner Bros. Burbank studios, where he'd been working at breakneck speed, 24/7, to finish cutting down the hundreds of hours of footage he'd shot for what was to be his cinematic masterpiece—*Renaldo and Clara*—to the slim four-hour commercial-release length.

The film was to be the epic that would make him into a movie star and director simultaneously, and there was so *much* to include. In part because of that, it's a film you may never see. Nobody has spoken of it recently in official Dylan world, which has lately been releasing every scrap of every variation of just about every song in "official bootleg" albums. It's as if the film never happened. It was such a commercial failure, such a sign that the tsunami of Dylan charisma no longer made waves, that it has been made virtually unavailable. I saw it two times, once as a kind of test before being granted an interview with Dylan to see if I could decipher it (it wasn't that hard). Yet the film did have its admirers. He still had his fans—but that's too pallid a word. Acolytes, fanatics, maybe.

Nevertheless, the rest of America wanted not the singer but the songs—and apparently not the film.

This is a tragedy, in a way, because the songs on the *Renaldo* soundtrack are rendered brilliantly, and any soundtrack album released now would prove it. I thought that, just in terms of music, it was the peak of his performances. I also think that, if the Dylan-world people listen to the argument I make in this book—how the film succeeded as a Village bohemian *Children of Paradise*—it would now be welcome both as artifact and as work of art. The time has come to rerelease it, and it will be hailed all the more for what might have been lost. Free *Renaldo and Clara*!

Dylan was seeking to do in film what he'd often done in song: to create an allegorical, phantasmagorical, pageant-like *experience* showcasing his songs, his confreres, and his love life. A love life that was at that moment perhaps why he looked back uncharacteristically dreamily to the snowbound visions in his hometown of Hibbing and the little house on the Mesabi Range where his father, Abraham, had moved his family from Duluth when Dylan was six.

We had been talking about everything from God to evil at the lunch counter, where greasy grill fumes mingled with Dylan's cigarette smoke. It was some sixteen years after he had left Minnesota, an unknown, to come to Greenwich Village to become part of the folk-music scene that captured his imagination. This was a scene—and the farewell—he was trying to recapture in the film, a scene that would be overwhelmed, overshadowed, left gasping in awe with his unexpected success. No one had seen anything like it.

What was it about his "projections"?

"The earth there [in Hibbing] is unusual," Dylan said, "filled with ore. So there is something happening that is hard to define. There is a magnetic attraction there." Filled with ore, filled with awe.

"There is something happening." There is something *magnetic* happening. But you don't know what it is.

"You know something's happening but you don't know what it is, do you, Mr. Jones?" he would later sneer in "Ballad of a Thin Man." He was trying to express that feeling—something happening and not knowing what it is, as is often the case in his songs, such as "Like a Rolling Stone" in which he was both the accuser and the accused. Identifying with that sense of dissociation and dislocation, that bewildered sense of being "lost in the rain in Juarez" when "my best friend, my doctor / won't even say what it is I've got," of being lost with "no direction home, like a rolling stone." He made that uncharted territory his own.

It's a signature Dylan trope. A mode he writes from, a mood he conjures up. Nameless dread, dreadful namelessness. Amazement, in the sense of being lost in a maze. Bewilderment, a sense of wonder at the world.

You never know entirely how earnest Dylan is being—he is not known for giving much importance to being earnest—but he sounded earnest, still a little amazed at conjuring up that feeling of magnetism in the air, that seductive, massive, magnetic attraction of the ore-filled Mesabi Range. It makes sense that Dylan would have a sensitivity to magnetism, doesn't it? He certainly became known for a kind of charismatic magnetism. Some might intuit he absorbed it in some inexplicable way from those magnetic fields near his hometown. (I wouldn't go that far; I said *some* would.)

But what do those "amazing projections" signify? They suggest something that is visualized, a destiny for himself that is imagined or "projected" the way a seer would. A sword-in-the-stone moment. They conjure the wonderful passages of ekphrasis in classical texts, Homer's Shield of Achilles, or even Milton's Raphael with his pictorial projections to a post-lapsarian Adam and Eve of the future testaments, culminating in the death and resurrection of Jesus.

These were "projections." Dylan's were undoubtedly more modest but sufficient to convince him he had a colorful destiny. This is what fascinates me: the sense that he *knew*, somehow, that he had a promised destiny.

It was a moment that came back to me, one of the first thoughts I had, when I awoke the morning of October 13, 2016, to the news that Dylan had been awarded the Nobel Prize in Literature. Nearly everyone else in the world had awakened with an opinion about it all. Was it a mistake to call Dylan's work *literature*? And even as literature, was it any good? Was it *that* good?

Was it poetry or was it song, but then, was it more than song? Homer was sung, and nobody is calling for the revocation of his status as a poet. Shakespeare had songs, perhaps one of the most perfect: "Full fathom five thy father lies / Of his bones are coral made" (a song about the making of poetry). The Old Testament offers Solomon's (or whoever's) "Song of Songs." Would it be disqualified for a literary prize? And oh yes, don't forget Blake's "Songs of Innocence and Experience."

I think the choice made by the Swedish Academy can be defended because, at bottom, all literature and song involve *words*: language— the composition, combination, and permutation of words. If it had been called the Nobel Prize in Words, it might be inadequate, but his being awarded it would not have been attacked so ferociously by those whose words did not manage to become more than words; it would not have touched an entire nation emotionally. One has to believe that the Academy was moved by the early power of Dylan's words to spur the civil rights movement and the antiwar movement. (Even if Dylan hadn't taken a stand on Vietnam himself, he did write "Masters of War" and "With God on Our Side.")

But the Swedes were probably thinking in particular of the two anthemic odes that he became most famous for: the sappy, Kumbaya-like "Blowin' in the Wind," and the genuinely thrilling and prophetic "The Times They Are A-Changin'." Or perhaps for some members of the Swedish Academy there was a moment when they felt perfectly in tune with Dylan's defiant sense of liberation, and when, as Wordsworth put it, "bliss was it in that dawn it was to be alive / but to be young was very heaven."

Just two songs! But what power they had. An urgent idealistic purity that transcended their moment in time to touch the place of eternal yearning that is universal. The power to instantly whisk one back in time to one's idealistic youth. A veritable fountain of youth. We could add a third song to this all-important list: "Like a Rolling Stone." Although it lacked the Scandinavian political advocacy of the other two, it captured the simultaneous contempt for and identification with the way being an outcast is liberating to the soul.

Yet his worldwide network of fans—all the Dylanologists, fellow songwriting poets, and especially musicians—were awed by the manifold, multitudinous body of his work, the hundreds of songs that spoke to them.

It was the demonstration of the power of words. And perhaps a recognition of the entirely unique and original way with words Dylan developed in his later (post-Jesus) period, when he produced more esoteric songwriting, and we could envision him as a kind of gene splicer of a sentence's DNA. Something akin to John Ashbery's verbal collage painting but with greater or more accessible depth, meaning, and—with the music—more emotive force.

One of the things I want to do with this book is offer one of the first (only?) close readings of the neglected gems of later Dylan and the way they've mutated the language (some would say mutilated, but not me). Those works are great achievements in finding a way to use common words, clichés, and once-empty phrases and pushing them to the limit of comprehension. Not a *narrow* close reading but one that embeds him in the historical context, the culture of his time, and the American tradition.

I find myself thinking of the great American poet Hart Crane, whose difficult but strangely exalted language I once described in a *New York Observer* column this way:

> Crane created his private lexicon of ecstatic
> apprehension, a witchy alchemy of sound and
> signifier both seductive and frustrating. A language
> somehow teasingly just short of yielding itself
> up, supremely intelligent but just shy of complete
> intelligibility, neither opaque nor transparent, a
> kind of crystalline translucency. I can't get enough
> of the *White Buildings* poems; lately, "For the
> Marriage of Faustus and Helen" has possessed me,
> sent me back to Ben Jonson's dazzling seventeenth-
> century play *The Alchemist* to trace Crane's
> alchemical inspiration to its source.

(And, of course, one could add "At Melville's Tomb," with its echo of "full fathom five" and its "calyx of bones.")

Yes, that was me, but the resemblance between Crane and Dylan is hard to resist invoking; they share some elusive genius with words and phrases whose resonance rubs up against each other. There is another analogy that I think helps clarify the literary source of the folk culture that originally made Dylan its chief expositor. No, it wasn't Aaron Copland, as biographer Sean Wilentz relentlessly tried to prove. (He wasted many introductory pages riding the hobby-horse that it was Copland who was Dylan's hidden source—but this would have been well hidden, since Dylan mentions just about every other composer from that period as an influence but, strangely, ignores this supposed mentor he never met.) So many critics, so many Dylans. Another example is Greil Marcus and his "old weird America" Dylan, the rootsy, choogling, ancient, blues Dylan, a Dylan that Dylan seemed to inhabit imitatively for a while. Few will let Dylan be Dylan.

I think the Swedish Academy did serve a curatorial function for Dylan, akin to Francis James Child's collection and preservation of pre-Renaissance folk tunes; otherwise, Dylan's brief moment of mega fame might have overshadowed his scores of other songs that display literary genius and that the celeb worshippers overlook.

Just as Greenwich Village folkie culture, so often ridiculed, preserved these beautiful Child Ballad lyrics for Dylan and Joan Baez and the like to pass on to generations to come, the Swedish Academy was bestowing not just a medal on a mountain but a hundred—perhaps hundreds of—years more to Dylan's singular achievement. Hundreds of years that may have otherwise left him among the lost.

Indeed, how long will Dylan's appeal last? I wager that it will be as long as or longer than any other contemporary singer-songwriter. (Sinatra never wrote a song.) Shakespeare is now four hundred years in the past. I recall one dinner I had with Sir Peter Hall, cofounder of the Royal Shakespeare Company. He lamented in his cups that comprehension of Shakespeare's language "in the original" would soon require translation or "modernization" of some sort for people to achieve a basic understanding—and of course what makes Shakespeare *Shakespeare* and all that will be lost. Even now, Shakespeare is at the point where a true understanding of his way with words and the way words play with words requires a "companion" or copious footnotes (often glorious) for the nonprofessional.

Will Dylan be sung, read, celebrated four hundred years from now?

My thinking in writing this book is that there are a hundred other greater and lesser conventional biographies on Dylan that can tell you about the acoustic versus electric guitar controversy. Does the world need another one? What would be most helpful, now and in the future, is a kind of companion to the songs whose secrets don't always yield themselves up easily. It would focus on the lyrics rather than the crude biographical criticism most books on Dylan indulge in. (Who *was* Queen Jane, the mystical woman, in "Queen Jane Approximately"?)

One thing I'd really like to do is something I've never seen in the dozens and dozens of repetitive Dylan biographies, which usually stop with his born-again period. I'd like to single out the Late Dylan songs that are seldom listened to, since Dylan lost his cultural capital in his Jesus-freak period. Songs that deserve to last. Songs he wrote when he discovered a new method of songwriting that would resurrect the respect he deserved for those few left to listen. I'd like to get you to make them part of your mental repertoire. I can tell you secrets about these songs.

There are some songs that never appeared in official release albums, or that Dylan dropped for mysterious reasons at the last minute: "I'll Keep It with Mine," "Up to Me," and "Blind Willie McTell" being the trinity. And there are some that were released but have lacked for attention, such as "When the Night Comes Falling from the Sky," "Ring Them Bells," "Series of Dreams," "Sweetheart Like You," "Emotionally Yours," "Dark Eyes," "Not Dark Yet," "Dignity," "Caribbean Wind," "Most of the Time," "Things Have Changed," and "Every Grain of Sand."

I would bet that most casual listeners are utterly unfamiliar with any of these. I know I myself stopped paying attention to later Dylan after the born-again Jesus freaks stole his soul for three years. (I will accept no temporizing about the theft; you just have to watch the YouTube tapes of his scolding, sermonizing "concerts" from that time to understand what I mean by "stole his soul." He's like a bad

Dylan simulacrum; it's terribly sad and frightening.) But he escaped somehow (see chapter eight, about the Sun Pie episode) and began reconstructing his songwriting in an utterly unexpected way.

He does something with these songs that has yet to be articulated or even given a name. The gene splicing of memes, perhaps. The unit of double helix sentences being the keyboard he played upon. It's not an Ashbery-level collage—verbal abstract expressionism. Rather, there is entanglement inference, not the utter refusal of coherence.

So I want to tell you about these songs as well as to single out those from his earlier period that I feel have not been looked at from the right angle or enough angles. I will do it chronologically, weaving emblematic stories from Dylan's life that I think have been untold or underplayed.

And I want to tell you more about *Renaldo and Clara*, the film Dylan was working on in that Burbank back lot where we took breaks for grilled cheese sandwiches at the smoky lunch counter.

But I don't want to leave Dylan behind, staring into the mind-altering whiteness of the snow. He had more to say about the snow-bound visions—imagining, perhaps, while gazing at the mountains the peaks of adulation and *power* he would achieve, the power to sway hearts and minds. Power: that is what distinguishes Dylan's body of work, not whether he was a songwriter or a poet, not what pigeon-holed category you want to put him in.

No, what distinguishes him is his ability to seize hold of the imagination of a nation with his *voice*. The primal instrument.

That's what literature does. Homer was *sung* and has lasted some three thousand years. The sound of his voice, the vibrato of his lyre defined the power of literature to span millennia.

Dylan's power at its peak wouldn't last much longer than sixteen years, as he proclaimed in 1977, the year he met me (coincidence?). Not the kind of power he commanded when the times they were a-changin', when his ship came in and the answer was blowin' in the wind.

There were always new acolytes who had the Dylan gene—the receptor not universally possessed but whose possessors were often strikingly obsessed—whose life could be changed by the way "things have changed," as a later, less anthemic tribute to change had it. But nothing changed about the certainty he was *right*, that the words and phrases he'd chosen and the way he played them seemed somehow to fit no matter what crazy jigsaw they constructed.

That's what genius can always do, what his did.

Could he have seen himself as he would be? As he would become in those "projections"?

Recently, in a book about the pre-Socratic Greek philosophers, I came upon a description of one of the earliest of the "seven sages," the Ionian sages, however you wish to address them. In this case, Thales of Miletus, a name I recognized but knew little about. Thales became famous for predicting a solar eclipse by means of mathematics as well as for using math in measuring the height of pyramids. What I didn't know about was Thales's early fascination with magnetism, before the property of magnetism was even attributed to lodestones; he was aware of the existence of the lodestone and was the first to be connected to knowledge of this in history. According to Aristotle, Thales thought lodestones had souls that had the power to attract other human souls.

Was Dylan aware of this ancient belief in the power of lodestones over souls? After all, he became a kind of human lodestone.

You have to wonder about the way he works *magnetism* of some sort into his description of human flesh and blood attractions. Of soul calling to soul as lodestar calls out to the lone star Dylan became. All his best love songs are about the magnetic bonds of love and why in the world they lose their mutually attractive power. All somehow speak of love as a magnetic attraction that can, tragically, lose its power. An attraction that is as palpable as the force one feels between two magnets with opposite or similar poles. That's what's unique about magnetism: the physical palpability of it, the weightiness. One feels in love the longing of lodestones to join from within their imprisonment in individual cells.

Somehow he knew. Knew he had that power, the magnetism within.

"BIGGER THAN ELVIS"

One early witness I spoke to suggests as much about Dylan's sense of his lone star, lodestar power. The writer Ron Radosh, back in 1961, was then head of one of the most radical factions of SDS (Students for a Democratic Society) at the University of Wisconsin. Radosh still remembers when he got a call from a friend in antiwar circles at the University of Minnesota asking him if he could find a place for this kid folk singer to stay on his way to New York City. It was Dylan, not yet twenty, on his way to his destiny.

So Radosh put him up, and the thing he recalls with great clarity is that, after hanging around drinking a few beers, Dylan told him with absolute earnest conviction, "I'm gonna be bigger than Elvis" and "I'm gonna play arenas." Elvis wasn't even big anymore at the time, giant though he was and would become, and who called folk music venues arenas? Radosh wonders at this still, recalling the feeling of someone who had an uncanny sense of his destiny.

Radosh, who is not given to overstatement and is no longer a radical, says, "It was like he *knew*."

That's the feeling you get watching the Martin Scorsese Dylan documentary, *No Direction Home*. It reminds you just how hostile, how angry, how tin-eared and *stupid* his folkie former fans were in their horror of Dylan "going electric." I should declare at the outset I *always* loved the rock-and-roll electric Dylan from the first moment I heard "Like a Rolling Stone" blaring out from a tiny transistor at a high school beach picnic. (Forest Hills was his first public performance of the song.) Offering the opposite message of its lyric. It was giddy, exhilarating, thrilling to feel like a rolling stone, not a source of schadenfreude but of the mad beatnik joy of pure rejection certifying one's artistic purity. Kerouac at the wheel and on the road.

But Scorsese captures the force of the animus of the world from which Dylan emerged at the time of his supposed abandonment—betrayal! "Judas!" they cried. Yet it never occurred to me—or Dylan—to take this biblical wrath seriously. How tunnel vision could you get: here was this astonishing fusion of every triumphant strain of American music in a glorious, gorgeous pageant (Dylan has said that as a youth he was thrilled by the traveling wrestling spectacles of "Gorgeous George"). How could anyone not want to go along for the ride?

But there it was, that visceral animosity, and I was struck equally by how Dylan was *utterly unperturbed* by the hostility. He didn't care if they hated his music. He just *knew* it was the right music to play, the only thing he should be doing. They were just wrong and they would realize it, but if they didn't, it'd be their loss. When you think about it, there are very few great artists who don't shock and dismay their public at one point or another—and keep on doing what they know they have to do.

The guy had confidence in his gift, at least before the Jesus freaks stole his soul; he had the confidence to shake off the animosity because he *knew*. How? Where did that confidence come from? Initially, I think, from the magnetic fields.

Magnetic attraction, more dramatic than the gravity we swim in, is invisible wavelike attraction at a distance. Even today, it's not entirely explained as an element of quantum theory; it's awaiting unification in the "final theory of everything." Like Dylan, an insoluble mystery.

THE MAGIC INCENSE

Before going further: a brief portrait of the artist as the consummate cigarette smoker.

Sitting across from Dylan several hours a day was a veritable immersion in his cough-inducing, unfiltered cigarette smoking. It left me with an ineradicable impression of an Oz-like wizard glimpsed through a haze of airborne ash, his face wreathed in drifts and tendrils of nonstop chain-smoking.

Thinking back on it, though, it gave me a feeling of his location in the hazy firmament of American culture. His location on the spectrum, the grid that divided dissident styles of postwar rebellion primarily into the Beat and the Hip.

We were speaking loudly over the background clatter of dishes, and along with the smell of grilled cheese, burning, fries, and cigarette smoke.

I rarely feel confident making character judgments on the basis of physical affects. But with Dylan, in retrospect, I felt I could.

The cigarette smoking is the clue, the smoking gun. It's the virtuoso cigarette smoking of a seventy-year-old ex-junkie beatnik.

I'm prepared to argue that no one today smokes cigarettes more *expressively* than Bob Dylan, waving the lit ember about with studied focus like a conductor's baton. Dylan, though still under forty then, had the signature moves of the great cinematic smokers of yore—Camus, Bogie, William Burroughs, Lillian Hellman. Weaving a hazy filigree around himself that garlanded his words with a smoky worldliness.

Setting aside the health danger, nothing becomes a legend more than a wand of smoke woven around their words with hypnotic authority. Gazing intermittently, searchingly, at the lit tip as if it could offer a clue to the mystery of Being itself, hidden somewhere in the pinpoint of incandescence. Zen smoking!

There's more to Dylan's cigarette smoking than stylistic accident. It was a clue to character, to his place on the stylistic spectrum of postwar dissident culture as the 1950s became the 1960s. A telltale sign more profound than the difference between acoustic and electric chords; rather, a sign of the larger modes of self-definition, self-fashioning, between the two poles of Beat and Hip.

Yes, that ancient schism, Beat versus Hip. Norman Mailer once ran aground and got it wrong, arguing that Beat was some pacifist feminist quietism and Hip all big and bold and masculine (like him). No, there is a classicist ascetic mode of smoking to be found in Beat culture that transcends pacifism and is reflected in a kind of digital (here betokening fingers) delicacy, the hand that holds the burning butt drawing delicate pictures in the air.

Beat tobacco consciousness. They're "on a whole other level" than wellness. A grizzled, granitic classicism, in sharp contrast to romantic hipster butt-flaunting. As things shook out—the way those crushed soft-pack tobacco-laden sticks would shake out when the pack was tapped as one of the superstitious rituals and single white cylinders fell out of their cellophane coffins—Beat lost out to Hip. But I've found that, for artists, Beat culture somehow bears the nobility—the respect—accorded to dispossessed aristocrats, hermetic monks, the weathered legion of the lost. Don't forget the jet-black shades. On the left coast, sunglasses are designed to keep light and gawkers out. For the Beats, shades are worn to keep the self in. Above all, those who fall on the Beat side of the Beat/Hip dichotomy would rather drop dead than abandon their bare-bones, deadpan, bleached-skull, high-desert, dry-like-you've-never-known-dry sensibility.

Beatniks were the lovely losers in the culture wars. The great artists wanted to be on that side of the line, not the opportunistic pop side. Need I bring up Leonard Cohen again?

"THE NAKED AND THE BRAVE"

S peaking of Mailer, Dylan, and Zen koans, I feel this is the appro-
priate place for an illuminating comic/cosmic digression about
Mailer, Dylan, and a deadpan shoot-out the two of them had, an
episode I still find a kind of Dylanesque mystery.

Let me begin by taking note of a memoir Anatole Broyard wrote
called *Kafka Was the Rage*. It was about the oh-so-achingly-lovely
flowering of postwar Village culture, a scene in which everyone read
Kafka and argued about the existentialists over double espressos at
the Caffe Dante, Figaro, and the like. Something that harked back to
the transcendentalists of nineteenth-century Massachusetts, only in
highly caffeinated face-to-face rather than epistolary form.

And after Broyard and Kafka there came a time when Mailer was
the rage. Not the Mailer of *The Naked and the Dead* but the Mailer of
the Lower East Side stories such as "The Time of Her Time" and "The
White Negro" and the attempt to identify the sensibility he called Hip.

There was a period when Salinger was the rage, and it will take a
separate section to illuminate Salinger's profound early influence on
Dylan. Suffice it here to say that his influence was more all-American
than parochial bohemian, though his attitude toward conventionality
was even more radical and long lasting.

The "Naked and the Brave" incident took place in the early 1970s
when Mailer was still the rage, fifteen years after Mailer wrote his first
columns for the paper he cofounded, *The Village Voice*, and then quit
in a rage over a copyediting error. But at the time he met Dylan in the
early '70s, Mailer was still the rage, though Dylan was on the verge of
superseding him. He and Dylan had never before met, and this is the
story of what happened when they did.

The buildup came from my friend and *Village Voice* colleague Lucian
K. Truscott IV, who had managed to become friends with "the Whole
Sick Crew" (which was Thomas Pynchon's name—in *V.*—for his beat-
nik cast of characters in the music and downtown literary world).

It so happened that Lucian knew both Mailer and Dylan. Dylan hung out at Lucian's loft at 124 Houston Street. (I lived around the corner for a time on MacDougal–Sullivan Gardens' south wall; Dylan was across the great interior garden in the quadrangle formed by Bleecker, Sullivan, Houston, and MacDougal, but I was regrettably too shy to introduce myself.)

The way Lucian tells it, he was talking with Dylan and mentioned Mailer, and Dylan expressed an interest in meeting the sage of a slightly earlier generation's rage. As it turned out, it was approaching the date of Mailer's annual Christmas party at his waterfront loft in Brooklyn Heights. These parties were a gathering of the downtown literati and the uptown glitterati, and they were famous for their all-night brawls and alcoholic excesses.

This was the time, about 1974, when Dylan was gathering up his "Children of Paradise" crew to set off on a journey to be filmed for something he called *Renaldo and Clara*.

The night of Mailer's party, Dylan's crew converged on Houston Street in a bus filled with revelers. Lucian had to straighten them out—this was no ordinary party. This was the peak of the year, bohemian revelry-wise.

But they made it across the river, a bus full, and this is how Lucian describes the meeting between Mailer and Dylan:

> A few minutes later we were filing up the narrow
> stairs to Mailer's place. Someone ahead of us was
> taking the stairs very, very slowly. I was in the lead,
> Dylan right behind me. A voice came from behind
> us down the stairs. "Hey, man! Get a move on!
> Who's holding up the show?"
>
> I stopped and turned around. "Who said that?"
> [Dylan said.] No one raised a hand. "All right,
> we're not going another step until I find out who's

the wiseass." A hand went up. Dylan glared at the guy and said, "That's Lillian fucking Hellman, asshole. Get back on the bus or go back to the hotel." Dylan had recognized her from behind. That was my first hint that Bob Dylan, though maybe not in his element, knew the territory.

Mailer greeted us at the door. I wisecracked that the big moment had arrived for the two most famous Jews in America. Tentatively, they shook hands, then Dylan looked up from under his flat-brim tour hat. "Nice to meet you," he said. "I really loved your first book, The Naked and the Brave." For a split second, Mailer thought he was being put on and his eyes narrowed, and then Dylan looked him full in the face and stuttered, "I meant The Naked and the Dead, man." Mailer broke into a broad grin and threw an arm affectionately around Dylan's shoulders as Dylan introduced the rest of the band. Mailer welcomed each warmly, then said, "Come with me, Bob. I'll introduce you around."

Dylan was clearly nervous. This may have been the first time in forever that he wasn't the most notable guy in the room. Over there stood Jackie O.

I'm not sure of Lucian's interpretation. This seemed like a duel of deadpans on the staircase. Was Dylan making a mistake? Does it sound natural to you—"I really loved your first book, *The Naked and the Brave*"? Do you think he actually read the book, forgot the title even though he "really loved" it? Or was it a Dylan put-on, a put-down put-on. And Mailer's canny reaction: to pretend not to notice or not to care, thus one-upping Dylan. Having absorbed with the speed of lightning what might well be an attempt to puncture the vanity of his host.

We may never know whether Dylan was fumbling in an attempt to offer a compliment or delivering a deliberate act of impertinence. I mention it because the Mailer-Dylan relationship is something I want to return to. Because I believe they share a similar theodicy despite their ego clash. And because it's an indication that Dylan transcended his hobo-hokey stage persona—he could play in the big leagues.

A FEELING OF WONDER

Today, when I think of Dylan in the greasy spoon looking back on what brought him to Burbank, I think of the snow. I think of Charles Foster Kane seeing his long-lost sled. *Renaldo and Clara* was/is Dylan's Rosebud.

Dylan spoke in awed tones of his original feelings of wonder, gazing into the impenetrable snowflake flurry—a surprisingly earnest-seeming discussion of a kind of initiation into a different realm, that of a sword-in-stone moment, which bequeathed him a sense of mission.

Those "projections"? "They were a feeling of wonder," he said. "I projected myself toward what I might personally, humanly do in terms of creating any kinds of reality. I was born in, grew up in a place so foreign that you had to be there to picture it . . . in the winter, everything was still, nothing moved. Eight months of that. You can put it together. You can have some amazing hallucinogenic experiences doing nothing but looking out your window. There is also the summer, when it gets hot and sticky and the air is very metallic. There is a lot of Indian spirit."

A feeling of wonder. "You can put it together," "very metallic." One might say *iron*-ic. And then he added: "Maybe thousands and thousands of years ago, some planet bumped into the land there. There is a great spiritual quality throughout the Midwest. Very subtle, very strong, and that is where I grew up."

The planet bump!

Yes, it's lovely and allusive in many ways, the hallucinogenic stillness, the metallic air (foreshadowing Dylan going electric?), especially that image of the planet bumping. Clearly something that stayed with him—he gave one of his albums the title *Planet Waves*, after all, suggesting (in the context of the planet-bumping quote) that those waves were sustained reverberances of the original big bump. Indeed, on the album cover you can see the hand-drawn radiant waves from an apparently just-bumped planet. And, in a sense, this very book is less a formal biography of Dylan than a biography of his *impact*. The impact of Planet Dylan bumping into ours. The impact of Dylan on our culture and consciousness from that first big collision (or planetary kiss): his meteoric apparition in 1962 and the sixteen years that followed, when the culture seemed to hang on his every word, sixteen years before Jesus (or, if you prefer, Jesus freaks) stole his soul and left him looking like the victim of a brainwashing for a full three years.

But the reverberations persist beyond that, even after he lost his original cultural capital to the Jesus freaks. After he lost the mantle of oracle, prophet, messenger—at least to non-born-again believers. We feel the aftershocks, the reverberations, even though many no longer realize the aftershocks' origin. Like the speculation that fish can't feel water, Dylan has created the zeitgeist we swim in. A bit hyperbolic, but I think I can make the case. And I think, too, that after he recovered, he was still capable of creating "a feeling of wonder," not as often but often just as powerful.

In addition to being a biographical essay about (and a memoir of) that impact, this book is an exploration of the source of that impact: How did Bobby Zimmerman, staring out the window into the still and snowy woods in that magnetic air, become Bob Dylan? And *why* did Bob Dylan have that planet-bumping impact on us? What chords did he strike?

What was the origin and nature of the magnetic charisma that "changed the world," as President Barack Obama put it, not entirely hyperbolically, while awarding Dylan honorary membership in the American Academy of Arts and Letters in 2013? Could it be found in the way he described the impact of the magnetic fields on him—their hallucinogenic effects? Those who have taken hallucinogens and have an inclination to Dylan also have an inclination to believe that Dylan *must* have taken hallucinogens himself. (In a very early interview he said he did, but spoke little about it thereafter.)

Or, to put it another way, you might recall from childhood the little plastic-encased iron filings that would—when a magnet was brought close—array themselves in coherent arabesque patterns.

THE WHOLE OTHER LEVEL

Dylan wasn't speaking idly when he talked about magnetic fields; he went into a kind of highly charged reverie, changing into a different being who could create "other levels" of reality. I think of this every time I hear that conspicuously mystical line in the otherwise straightforward, nonmystical protest song "The Lonesome Death of Hattie Carroll." She was the murdered hotel maid who, as Dylan puts it, "emptied the ashtrays on a whole other level." Here is your exceptionalism—that whole other level. The ability to think of one of life's poor players and victims as finding the ecstatic in the mundane. That "other level" is where Dylan lived in his best work, and somehow he wanted to unify his world to capture the clash of the impoverished and the nobility.

But I think there's more to his account of the hallucinogenic visions. I think it was not merely the invisible presence of magnetic ions in the air. Admittedly this is a bit speculative, but I can't help wondering if his primal sense of wonder had something to do with the way the northern lights lit up that magnetic atmosphere—like a jukebox in the sky. One whose flickering neon Sistine Chapels in the dome of the night sky would evoke, perhaps provoke in the first place, some elements of the Dylanesque. Of "that thin, that wild mercury sound" he later spoke of to me. The sky "going electric," lighting him up in a frenzy of mercurial synesthesia. Yes, there is evidence Dylan, like Nabokov, like dozens of other lesser-known artists and civilians, enjoyed the facility of synesthesia, which, you may know, is the ability to experience one sense as another. The way Dylan "sees" sound in "My Back Pages" when he experiences the "chimes of freedom [sound] flashing [light]." Chimes don't ordinarily come across as light.

Dylan would have seen in those long Northern nights the visual equivalent of celestial chords, the music of the atmosphere. This helps to explain, for example, the line from "Mr. Tambourine Man," "to dance beneath the diamond sky." And you can think of Dylan "going electric" in terms of the sky "going electric" in an aurora (ore-aura) borealis frenzy.

I wouldn't have known what to think about his expostulation on the Northern visions he had as a youth—and one characteristic of Dylan always worth remembering is his ineluctably Northern sensibility. It's there, in the beautiful "Girl from the North Country," a song Mikal Gilmore once characterized as American transcendentalism. It's a term I might not have fully understood if I hadn't seen the northern lights myself. And I wouldn't have seen the northern lights myself if it hadn't been for Dylan and "love at first cite" with a Dylan girl from the North Country.

Do I know absolutely Dylan was moved by the northern lights? But I'm willing to go out onto a limb. And if he wasn't, he might as well have been.

When I say I saw them because of Dylan, I mean the way his magnetic field had an element of yet another kind of attraction: erotic. I tell the following story because it's a case study of the kind of influence that surrounded him, at least in his prime. It's not only about his impact on my romantic life, but also about his impact on the romantic life of generations.

I think it's worth looking at the way he inscribed a certain kind of romantic connection—romance on "a whole other level." It is in this very personal realm—not the protest songs or the druggy surrealist epics (unless they were love songs, too, as they often were)—that the Dylan impact was often most powerfully felt.

I first saw the northern lights at a place not far from Dylan's Hibbing, across the Straits of Mackinac at the top of Lake Michigan in the snowy wilds of the Upper Peninsula of Michigan. I was there because of a woman I met through Dylan, or through Dylan songs. Or through the incident I call "love at first cite." This snowbound setting was her parents' abode, where we spent below-zero winter holidays doing cross-country and snowmobile things during the day and watching the northern lights at night.

This epiphany probably represents the peak of my Bobolatry—the erotic peak, when everything was so highly charged by Dylan magnetism that "love at first cite" was possible.

Then, in the early 1970s, there was a garret party in the Village, an Edna St. Vincent Millay–type bohemian crew. As a new staff writer for *The Village Voice*, I had written about avant-garde musician La Monte Young (whose show consisted *entirely* of him emitting a vocalized "sine wave drone"—to the accompaniment of his wife, Marian Zazeela, on sitar—for hours at a time; you had to be there), and it was my job at the *Voice* to keep track of avant bohemian downtown culture, which was also very Dylan conscious. At this moment, Dylan was the rage, and everyone seethed with secret theories about his disappearance from the scene after the (later debunked) "motorcycle accident." It was like he was the Absent Guest at every party. Or an absent God.

No one knew why he had withdrawn from the world. Had his death been covered up? "The withheld work of art is the only eloquence left," Don DeLillo had written in *Mao II*. And, DeLillo wrote, "When a writer doesn't show his face he becomes a local symptom of the famous absence of God."

"The famous absence of God"! It was the moment when Dylan was like unto an absent God in that time and place, everyone awaiting "the withheld work." And, as I will argue in my "crazy sorrow" theodicy theory, the absence or, worse, the passive presence of God in the face of evil became a preoccupation of Dylan's.

But to return to "love at first cite," I speak of it not (only) because of my personal stake in it, but because it gives a hint of the impact Dylan had on a generation of vulnerable souls. The atmosphere at that party was charged like a magnetic field with Dylan, an electric subject for those on his wavelength. Many women in the Village were *deep* into Dylan in a genuinely profound and soulful way, a "whole other level" that the mostly male Dylanologists never got to—except, if they were lucky, through such advanced women. (You can still find a hive of Dylan-struck young women on Twitter today. One calls herself "Mrs. Bob Dylan," another "Rainy Day Woman," and another "Isis [a song from *Desire*] Zimmerman," to name just a few.) Oh my god, there were Harvard Phi Beta Kappa Dylan girls in the Village, and there were Bohemian goddess Dylan girls in the Village. It was a sea of mermaids, swayed by his tunes, dancing in the waves. Forgive me if I found myself wanting to share their intellectual and emotional passion. It was so *attractive*!

In any case, the whole thing about Village bohemian parties, I was learning, was to strike a defining pose that would differentiate one from the other poseurs. In this instance, I was framing my persona at the party as Dejected But Romantic Loser in Love, and I was quoting Dylan's insidiously weepy ballad of regret, "I Threw It All Away," to all who would try to offer comfort.

My girlfriend of three years—an adorable West Texas drawl of a girl—had suspected correctly that I was not mature enough to settle down and start a family. (I was still under the spell of Mr. Tambourine Man: "In the jingle jangle morning I'll come following you." I wanted to follow something somewhere someone had never been. Somewhere "far from the twisted reach of crazy sorrow.") After a sheltered childhood and education, I *liked* being on my own, "like a rolling stone" (with all its insecurities). Thus, she had just left for London to marry a British investment banker and live in Cornwall. I could summon up, for shameless self-dramatizing purposes, the profoundly wistful, deeply bleak and beautiful "Girl from the North Country" with its haunting American transcendentalism. (Wish I'd known the phrase at the time, I'm sure I would have used it.) Or "One Too Many Mornings"—Dylan is so *good* at leave-takings and farewells and regrets and goodbyes! Half his best work is about heartbroken separations. "Crazy sorrow."

But I chose—for self-identification purposes at this party—the song that may have been the ultimate self-torturing Dylan regret ode: "I Threw It All Away." Sometimes, in his farewell songs, he's sarcastic or ironic ("Don't Think Twice, It's All Right") or he sees it all as "complicated" ("You're right from your side / I'm right from mine" in "One Too Many Mornings"), but this one, "I Threw It All Away," is just utterly, devastatingly, nakedly unsparing of the self. It twists the knife of self-reproach into "a corkscrew to my heart" (that memorable phrase from "You're a Big Girl Now," perhaps his ultimate—but then yet to be written—regret ode).

"I Threw It All Away" is a killer country ballad (from his album *Nashville Skyline*) that—courageously at the time, something he took flak for among the bohemians who had never been to West Texas—took country and western male emotionalism seriously, something he'd learned from Hank Williams and Johnny Cash. The song deserves to stand with the best of Hank and Johnny and Willie Nelson. It summons up all of the (almost biblical "Song of Solomon") joy he had, when "Once I had mountains / in the palm of my hand," and then he relentlessly lacerates himself with the refrain, "I must have been *mad* / I never knew what I had . . . / I threw it all away / I threw it all away." The repetition is so powerful.

I don't know how good I was at staging the sensitive guy thing at the party. But the more intoxicated I became with the intoxicants available and the self-pity on tap, the more belligerently (and sort of boastfully) I refused the possibility of solace that people were offering: it would have spoiled the effect. And I realized I was playing (or overplaying) this role for a particular young woman in the crowded room, who sat on the far end of the couch I was standing at. It did not escape me that her raven tresses, her dark lashes, gave her an un-avoidable resemblance to folk goddess (and Dylan consort) Joan Baez, if Joan Baez had been wearing a rust-colored velour mini-shift and an amused smile. Amused at clearly seeing through (but not really de-spising) my act. And it so ensued that when she heard another iteration from me of the phrase "I threw it all away," she piped up in response,

"Yeah, but 'don't think twice, it's all right.'"

Love at first cite. We spent the next three years living together.

It was a real connection at that time, being together on that Dylan wavelength. I think there is—or at least once was—a kind of tele-pathic or extrasensory communion between Dylan lovers, especially between Dylan-*lover* lovers. One of the more unexamined aspects of the Dylan impact, I believe, is the romantic connections it created.

It used to be a truism of the dawn of the age of Dylan, the Beatles, the Stones, the Doors—an apocryphal quote from Plato's *Republic*: "Only change the mode of music and the walls of the city will fall." (Analog in Joshua and the Fall of Jericho?)

For many people, listening to Dylan changed, for a brief moment, anyway, our mode of romance. A greater, perhaps more urgent mu-tuality; a matter of mutual recognition rather than manipulation; a common bond established on "a whole other level." And on the other side of the matter, I know of a marriage (not mine, I married a Willie Nelson girl) that broke up because the wife conceded she had lis-tened—*just* listened—to Dylan's ultimate killer love song, "I'll Keep It With Mine," with another man.

Somehow it was a breach of faith worse than—or more aggravated than—garden-variety sexual infidelity. Dylinfidelity.

This may be part of the secret of the "whole other level" that bound Dylanophiles together: when I say he changed the mode of romance, I mean he brought it into the post-Sinatra and post-Elvis era; he gave it a complex depth that probably was a fig leaf for the old verities, you could say. But one of the ways a society defines itself is by what and how it fig-leafs things, isn't it? There have been essays written claiming Dylan's achievement was somehow to overthrow the Brill Building school of songwriting. But that's all wrong. There were two Brill Building eras (named after the old Broadway music biz office warren). The early Brill Building era, yes, was to my mind bland and simpering Doris Day moon/June stuff. But the later Brill Building era, in the early 1960s, gave us immortal Phil Spector'd girl group anthems by the Ronettes and the Crystals; it made Motown possible, and Carole King and the like. I think what Dylan did was build upon the Brill Building foundation and take it to "a whole other level."

I'm not saying that this sort of romantic connection doesn't happen to people who listen to Sinatra or the Beatles, but I think the parents of those Dylans now come of age and having Dylans of their own would agree that there was a connection on "a whole other level." And I know that the two of us—the girl from the North Country and I—found it with that "first cite," but it may have reached its peak watching the northern lights together. Once you've been to *that* level, it's hard to come back to earth.

The popular image of Dylan—facilitated by honest, if narrowly focused (on celebrity), films like *Don't Look Back* and *I'm Not There*—fixates on his sneering hostility to the world, his cynicism and sarcasm. But there was more to the story. It would be an incomplete picture if we didn't recognize the powerful romanticism of Dylan's music, his contribution to the cult of love, and the way he became a powerfully romantic figure from whom many of us learned the modes and rhetoric of love. After all, sex is conventionally more biological than cultural, and love is conventionally more culturally shaped and conditioned. Clearly, however, one of the powers of song and poetry is to school us in what love is. Who wrote the book of love, indeed. Dylan has his own chapter. And you can't tell his story without explaining the way he changed romantic sensation and the rhetoric of love. The change he made in such rhetoric was comparable to that of the debuts of Byron and Pushkin.

CHAPTER 3

"SCREAMING SOUNDS INSIDE THE BARN"

What makes Dylan Dylan? It's worth noting that, even though he caused a tempest in a cappuccino cup when he shifted away from conventional political protest songs, he did not abandon his profound metaphysical protest at the way of the world: his running argument with God over the way God made the world and human nature. In fact, the roots of this more profound protest could be traced far back—probably, I'd argue, back to a horrific incident that took place twenty years before he was born.

It was a hot night in Duluth, Minnesota, on June 15, 1920. The workers for the John Robinson Circus were folding tents behind the big top after midnight. A couple of teenagers, a boy and a girl, stood watching.

By the end of the night, rumors raced through Duluth, the northernmost port city in continental America, that eight black circus workers had been arrested for the rape of the teenage girl and were being held in the police commissioner's jail.

By dawn, an agitated crowd of more than a thousand—some estimates had it as high as ten thousand—stormed the jail. The police commissioner refused to use firearms to stop them, and the lynch mob dragged three men—three black circus workers—out into the street.

What happened next occurred just two blocks from the home of then–nine-year-old Abraham Zimmerman, who would become Bob Dylan's father. It was an atrocity, a nightmarish American-style pogrom that would haunt Abraham and his son Robert, born twenty-one years later.

No one could have known the full dismaying political context beginning to unfold back in 1920, but it was one of the first outbreaks of what became known as the Second Ku Klux Klan, the movement that raged in the early 1920s in the North as well as the South and came to exercise great political power, particularly in the Democratic Party.

For the Zimmerman family, the memory of the lynching was a nightmarish shadow that hung over their assimilated all-American small-town reality—the sense that, beneath the surface of the American landscape, this sort of savagery burned like one of those inextinguishable hundred-year-old coal fires that smoldered beneath the surface of abandoned mining towns.

Nor should it be forgotten—few Jews did—that a young Jewish man, Leo Frank, had been lynched several years earlier in Atlanta. Jews had not escaped the Old World hate.

This was the dystopian American landscape that Bob Dylan seemed to have internalized. The subterranean delegitimization of all-American propriety. How do we know it affected him, that horrific story? One way we know is that some twenty-four years *after* he was born, he gave the first public performance of "Desolation Row," one of his two or three greatest songs, that surreal, absurdist funeral procession for Western culture, his "Waste Land." "Desolation Row" is—though it is not often or ever referred to as—a lynching ballad.

The song begins with an image of a lynching: "They're selling post-cards of the hanging." The line refers to the revolting habit of KKK lynch-mob partisans taking photographs of their evil handiwork—Black men hanging broken-necked from tree limbs and lampposts—and turning the photographs into postcards for sale at the bait-and-tackle shops of the lower Mississippi.

I once saw one of those postcards as the YouTube title card for "Desolation Row" (it's been since taken down). If you take a look at the expressions on the row of dead men's faces, there's your "desolation row" for you. That first line, whether or not anyone at the Forest Hills concert knew it—Dylan knew it—was about lynching. Every word, every line that follows bears the weight of those bodies, gravity bending the tree limbs they were hanging from.

What is it about lynching, as opposed to other forms of homicide? Is it that it's an evil so personal—so face-to-face, placing the rope around the neck? Or is it that the true "wickedness" (the formal philosophical term for *knowing* evil) is somehow more floridly disclosed by the practice of postcarding it? As Satan puts it in *Paradise Lost*, "Evil be my good." They made postcards of the lynching in Duluth that night, proud of their deed, and I've seen one online and it's sickening. I also came upon a quote eighty years later that discussed the representation—and profit-making—aspect of it. Richard Lacayo, writing for *Time* magazine, noted in 2000:

> Even the Nazis did not stoop to selling souvenirs
> of Auschwitz, but lynching scenes became a
> burgeoning subdepartment of the postcard industry.
> By 1908, the trade had grown so large, and the
> practice of sending postcards featuring the victims
> of mob murderers had become so repugnant, that
> the U.S. Postmaster General banned the cards from
> the mails [which, of course, did not disrupt their
> lively retail trade].

And mirabile dictu, lynching is still with us in the twenty-first century, in digital forms of lynching postcards. In early January 2018, almost a century after that Duluth lynching, this item appeared on Twitter from the aptly named Raw Story website: "White girls from Utah stage mock lynching on social media to mark 'national n*gger day.'"

It's even more sickening, isn't it, that they're paying tribute to it. One thing I've found fascinating about Jewish thinking and writing, secular and sacred, is the microscopic attention it gives to the origins and the distinct gradations and degrees of evil.

One hears an echo in the famous Tolstoy line that "happy families are all alike; every unhappy family is unhappy in its own way." Good is unitary; evil is elusively multifarious.

Dylan's four lynching songs—"Desolation Row" and three others I'll discuss below—offer an instance of a particularly Jewish exegesis of evil. He goes at evil from different angles. Or, to use another epithet of a different culture (Dickens's *Our Mutual Friend*), "He do the police in different voices." He does evil in different voices. His were rarely generalized folkie denunciations of evildoers; they were specific and personal.

Dylan has much more to say about the nature of evil than he does about God here. About why evil exists, if it does exist apart from its relation to God.

It's telling that the uncontestably ludicrous low point of Dylan's career—his three years as a Jesus-freak scold—demonstrated what a botch he made of ventriloquizing the voice of God scolding people.

Dylan seems, in his lynching songs, to share some sense of the mystery one finds in those Jewish philosophers descended from Spinoza on evil and on good: one can't exist without the other. Or the antinomian sinners and rogues in touch with dark spirits in I. B. Singer who glimpse God through the shadows of their own sins. At times I feel that the truest analogy in literature to Dylan is Singer: a rascal, a rogue, but someone acquainted with a God in the shadows. If Dylan wasn't like the demon-entangled figures in *The Magician of Lublin* or *Satan in*

Goray, he conjured up Singer's wonder rabbis of the fourteenth century who had been to the heart of everything. No wonder, as we've seen, the affinity of Kabbalah scholar Daniel Matt with Dylan.

Early on, Dylan seemed to want to explore both the unimaginably good and the irredeemably evil. In his lynching songs, he offered a panoply, a spectrum, a hierarchy of evil that seems carefully thought-out and is a feature of his serious later work. But nowhere is this parsing evil more evident than in his four lynching songs. One every year starting when he arrived in New York City in January 1961.

He gives us portraits of the passive spectator, the enabling by-stander, and the actual perpetrator. This is a spectrum that reflects—in a dark mirror—Hannah Arendt when she abandoned her "radical evil" concept to focus on the other end of the spectrum, the so-called "banality of evil."

The beginning of "Desolation Row" ("They're selling postcards of the hanging") may be an early if not the first instance of Dylan exploring the degrees and nuances of evil. Just what was it that distinguished lynching from a merely bad act? This is an abiding question that can be seen to pervade his work. Where does the shadow of ordinary evil fall, and what makes for the extraordinary evil measured against the original sin his father witnessed in person?

"A BOLT FROM THE BLUE"

One could feel in "Desolation Row" the weight of tragedy in the bizarre, surreal, and carnivalesque funeral procession of Western culture—from *Hamlet* to the *Titanic*.

I know. I was there that night, in Forest Hills, when Dylan debuted "Desolation Row." I was there, and it struck me like a "bolt from the blue," to use Mary McCarthy's phrase for her initial reaction to her first reading of Nabokov's *Pale Fire*. When I say "I know," I mean it felt like I'd heard something that had the power to change everything else I'd ever heard. The power to throw everything else into question.

I know I'd never heard anything like it. In my brief life thus far, I'd listened to the corny pop music of the 1950s and I'd listened to early rock and roll with almost illicit-seeming excitement as it came crackling with static over the air from Alan Freed in Cleveland and Murray the K in New York. (Murray the K, in fact, introduced Dylan at this Forest Hills concert.) I'd also listened to folk music—Pete Seeger, the Weavers, and the like—supplied by the fellow-traveler ex-communists in my suburban hometown. They'd even tried to introduce me to Dylan; I first heard him sing on the TV broadcast of Martin Luther King Jr.'s DC March "for jobs and freedom" in their living room. Heard Dylan's shockingly raspy, unfriendly-to-the-ear, but somehow liberating voice, that rasp that cuts open prison bars. But even after he'd become a star with "Blowin' in the Wind," the version he wrote for Peter, Paul and Mary that was an international smash, I had never heard *this* Dylan, the "Desolation Row" Dylan.

I would venture to say that this song, "Desolation Row," was, more than any other, responsible for Dylan getting the Nobel Prize in Literature. Some might disagree and say it wasn't the very peak of his work, but it could be said to be the most literary of his major works, including the slightly cringe-making sophomoric line "Ezra Pound and T. S. Eliot fighting in the captain's tower / while calypso singers laugh at them and fishermen hold flowers."

It was like reading Kafka, Borges, or Calvino for the first time.

I thought I knew Dylan, but this was unlike the Dylan I thought I knew. It's often forgotten now, the radical newness one can hear in "Desolation Row"—the strange realm, the ghastly surreal parade he conjured up, wreathed with the eerily soothing yet subtextually threatening muted mariachi-like musical undergrowth. I had that sense, a dreadful sense, of "exploring the unimaginable"—a line someone says in Errol Morris's haunting *Hamlet*-obsessed *Wormwood*.

Part of the attraction of Dylan (for men, anyway) has always been the desire to *be* Dylan for just one moment. One moment at the peak of joining him in song, the way one joins *him*, becomes him, assumes all that black-clad sneer of a persona that is or was the essence of cool.

Dylan as Hamlet, yes. The younger Hamlet of the so-called Bad Quarto, bequeathed to us by the brilliant scholar Terri Bourus. The younger Hamlet of the First Quarto, or, as I called it in an essay in *The Chronicle of Higher Education*, the "Badass Quarto." One of the things that undoubtedly, initially, made Dylan so magnetic to so many was the majesty of his sneer and the daring of his defiance of conventional pieties. He knows "something is rotten" from the get-go.

How new was whatever it was Dylan was doing? Or how old?

Old in the sense it was more like the seductive complexities and strangeness of the early-seventeenth-century metaphysical poetry, which had come to be my focus in my literature classes at Yale. (In fact, when—on a postgraduate fellowship in Yale graduate school—I'd taught an undergraduate literature seminar at Yale, I sought to get my students to see the similarities between Dylan's farewell songs and Donne's "A Valediction: Forbidding Mourning.")

But nobody had done Donne for four centuries. I have always thought that Dylan achieved something Eliot felt had been missing from poetry in English since the time of Donne and the metaphysicals: he had repaired the rift in the "dissociation of sensibility" between the abstract concept and its carnal embodiment.

New or old, this was something one didn't hear in popular music, in rock, in folk. Rarely in contemporary poetry. What was it? The Swedish Academy had a word for it: literature.

You might call "Desolation Row" the signature song of the literary Dylan, as opposed to the liberatory Dylan of, say, "Hey, Mr. Tambourine Man," a call to follow a pied piper on a quest for an escape from the ordinary. The literary Dylan in "Desolation Row" is a Dantesque excavation of the Hell beneath the ordinary:

They're sellin' postcards of the hanging
They're painting the passports brown

It was as if there had been a macabre reunion of the figures from the 1920 lynching: the circus worker and the police commissioner, blind to the horror his trance of inaction was permitting. The tightrope(s) from which the murdered men hung. (A clever touch, the tight ropes around the necks of the victims of the lynchings resurfacing in the tightrope walker, as if the word "tightrope" became unmoored from its context.) A bitter coven summoned by the song's trancelike séance. And it is not without significance, I think, that when Dylan first came to New York City in 1961 and created his train-hopping hobo/Guthriesque persona for himself, he would almost invariably say that every year back home he joined some traveling circus.

It was a nightmarish return of the repressed. The song recalls the Nighttown episode of *Ulysses*, hovering ominously between this world and the underworld to which so many of its characters from literature and culture have been consigned.

THE DYLAN EXPERIENCE

Another Dylan song had its performance debut that night in Forest Hills, a more famous one, instantly recognizable: "Like a Rolling Stone." It was more widely celebrated for its newness yet was not really as new as "Desolation Row." It was closer, in a way, to the Stones' "19th Nervous Breakdown," the put-down of a party girl (raised to extraordinary heights of ecstatic schadenfreude, of course, but not as strange a surreal landscape as "Desolation Row").

It's true, in a sense, that "Like a Rolling Stone" could be said to be more central to the Dylan *experience*—the life experience of his listeners—something that should not be discounted. By "the Dylan experience," I mean the exhilarating feeling one had in the shotgun seat of a fast car driven by a fast girl, punching the radio buttons and coming upon "Rolling Stone" and shouting the chorus—"How does it *feel*? How does it *feel*?" madly into the oncoming traffic. An ecstatic ode to introspection, not your ordinary moon/June American Songbook blah-blah. "How does it feel?" The signature Dylan question.

I remember visiting the great litterateur Christopher Ricks, Oxford professor of poetry and the biographer of Keats and the young T. S. Eliot, when Ricks was a visiting lecturer at Boston University; I listened to his exegesis of the scansion of "The Lonesome Death of Hattie Carroll" (his party piece, I later learned—something he used to intimidate nonversification-savvy rock critics). And then he took me to his Dylan room, which was packed with bootlegs and where he summoned up variant versions of the great songs. And I thought, yes, this man knows more about Dylan than I'll probably ever know— he's the world's most erudite Dylanologist. And yet he had not had the exhilarating Dylan experience. I wonder how many have or do these days.

And I wonder whether it is a mostly male phenomenon. I know— and elaborated in my discussion of Dylan and second-wave feminism— that there are quite a number of superbly intelligent women who have become heartfelt Dylan fans long after the first gush of motorcycle-black-leather-jackets-and-shades Dylan of the early album cover. Long after the photo of Dylan and first girlfriend, Suze Rutolo, arm in arm in the snow of the Village radiating love.

I found myself fascinated when I asked one of these later-generation women, Catherine Nichols, a feminist essayist and contemporary Dylan fan, what the attraction was for a woman and received a remarkably thoughtful, eloquent answer not just about women but about men, too: "Well—you know there's a big part of my psyche that believes I am the Bob Dylan of my own life, whatever I'm doing. Not that I have his same talents, but the way that his center of balance is always right in the middle of himself. He may fall in love, but he never loses himself in love. I don't lose myself either." There's an echo here of Ellen Willis, the first female rock critic (for *The Village Voice* and *The New Yorker*), who wrote complex and sensitive essays about Dylan and women.

When I asked Nichols to expand on this, she spoke of the way she finds Dylan so radically "present" in his voice, so uniquely truthful, a gateway to that feeling that was beyond male and female. For so many men and women, it was/is something about the voice, something about where it came from inside of him that made it "magnetic." It drew at least some impassioned adherents to him.

But it was not always an unmixed or ungendered feeling.

I got the sense she was saying that women—so used to lies and masks and guises from men—found, in Dylan, one who was emotionally naked and truthful:

> So—yes, I do have that feeling. But I also know that he's not always a friendly place for chicks, and I think a lot of the women in my gen. that DON'T connect with him feel that way because the whole Dylan-world landscape is often a place where a woman won't feel like a full citizen, she'll feel like she's there on a temporary visa, as long as she's cute. I know there are counterexample songs, I'm just explaining why, but when I wrote an essay about Dylan, most of my mentions are from men.
>
> But you know my dad's theory of Dylan was that many boys of that generation were profoundly alienated from their own feelings, and Dylan gave them a way of talking about and experiencing emotion that was also masculine. Not WWII PTSD, John Wayne, Strong Silent Type, but a true alternative to that. That's what he observed among his friends anyway.

This helps to explain the magnetism: Dylan drew out the men's true emotional selves, their own "radical presentness" (to use his daughter's phrase), which once drawn were never really withdrawn.

If you go to Dylan concerts, people still want that communal thrill he offers. This is evident in his worldwide Never Ending Tour, which has taken him from the Balkans to Auckland and many large and small nations in between. Not long ago I was sitting next to a fellow in Starbucks who saw I was reading a Dylan book; he told me the people of his country were big Dylan fans. The country? Ecuador. He said he was surprised when he came to America and discovered that "Dylan was bigger in Ecuador than he was here."

One could mention, too, the Turkish radio station where two philosophy professors do nothing but discuss Dylan all day long.

THE UNSUNG LYNCHING SONG

Desolation Row" wasn't Dylan's first lynching song; there was an earlier "lost" lynching song, one that he recorded on a demo tape (*The Witmark Demos*) for a music publisher in the summer of 1962, just a few months after he arrived in New York.

It was called "The Death of Emmett Till," and for some reason—perhaps because the atrocity that gave rise to it was so searing—Dylan never sang that song again. Why? Why never? I have a theory about Dylan and lynching and what was revealed in his four lynching songs.

"The Death of Emmett Till" was followed by "Only a Pawn in Their Game," about the murder of Medgar Evers in 1963, a song written in the voice of the murderer in what *seems* like an Eichmann defense of the perpetrator, akin to Hannah Arendt's contemporaneous, misguided "banality of evil" argument that the "little men" who facilitated the crime of genocide were "only following orders." They did not have the feral racist animus of their superiors (though, contra Arendt, this was untrue of Eichmann, who memorably boasted he would go to his grave happily knowing he had sent five million Jews to theirs).

Dylan seems aware of the discourse over the enablers of the Holocaust—to the point of *possibly* satirizing that position in "Only a Pawn in Their Game" and robbing the perpetrator of moral agency. The fact that the Medgar Evers song can be taken both ways—as a reprise of the standard defense of the "banality of evil" and as a critique of that defense—makes it more than a folkie lament but rather a sophisticated work of art.

Then, in 1964, came the penultimate lynching song, "The Lonesome Death of Hattie Carroll," about a hotel maid beaten to death with a cane by a wealthy patron. A lament followed by 1965's "Desolation Row." And for all the ambiguities, Christopher Ricks's scansion could not deepen "Hattie Carroll," which rang out unambiguously like a prosecutor's death penalty jury summation.

(I should mention that I categorize Dylan's songs about the racist murder of Black people as lynching songs, though "lynching" is more commonly confined to cases in which the murder was committed by a collective mind: it was a mob and a rope. Dylan seems to be arguing in his lyrics that all racist murders are the work of a mob—namely, the white supremacist oligarchy.)

But that first one, the nearly lost one, the Emmett Till song, was his most raw, unpolished, even revealing evocation of the crime. Perhaps, you might say, it was the linchpin between that night in 1920 and "Desolation Row" and everything that came after it.

If "Like a Rolling Stone" was truer to his listeners' experience, "Emmett Till" might be truer to Dylan's inner experience and to the quest that runs through his work, the attempt to imagine, to explore, the "unimaginable" level of evil or love. Truer to the question raised by that first lynching long ago: What—metaphorically—was "the screaming" inside Dylan?

(It's hard not to allude to the line in the Dylan Thomas poem about the death of a child by fire in the London Blitz: "After the first death, there is no other.")

We have only heard Dylan sing the lost lynching song because of the demo tape that was rediscovered in 2007 and released as one of Dylan's "official bootleg" series.

Why would he never perform it again after that one recording? Does it have something to do with the fact that Emmett Till was murdered in 1956 when he was about the same age as Dylan?

Emmett Till was a Black teenager from Chicago visiting relatives in Mississippi. He was accused of the "crime" of whistling at a white woman (apparently without any truth to it, however little that mattered). This is how Dylan describes what happened to Till:

> They tortured him and did some things too evil to repeat
> There were screaming sounds inside the barn, there was
> laughing sounds out on the street

The primal terror in these lines is one he tries to feel, though he knows he can't. He's outside the barn. But in that image, "There were screaming sounds inside the barn," he tells us more than we want to know.

There are "things too evil to repeat." What is the difference between an evil deed and a deed too evil to repeat? Dylan is implicitly asking us to make fine-tuned philosophical distinctions, such as the academic moral distinctions philosophers make between ordinary evil and wickedness and between wickedness and the ne plus ultra of malignant wickedness— wickedness for the sake of being wicked. Evil for the sake of evil.

Highlighting the difference between an evil deed and an evil person reflects Dylan's conflicted insider-outsider sense of the evil things in the song. The onlooker persona in the song has heard tell of them but can't repeat them, so evil are they, thus conjuring up our worst unimaginable visions of the proceedings—not merely unspeakable but unimaginable.

The person narrating "Emmett Till" is like the Polish neighbors who stood by while the Jews in their town were burned alive in their church. The Poles were not direct participants but inculpated observers. They let the Jews burn.

In the song, the closest Dylan can get to the unimaginable is outside of the barn: the narrator is outside of the barn but is perhaps passively complicit in the evil deeds inside.

It's in his next lynching song, his response to the murder of Medgar Evers, "Only a Pawn in Their Game," where he seeks to go inside the head of the murderer. It's a daring move—and a controversial one.

In each song, the question of complicity is raised. His own father was, after all, a passive observer of a lynching. Is the bystander outside the barn complicit in his passivity? Is the murderer of Medgar Evers "just following orders," exhibiting the "banality of evil," not thinking he is doing evil at all?

Dylan's Medgar Evers song does seem to suggest on the face of it that he buys into the Eichmann defense of the killer, the one that Arendt offered in her infamous "Eichmann in Jerusalem" essay, which misleadingly portrayed that feral genocidaire as a mere bureaucratic tool or cog in the wheels of the Holocaust machine (and which abandoned her earlier conception of what she called "radical evil"—knowing, willing evil, not automaton-like obedience to higher-up evil).

It is notable that so much of Jewish philosophical speculation is less about the nature of God and good than about evil and its enablers, its varieties. There is a difference between passive evil—the farmhand listening to what is going on inside the barn—and the perpetrators of the lynching inside the barn doing the deeds "too evil to repeat." What makes a deed "too evil to repeat"? Is it in the nature of the deed or the nature of the repetition? Or in the nature of the perpetrator?

Dylan seems alive to these questions, which are shared not only with Jewish philosophers but also with those of other faiths seeking to distinguish ordinary evil deeds from conscious evil.

Evil isn't just one thing in Jewish philosophical discourse but a panoply, a spectrum, a gradient. One whose peak is the endpoint: evil deeds too evil to be repeated because repeating in some way replicates the actual deed.

"Only a Pawn in Their Game" is the first instance of what I suggest is a far deeper engagement of Dylan with Holocaust discourse in his own way, whereby the Holocaust and those who collaborated in it had been almost forcibly forgotten for the first twenty years of his life. It existed only as "screaming sounds inside the barn," you might say, encapsulated from public discourse, set off in a separate part of the cortex, at least in America. Inside the barn? Inside him?

The more I thought about the "Pawn in the Game" defense of Medgar Evers's murder, the more it seemed that in fact Dylan was *not* buying into the Eichmann defense. He was *presenting* what passed for a sophisticated account of it, but ultimately he was satirizing through mimicking it. Or perhaps, as will become a subtext of his songwriting, he was entertaining *both* contradictory reactions at once. As F. Scott Fitzgerald, defining Keats's "negative capability," put it: "The test of a first-rate intelligence is the ability to hold two opposed ideas in the mind at the same time, and still retain the ability to function." Or as Keats originally pleaded: No "irritable" reaching for certainty, please.

Like both Fitzgerald and Keats, Dylan expresses his inability to imagine (fully) the unimaginable. He's outside, not inside, the barn; outside, not inside, the murderer's brain. He knows what the "evil deeds" are, but he can't utter a description of them. To do so would be to amplify the evil, presumably. Better to highlight the difficulty of representation of evil, its indescribability, unspeakability, unimaginability. Why his generation kept quiet about the Holocaust—until the Eichmann trial—is where words fail.

The year before Emmett Till's lynching, 1955, saw the Montgomery, Alabama, bus boycott sparked by Rosa Parks's refusal to be segregated, and the year before that, 1954, saw the US Supreme Court desegregation decision. Suddenly, race was on the front pages and the norms of racial justice were changing, not without violent opposition. When Dylan went down to Mississippi in the summer of 1963, it was in the wake of Medgar Evers's murder in his hometown, the response to his successful activism. To go down to the part of Mississippi that lynched Emmett Till and murdered Medgar Evers suggests that Dylan's commitment to civil rights causes was not merely a bien-pensant gesture. It was, in some way, *personal* to him.

Look at the photos of Dylan in Mississippi, playing his guitar for the Black activists and the sharecroppers they were trying to register to vote—virtually under the gun of the Klan who not only murdered Medgar Evers but would, the following summer, murder three civil rights workers—Goodman, Cheney, and Schwerner—volunteers from New York City who were kidnapped, beaten, and buried in a dam.

Yet at the time Dylan wrote and recorded and curiously left behind that song, "The Death of Emmett Till," there was a kind of turning point. Historically, the 1956 lynching of Emmett Till and what was done to him in that barn that made him scream was a kind of pivot point in America's self-awareness, an act of revealing unveiling. It was an unforgetting of the post–Civil War racist Jim Crow regime in the South because Till's mother demanded an open coffin "so people can see what they did to my boy."

A photo of Till's horribly disfigured face and head, bashed in beyond recognition, was published by the Chicago Black press, and eventually the horror came to the attention of the nation as a whole. That picture has been credited with a turnaround in the passive acceptance of lynching as not just another crime but specifically as a civil rights atrocity, a betrayal of the millions who died in the Civil War to right these wrongs. Perhaps Dylan never felt he was equal to the depiction of evil in that photo.

Dylan concedes implicitly that he lacks the moral fortitude to do what Till's mother has done or the empathetic ability to respond to it with the screams it deserves.

Once I'd rediscovered the song, I found myself fixated on those words, "There were screaming sounds inside the barn." Dylan had expressed the unimaginable in a way that did justice to the scale of the horror and yet did not pretend he could ever reach an empathetic communion with the youth being tortured and mutilated in it.

It is almost an instance of *tact*—sparing Till's mother from another repetition of this primal horror, refusing to make her think about the extinguishing of her son's life. She did not need a reprise. We did—everything was personal with Dylan.

But there's more to it, I believe. To think about lynching, the extinguishing of life at the end of a rope, is to think not just of that brutally mutilated man but also of the crowd, the strangely blank expressions on the faces of the lynch mob and witnesses in the "postcards of the hanging."

And the horror that precedes it is a reminder we are all hanging an instant away from extinction. Or so it seemed when Dylan wrote this song and his several nuclear war songs. We are all subject to a kind of unimaginable horror: the horror of nuclear extinction, the horror of another genocidal eruption. As a youth, Dylan's world was saturated with horror. After the first lynching, there is no other.

No wonder the image of screaming inside the barn resonates. Think of it as a self-image of Dylan's psyche: the barn being the flimsy permeable structure of his psyche barely able to contain the horror within. There is more to Dylan, of course. But there will always be the echo—the screaming inside the barn—and Dylan's role in the great unforgetting of the racist murders, the great unforgetting of the Holocaust in the immediate postwar era.

One could almost see Dylan's construction—some screaming came from inside the barn—as way of describing his own awakening and that of his generation of Jews. What was the screaming inside the barn for generation zero if it was not screaming within about the evil deeds that had been done to his people and that had been muted for reasons he was no longer going to put up with?

Dylan's lynching preoccupation helps explain at least one of the mysteries that have perplexed observers. One such mystery is how he avoided any identification in reality with the antiwar movement and yet it was *assumed* by the millions marching in the streets in the 1960s and 1970s that he was not only one with them, he was their prophet. After all, Dylan once said, much later, with a sardonic sense of humor, "I own the sixties. Does anyone want to buy them from me?"

After all, hadn't he denounced war in general in "Masters of War"? And he certainly wrote varieties of apocalyptic prophecies about nuclear war.

And yet, Vietnam. I've never seen a single interview in which he didn't mumble and avoid any commitment one way or another.

This is particularly fascinating because the sharpest minds and most radical postulants of the antiwar movement *named* themselves after a line in a Dylan song. The so-called Weatherman faction of a radical student group (SDS) took its title from Dylan's "Subterranean Homesick Blues," in which he rapped, "You don't need a weatherman to know which way the wind blows."

Members of the faction not only named themselves but *renamed themselves*, reversing their ideology of violence. A few months after they blew themselves up, killing two of their inner circle while trying to build bombs in a Greenwich Village townhouse, they issued a pamphlet called "New Morning," named after Dylan's new pastoral album, *New Morning*. In that pamphlet, of which I was at the time an early recipient (and I think I know who wrote it), the Weatherman faction not only changed its name (to the purportedly nonsexist Weather Underground) but also did a radical 180-degree reversal of its ideology and called for a *nonviolent* breathing space in its war against the war.

It was assumed that Dylan was somehow guiding the group. And the rest of the Left meekly followed, mumbling something like "Well, Dylan said . . ."

In fact, I was underground with the Weather Underground the day the US helicopters took off from the roofs of Saigon and the United States surrendered. I had been blindfolded and "kidnapped" with a videocam-equipped journalist for a super-top-secret interview (which appeared on PBS), and, believe me, the Weather Underground was all about the war and believed Dylan was with them. (Maybe he was, secretly, thus the mumbling?)

And then came the *New Morning* album and the "New Morning" pamphlet, and it's like a nonexistent Dylan, a Wizard of Oz (or a Moses), had waved a staff over an entire radical movement and calmed the waters with his authority—or what they thought was his authority.

Dylan himself was nowhere to be found when hundreds of thousands of antiwar youth converged on a scene (Woodstock), which they thought was Dylan's welcoming home to "his" movement, whereas he had jetted away from the whole phenomenon to play at the U.K.'s Isle of Wight Festival where the war was just not an issue.

And the reason: I think Dylan just didn't want to play to everyone's expectations, didn't want to be taken for granted in a knee-jerk way. Just because he was for civil rights and went to Mississippi and sang for Reverend King didn't mean that he agreed with the fractious Vietnam War opponents.

Somehow lynching—the "screaming sounds inside the barn" and the screaming inside himself—made civil rights *personal* to him in a way that, for better or worse, the war wasn't.

CHAPTER 4

"HITLER WAS HISTORY": DYLAN'S ARGUMENT WITH GOD

I am not alone in thinking that Dylan evoked a response on a "whole other level." A mystical level—Daniel Matt's "Gateway." It was my email exchange with Daniel Matt that validated for me the supernatural aura of Dylan's songs—my sense that they were speaking a lyric language on "a whole other level." It was Abe Socher, editor of *The Jewish Review of Books*, who put me in touch with Matt. Socher had asked me to review a biography of Dylan for the first issue of the *Review*. I was probably unduly harsh in writing about it because it represented a trend among Dylanologists (here I use the term I deplore advisedly) of a certain stripe to force Dylan into a strictly Jewish mold, a Jewish procrustean bed, to look at everything he's done through the lens of Jewishness. To make him seem like a nice Jewish boy. Norman Mailer wrote of this problem, and of course Philip Roth did, too.

Yes, certainly Dylan's father had gone to the length of paying for a Brooklyn rabbi to come to Hibbing and live under the northern lights for a year there, just to give his son, Robert Zimmerman, his bar mitzvah lessons. Yes, Dylan had become, briefly (in the 1970s), interested in Zionism under the tutelage of a wild-eyed Israeli (I once met him) known as One-Legged Terry. And, indeed, recent stories have him returning to the faith through the medium of a Chabad sect often referred to (mostly affectionately) by other Jews as "the hippies of Hasidism."

But of course he had also changed his name—and, it must be said, whether or not it was a motive, it cannot be denied that this change effaced one key aspect of his Jewishness. It is often forgotten that, in the early 1960s, it was still the practice of many Jewish artists who wanted a mainstream national audience to change their names to something "less Jewish." One can still find examples today (Jon Stewart was Jon Liebowitz). I know that when I first began getting bylines, my father made a point of telling me he was gratified I had not changed my name. The name change remains a cultural marker in the course of Jewish assimilation—and one of the persistent stumbling blocks to those who seek to undermine Dylan's pretense to authenticity. He still gives evidence of being sensitive to the matter, never (as far as I've seen) accepting the widely held view that he changed it in a kind of tribute to Dylan Thomas.

And then there was the satirical mockery of the foundational story of the Jewish faith, the story of Abraham and his willingness to sacrifice his child, Isaac. Dylan famously reframed it this way (to the tune of a carnivalesque kazoo) in "Highway 61": "God said to Abraham, 'Kill me a son' / Abe says, 'Man, you must be puttin' me on.'" It was the 1960s, and nobody took it too seriously, but in retrospect, in the context of what I will characterize as Dylan's argument with God— an argument over theodicy, the problem of evil, and the source of his "crazy sorrow"—too little attention has been paid to this radical rethink of that story. Even Lord Buckley, the predecessor to Lenny Bruce and Dylan and responsible for the amazing riff on Jesus called "The Naz," went pretty far but never that far.

Like the best satire, this sort of mockery really makes one reconsider that which has been taken for granted or not taken seriously enough by anyone since Kierkegaard in *Fear and Trembling*. Even Kierkegaard could not defend it on rational grounds; he argued that it could only be defended by an "absurd," irrational "leap of faith."

It seems reductive to me to look at Dylan solely through the lens of his Jewishness, as Rogovoy did, even straining to interpret Dylan's conversion to Christianity as a very Jewish thing to do. As the great litterateur George Steiner has pointed out in an essay called "Why the Jews Rejected Jesus," not becoming a Jesus person is one of the few things that irrevocably defines Jews. Steiner calls Jews "children of Eve" because of their curiosity: they wouldn't stop searching for the Divine. Dylan was indeed a singular child of Eve.

In any case, I found myself fed up with all the knee-jerk Judaizing of Dylan. I had been reading about the period before Dylan's conversion to born-again Christianity, and I had come upon two interviews from about that time in which the interviewers were virtually *hounding* Dylan into admitting his Jewish influences. Poor Dylan, you can imagine him squirming and trying to listen politely as the erudite Jonathan Cott pelted him with long, tedious (to me, anyway), and less-than-top-notch Hasidic tales and then asked Dylan whether they "explained" his work.

And then the Australian writer Craig MacGregor, in a less learned way, drove Dylan to speculate that his grandmother had been raped by Cossacks in Odessa and his resultant un-Jewish blue eyes proved he was only *part* Jewish genetically. As if that were the preferred attribute.

It was all particularly galling or guilt-inducing because I, too, had begun my grilled cheese lunch-counter conversation about God with Dylan—the one in which he told me about the magnetic fields—by asking him if he "felt Jewish." It wasn't my *first* question; it was on the last day of a full week talking to him. I will get to his extraordinary reply to me about his view of God at the time, just before he succumbed to the Jesus freaks who took advantage of the unholy pressures in his life.

Looking back, I still feel somewhat guilty about perhaps having started Dylan down the path that would have him end up a born-again convert—the only way he could escape being *hondled* (wonderful Yiddish term for "hassled") by those trying to cram him into a box the size of a mezuzah. The only way he could escape the relentless Judaizing was to become a Christian.

Daniel Matt's work on the translation of and commentary on the *Zohar* is another intersection, I believe, with Dylan. Now, so many excessive things have been said about the mystical power of the *Zohar*—a collection of visions and platonic dialogues and philosophic explanations—that I had tended to be suspicious of the way it had become a go-to mystical text that answered all your questions (if you're Madonna, for instance).

But, as I was working on this chapter, I came upon a U.K. *Times Literary Supplement* review of Matt's ninth volume by Jeremy Adler. The review was a tribute to Matt; Adler makes the case that the *Zohar* must be incorporated into the sacred circle of mystical texts that mediate between God and man. In fact, there may be a light—"a dark flame"—within the *Zohar* that exceeds in its innerness the Bible itself, even quantum physics. The modern big bang theory seems to be anticipated in the *Zohar*'s creation myth: the dark flame issues from the interior of the inner light.

Indeed, if you were to seek an analogy to later Dylan's esoteric lyrics, there is none better than the attribute of quantum physics that Einstein called "spooky action at a distance" and that contemporary quantum adepts often refer to as entanglement. There seem to be so many instances of spooky action at a distance in Dylan lyrics—the relationship between Dylan's recurrently separated lovers, for instance. And of course entanglement in the quantum sense suggests separated lovers and is everywhere, not just in the time shifts of "Tangled Up in Blue." In the fuzzy math of songwriting wherein a connection is felt that transcends logic and causality, a connection is implicit but not fleshed out.

Nonetheless I found myself fascinated by Matt's eagerness to proselytize for Dylan. I had a sense that Dylan struck a chord in him much like the chord he struck in me. There was something eerie, an uncanny something that resonated with a mysticism susceptibility receptor. (I'm fond of neuroscience metaphors, though not the overly deterministic neuroscience worldview itself.)

I have implied that Dylan's born-again conversion was the product of his life circumstances, the divorce, the exhaustion from the doomed movie edit, the guy (me) with the yellow legal pad asking questions about his Jewishness. But I think there's a neuroscience explanation for his vision in the Tucson motel room, the apparition of Jesus that would make this event seem less a studied deception than a kind of lightning strike.

A few years later I found myself talking to a Berkeley neuroscience professor in the lobby of the fabled American Hotel on the Green Line in Jerusalem. (Lawrence of Arabia had been a frequent return guest.) I had been early for an appointment with a Dead Sea Scrolls scholar and was talking about my experience climbing into one of the bat-infested Dead Sea caves out where the Judaean desert meets the Jordan River.

I asked the neuroscientist what brought him there, and he told me that the year before, while attending a conference, he had been out in the pitiless heat of the Judaean desert, and though he had at the time no religious conviction, he had what he called "a direct personal experience of the Presence of God." It was instantaneous, total, and to him irrefutable. Who knows if the desert did this to Dylan in Tucson? I think it's important to allow for the possibility of explaining his conversion as a neurological event rather than the result of some born-again catechism—or, worse, calculation.

So what was it exactly? What made people like Matt and me and millions of others respond to the core and the chords Dylan struck in such a resounding way?

To me it was the mystical spiritual streak in Dylan, one that—as we've seen—was there from his childhood in the magnetic fields, under the northern lights. Not one that was explicitly Jewish, but it could be found in Jewish mysticism and in Sufi mysticism, too. As I write this, I'm listening to a collection of Sufi mystical chants called *Gateway to Heaven* and thinking about Matt telling me he once thought of Dylan as "a gateway to truth and wisdom."

All religions have this mystical aspect, though it's not always mainstream. The phenomenon of speaking in tongues, for instance, suggests it is a form of singing—sounds—without words. Similarly, I—and apparently others—had the feeling that Dylan was channeling not an unknown language but an unknown *syntax* and unknown metaphorical frame of reference that gave unity at some level to the apparently utterly enigmatic lines in his songs. In fact, he told me, before the Jesus freaks stole his soul, that for most of those magical sixteen years when he made his impact on the culture he had written "unconsciously." He didn't have to think up lyrics and stanzas; they came to him. And that he had to learn to write consciously—though I would argue that, at his best, even in the post-Jesus period, there's an unconscious component, an unconscious unity there. I will make the case.

Interesting that Matt felt himself inspired to articulate his ecstatic apprehension of Dylan to Scholem while he was high in the Himalayas, where atmospheric displays and ionic electricity seem to stimulate a similar sense of the spiritual. Attuned to Jewish mysticism, Matt heard a kind of dog whistle in Dylan's songs: one mystical soul signaling to another. Perhaps Matt's was a more Jewish-inflected mysticism than it was for Dylan, at least consciously, though he definitely seemed to be one of the "children of Eve," or those who want knowledge "on a whole other level" through some esoteric gate or gateway.

I could go on—for instance, about the gates in Dylan from song titles like "Gates of Eden" and perhaps the most enigmatic, exegesis-resistant line to be found in the work of an artist who is nothing if not relentlessly enigmatic. I'm speaking of those lines from "Sad Eyed Lady of the Lowlands": "My warehouse eyes my Arabian drums / Should I leave them by your gate." (Is "eyes" a verb here? Enigmatic indeed.)

But those Arabian drums, I hear them now listening to the *Gateway of Heaven* chants. There is an even more direct connection between Dylan and the Whirling Dervishes. It was Dylan, after all, who titled his first and only novel *Tarantula* (though many argue there's a lot of fiction in his autobiography, *Chronicles*). That first book (or non-book), *Tarantula*, left behind an enduring mystery, beginning with the title.

There are no spiders in the book, and it's hard to tell whether it's deliberately obscure. After half a century of argument, I've found only one explanation that makes sense—a connection discovered by Craig S. Karpel, a friend and former colleague, in a self-published pamphlet several decades ago. He pointed out the connection between tarantula the poisonous spider and the tarantella, a wild, crazed, communal dance that afflicted Renaissance Italian farming villages from time to time. The frenzied dance was called the tarantella because its origin was often (mis)attributed to the bite of a poisonous breed of tarantula. Some of the "infected" dancers were unable to stop and danced themselves to death.

Karpel argued that Dylan was referencing the tarantella—"on a whole other level"—really a metaphoric reference to the ecstatic power of music that drove the Dervishes as well. So the title could well be Dylan the autodidact's fascination with the seductive, even deadly power of music. Of course, as we shall see, there is more to *Tarantula* than a communal dance of death.

Elvis had devotees as fanatical—I've spent time with them—but few would make claims that "Viva Las Vegas" was a "gateway to truth" or "penetrated to the core of everything" (and I love both Elvis and Las Vegas). Even Salinger, whose voice—the voice of Holden Caulfield, anyway—had a lasting hold on generation after generation struck what might be called a psychological level of affinity, but not Dylan's kind of mystical metaphysical "gateway to truth and wisdom." A "whole other level" beyond psychology. (When Salinger tried to force-feed mysticism to his readers in his Glass family stories, it never *sung* to the reader the way Dylan's mystical streak did.)

THE CATCHER IN THE WRY

There's more to the Salinger/Dylan connection than you've been told. No Dylan biography I've seen captures the profound effect that Salinger had on the formative stage of the young Dylan, his psyche, his voice. (Voice in the sense of the eye-roll attitude he imbues his lyrics and his listeners with.) I might have missed the Salinger connection as well if it had not been for a lucky find in New York City's legendary Strand Book Store.

The grail, the Rosebud, for anyone writing a biography is the origin story. For Dylan there could be said to be more than one origin story. There are the "projections," the pale visions he saw through the raging snow. There is the subtextual presence of the Shoah. And there is another influence, as we'll see, indirectly derivative of the Shoah. An influence equally neglected. So I will begin with a discovery (or rediscovery) I made late in the process of writing this book: the neglected influence of Jerome David Salinger.

Yes, I know, it lacks the gravitas, the spectral horror of the Shoah. Yet, for Dylan, little else compared with the way Salinger influenced his voice and reflected his attitude toward the world. He said so himself, he told me in person. But few paid attention. It was a sensibility, a mindset that more than anything (more than any single love song or any sad farewell song Dylan created) shaped his impact on American and, indeed, on world culture. It was a mode of speech that left a mark unlike any other. What is "subterranean homesick blues" but a reworking—"on a whole other level"—of *The Catcher in the Rye*?

I think I've made the case earlier in this book that you can't understand Dylan without understanding the rage and grief over the

Shoah, the argument with God that underlies—is the undertow—of the sensibility heard in Dylan's voice. The rage undermines belief in conventionality and drives his subversion of pietistic language. Bridling at propriety.

But the unexpected surprise for me in digging down deeper into Dylan lit was how much he shares this metaphysical disrespect with an artist just a decade older. A disrespect that shares the same source: the horror of the Holocaust. Salinger has recently been revealed as one of the American GIs who liberated Dachau concentration camp and saw the wretched survivors and the crematoria that consumed the rest. He wrote about it only glancingly in two short stories, "For Esmé—with Love and Squalor" and "A Perfect Day for Bananafish"—though it pervades subtextually the rest of his work and especially the odyssey of Holden Caulfield.

I should have seen it earlier. In fact, I should have seen it several times. First when Dylan himself straightforwardly *told me* that he'd been influenced as an adolescent by *The Catcher in the Rye*. That's not a casual influence; it's a lifetime side-eyed eye-roll look askance at the world and its pretensions to propriety sustainable only by turning its back on what happened in 1939–45. Turning every complacent utterance into a potential ironic subversion of itself. So we always have to "think twice" about what we say and what is said to us, kicking the tires for the irony within. I should have seen it when I spent time looking for Salinger's New Hampshire fortress of solitude and suddenly saw how much—how very much—his most celebrated short story "A Perfect Day for Bananafish," whose mystery confounded critics for half a century, could be explained by a wartime nervous breakdown. Salinger's breakdown was one that forever inflected his vision and his voice.

I should have also seen it when, a couple of years after Salinger's death in 2010, writers David Shields and Shane Salerno presented enough evidence to convince even those who objected to their literary reductiveness to make the connection between Salinger's horrific wartime experience and Holden Caulfield's odyssey through Manhattan. What Salinger saw in the war forever imbued him with a black comic view of human nature, one that can be found in his deadpan voice.

Salinger's Holden was a kind of homesick war poet trying to find his way home, akin to the plot of the *Odyssey*. Salinger did, after all, tell his daughter Margaret that never for the rest of his life would he be able to "get the smell of burning flesh" out of his nostrils. Read that sentence again. It is there in his view of the material world and drove him to the far edges of Eastern mysticism in life and to the deadpan inversion of language in his fiction.

I think Dylan heard that voice and was responsive to that sub-textual experience. Not all Midwestern adolescents are responsive in that way when they read *Catcher*. I know that, for me, the Shoah was initially just an abstract number, six million. I know of no family member lost to the flames. Neither did Dylan directly, so far as I've been able to find out. But, as we'll see, six million seemed to hit him with an especially personal force.

Yes, I should have seen it sooner, such as in a remarkable story about Salinger that was lost for a long time, buried in a cheap mass-market paperback I was lucky to unearth deep in the stacks of the Strand Book Store among scores of other Dylan-related titles. This one was called *The Mammoth Book of Bob Dylan* and was assembled by an Aussie Dylanologist who seemed to specialize in little known Dylan lit.

The *Mammoth Book* contains a now-long-forgotten early 1960s essay by Jules Siegel that originally appeared in *The Saturday Evening Post*. His story was given the hipsterish title "Well, What Have We Here?" Arthur Kretchmer (who would, ironically, later become articles editor of *Playboy* and assign me to interview Dylan) is a figure in the story and describes a scene in a Beat/hipster/downtown/Village party sometime around 1965 or 1966:

"There was this crazy reckless little kid [Dylan would have been about twenty] sitting on the floor and coming on very strong about how he was going to play Holden Caulfield in a movie of *The Catcher in the Rye.* And I thought this kid is really terrible, but the people whose party it was said, 'Don't let him put you off, he comes on very strong, but he's very sensitive, writes poetry, visits Woody Guthrie in the hospital' and I figured, 'right, another one.'"

"Right, another one," meaning another Hip poseur?

The story ends with one of the Clancy Brothers, Irish folkies, foundational figures in the Village folk scene, coming upon Dylan and saying "Well, what have we here?"

Siegel captures the "yeah, sure" response Dylan was already evoking (and seemingly hoped to evoke). Put you off, put you on. The foundational Dylan trope, the put-on. It's there in one of his breakthrough songs, "Don't Think Twice, It's All Right." But of course he *wants* her to think twice—he's only putting on indifference. This is what I mean when I argue that Dylan changed the tone of the language we speak, giving everything a second layer of sarcastic meaning that subverts the first.

When I speak of the originality of Dylan's voice and the way it insinuated itself into your consciousness and *your voice*, I think it's fair to consider the theory (my own) that Dylan was echoing on "a whole other level" the tormented voice of Holden Caulfield: deadpan on the surface for both of them, and for both of them a rage—that "screaming inside the barn"—simmering beneath it, subverting every utterance into its opposite. It is Dylan's voice, no doubt, but in a harder, more embittered register than Holden. Nonetheless, in the beginning there was a rage against "phonies" that seemed to be energized by something deeper.

The subject of repressed rage in Jewish artists of all kinds is one I found echoed by some critics attuned to it. Naomi Seidman's "Elie Wiesel and the Scandal of Jewish Rage" in *Jewish Social Studies* in 1996 is a good place to start. And note the archival discovery of Elie Wiesel's early draft of his death-camp memoir, *Night,* in May 2016 shortly before his death; this draft shows him prosecuting God in far more explicit terms than the fudging done previously (see my essay on the new discovery in *Tablet*'s 2016 hard-copy magazine).

Not that Dylan is Wiesel, but it explains a lot. They have a similar quarrel with God.

"HITLER WAS HISTORY"

I want to return to Salinger as a bridge to a greater preoccupation of Dylan's: Adolf Hitler. Here again, it seemed at the time as if it were an instance of happenstance, pure luck that alerted me to perhaps the most salient two-line couplet Dylan ever wrote. It appears in his book *Tarantula* (a demonically difficult work that few can agree on—and that I spent many hours trying to decode, with limited success). This terrifying couplet opened an otherwise gibberish-filled "poem":

> Hitler didn't change history
> Hitler WAS history.
> [caps in original]

This is an utterly stark, sweeping devastation of this embittered cry not just against Hitler but against human nature and human history. And I will argue that it reflects Dylan's rage, not just at the Germans but also at human civilization as nothing but a thin veil covering slaughter. And, finally, it reflects his most heretical rage: against the God who presided over such a relentless record of savage blood and murder. Hitler *was* history! And if there is a God, he was doing Hitler's bidding. Or vice versa.

Dylan was, most likely, only in his mid-twenties when he wrote this. Perhaps it just came and went, that epiphany about Hitler, a lightning flash, a dark flame. But I believe that, as for many Jews of his generation, the timing was important: the Eichmann trial, which began in 1961, was an awakening, an unforgetting. It was the moment when "six million" became a kind of watchword in one of Dylan's songs. I believe that traces of this bitter heresy are the subtext of many of his most heartfelt songs, and they can't be properly understood without reference to Dylan's argument with God.

Whereas Salinger had inhaled the smell of burned flesh from the still-smoking bodies at Dachau's crematorium, it could be said that Dylan inhaled "the secondhand smoke"—a phrase used by my friend (unrelated) Thane Rosenbaum, himself a second-generation descendant of Holocaust survivors. If one thinks, as I do, that victims of the Shoah were one extended family once awakened to what happened, it's impossible not to feel a relationship—and a rage—about their fate. How one reacts to it is not always predictable. Nor does one have to be Jewish. The German writer W. G. Sebald, referring to the Holocaust in deliberately provocative hyperbolic terms, wrote, "No serious person thinks about anything else."

Yet growing up (as I did, too) in a mostly non-Jewish small town in the 1950s, Dylan's awareness might have come from reports of distant relatives' fates. More likely, he might have had relatives from the Pale. (Recall that bad-taste joke about his blue eyes being the product of his grandmother being raped by Cossacks.) Clearly he had not "processed" the trauma of being Jewish in a non-Jewish world that slaughtered half his people. And so he hid behind his eyes and his name change. He would ultimately decide that renouncing his religion of birth completely and accepting a supersessionist theology—Christianity was the necessary logical step that superseded the Hebraic faith.

I never felt that way; I was (perhaps deliberately, I don't know) kept in the dark, or perhaps I was less sensitive, didn't embody the dead the way Dylan's imaginative consciousness might have. I had no faith to abandon. And then I wrote a five-hundred-page book about Hitler that left it further behind. Yes, there was a generalized awareness in my town of the totemic six million, but the incomprehensibility of the number had an abstracting, distancing effect. It was perhaps only in 1961 and 1962 when Dylan came of age as a songwriter that I (and perhaps he) had what might be called a post–bar mitzvah lesson: the sudden apparition of the Eichmann trial and the man in the glass box on TV. The box in the box that could not contain but did help make plain the face of evil.

There is an echo of the Eichmann debate in one of Dylan's early protest songs, his unconventionally oblique take on the murderer of Medgar Evers in the song called "Only a Pawn in Their Game." Instead of directing his wrath at the killer of Evers, the Mississippi civil rights leader, Dylan focused it on the "Eichmanns" of the lynching South, those who gave the orders to the hands-on murderers, who were "only a pawn in their game." Some saw it as exculpating the murderer, but no, he was just pointing at the true source of evil on a "whole other level." Or was he satirizing the argument that those who gave the orders are more culpable than those who carried them out?

Indeed, this question of the origin of evil seems to be an early preoccupation of Dylan's, because you hear the structurally very similar shift to whole other levels in his angry, insistent "Who Killed Davey Moore?" The boxer, battered to death in the ring, is examined forensically and metaphysically as Dylan's barrage-of-punches verses run up the ladder from the bloody ring to the blood money behind it all. All the while asking, "Why, what's the reason for?" That's the unanswered question in so many of these songs, the question at the heart of his work: Why, what's the reason for? What was God doing when this evil was transpiring? What purpose did it serve?

Salinger reacted to the Dachau crematoria by fleeing into a depersonalized mysticism, a nonpersonal God, a cosmic deadpan. Dylan reacted—and so much can be understood about him from recognizing this—by taking it *personally*. By reacting with defiant rage, at least at first. You can hear it in the Holocaust verse in "With God on Our Side," where he rages at the way "we forgave the Germans" after World War II, after the Holocaust, even though

They murdered six million
In the ovens they fried

The Germans now too
Have God on their side.

You could argue that he's talking about the *misuse* of God. But it's impossible not to feel he's also talking about God's misuse of humans, if there is a God. Who looked on passively while his children "fried."

Fried—it's such an ugly term, and it has attracted detractors. One critic, Craig MacGregor, found it offensive and berates Dylan for its savagery. I felt that way, too, for a long time, until I saw it from a different angle. I saw that it comes from the same bleak anger, the same black-humored muse that "Hitler WAS history" emerged from. The smell of burned flesh—on some whole other level—always in his odes. (It's no accident, perhaps, that Hattie Carroll emptied "ashes" on "a whole other level." We can imagine what ashes are being referenced.)

Fried. Horrible, barbaric, cruel intensifier: "fried." Not poetic, at least not traditionally poetic if poetry is always about finding the beautiful or allusive phrase. Unless one thinks of the concept of "conspicuous irrelevance," which I picked up from the New Critics at Yale and have often found valuable in understanding an apparent anomaly in poetry—or song or prose, for that matter—where a deliberately jarring, seemingly out-of-place word or line is designed to make one stop and see things, reconsider things, even terrible things, afresh. Clearly designed to evoke "the stench of burned flesh" in all its nakedly fried ugliness. In a way that makes other descriptors mere euphemisms. In a way that could not be ignored.

Such a provocation returns you to the realization of how raw, how buzz saw-like Dylan's voice—and his words—could be when he came on the scene. We've made mental adjustments for it but—like Holden Caulfield's voice—it was something that cut through the white noise of the culture with a kind of lightning, crackling, electrifying dissonance. Though of course they come from different context, modes, and genres, Dylan's voice makes Holden's look like the adolescent, immature (however romantic and appealing) version of his.

There's something about the voice, its ironic tone that comes through even on the page, the edge of irony one hears in the voice on the stage, the voice that is both pleading and declamatory, serious and tongue-in-cheek seductive.

More of a shakeup than Elvis. Only Little Richard, one of Dylan's early rock-and-roll idols, had a voice so otherworldly *strange* that *its* "conspicuous irrelevance" made you think twice about what was what. ("Don't think twice, it's all right" means, of course, the ironic opposite of what it says.)

The first time I heard Dylan's voice was on the TV broadcast of his appearance at the March on Washington in 1963. It really *rasped* in a way I found distinctly unpleasant at first. There was a kind of untamed wildness to it that you rarely heard on TV, rarely heard in popular culture before. I remember he sang "When the Ship Comes In," which is still one of his best apocalyptic jeremiad-like warnings, and it had an edge I hadn't heard in music—indeed, in anything—before.

In my small-town suburbia, there was a nest of, let's say, *very* left-wing types, if not party members: "fellow travelers." It was after the early Cold War Smith Act prosecutions, which caused the entire party to go underground, formally dissolve. Many urban fellow travelers moved to the suburbs, the new suburbs where they applied old-world skills like watchmaking to survive. But they remained true to the party and its culture. From one family in particular, jewelers, I was introduced to the Weavers, Pete Seeger, *I. F. Stone's Weekly*, various newsletters, eventually Joan Baez—and, through her, Bob Dylan. I listened to her album of Dylan covers, the one that includes the superb heartbreaking songs "One Too Many Mornings" and "Boots of Spanish Leather," but I hadn't heard *his* voice until the March on Washington.

He was an un-American in the narrow definition of the House Un-American Activities Committee. His voice was a rasp like the sound of rust on rust ones hears in prison escape movies when the inmates are cutting through the bars; it was a break-out-to-freedom rasp.

I don't bring up the HUAC casually; indeed, when HUAC's minions came to our town, summoned by local members of the John Birch Society, I stood up in my high school auditorium alone and sought to discredit the propaganda film HUAC was showing, *Operation Abolition*.

Later I would learn that Dylan had come to be embraced by fellow travelers in their homes, and it was they who made him a folkie. Although he told me that it was first listening to Odetta that had done it.

It's sometimes amusing: no one would argue that Odetta's voice isn't beautiful, but its power might be lost on those who lack the receptor to the right chord. Like David in the Bible, Dylan was always finding the lost chord. People went into a frenzy when Dylan traded his acoustic guitar for an electric one, but it's not well known that, back in Minnesota, he was playing electric guitar until he heard an Odetta record and traded in his electric for Odetta's favored acoustic model.

The proto-rock-and-roll "race records" that Dylan listened to after midnight in Minnesota—finding a clear channel for their fifty-thousand-watt below-the-Mexican-border stations—would electrify him. Until he heard the depth of that acoustic sound. He seemed to be, early on, a guy who adopted a new identity when he came upon a new sound that appealed to him.

I find it so interesting that Dylan's voice is *still* controversial to some. Still heard as unpleasant rasping. If you look at the voluminous YouTube comments sections beneath various iterations of his songs from almost any period, there will *still* be trolls entirely fixated on the idea that he *can't sing*, the voice is "terrible." Again, in charity, I don't think it's mere intolerant lack of sophistication (well, I guess I do) but that they can't abide (or even imagine) the notion of a different *kind* of voice from Herman's Hermits, Billy Joel, or Barry Manilow, an inability to appreciate some of the songs as *declamations* rather than tuneful ditties (though the best are intoxicatingly tuneful). It's a kind of handicap, a "differently able" thing, a missing receptor thing. However, I would agree that in some cases patience is required, as it often is with unfamiliar art, and great art is almost always unfamiliar at first.

Stravinsky and Picasso were abrasive when first exposed to the world. I found myself gradually getting over my distaste for the rasp, eventually not being put off by it at all but finding it appealing.

But there was something more to this rawness. Something spiritual, even God-maddened or, as I'll suggest, God-angered.

Some whole other level.

THE DIFFERENCE: THEODICY

I suppose this is as good a time as any to offer an answer to the Passover night question ("Why is this night different from all other nights?") regarding this book: Why is this book different from all the other books on Dylan? What new perspective am I bringing to the Dylan enigma? As I say, this is less a formal biography than a biography of his impact on the consciousness of the culture. It differs, too, in that I suggest a different source for that impact—in theodicy. Yes, theodicy, which I probably don't need to remind readers is not the same thing as theology. Theodicy is a subdiscipline of theology (and philosophy) devoted to the problem of evil, most often the attempt to reconcile the persistence and presence of catastrophic evil and suffering in human affairs with a purportedly just and loving God, an omniscient God, we're told, one with the power to intervene in human affairs.

It's no easy problem; the best intellects of the past three millennia from Socrates to St. Augustine (whom Dylan dreamed he "saw, alive as you and me"), from Leibniz to Dostoevsky and Isaac Bashevis Singer—all have virtually dashed their brains out trying to get their mind around it. No surprise it should bedevil a singer named Dylan. What's surprising is how what I call the "crazy sorrow" in his work (a phrase from "Mr. Tambourine Man") can be traceable to it.

It was Dylan's argument with God over theodicy, his rebellion against the Jewish God, his subsequent sacrifice of his soul to Jesus (or, more precisely, to what I regarded as a Jesus-freak brainwashing that took advantage of his "crazy sorrow") that nearly killed his career, obscured his impact, and bankrupted his cultural capital (in the phrase made common by Pierre Bourdieu). Indeed, another thing that makes this book different is that I don't tiptoe around the catastrophe, the cultural crime, that almost erased him entirely before he pulled out of the death spiral of robotic dogma-spouting after three years. An escape that he describes allegorically, as I suggest, elsewhere in this book.

Unlike some of his sycophants, Dylan himself came to realize the near-fatal fall into Bible babble he suffered after (as he claimed) Jesus visited him in a motel room in Tucson and asked for his soul. Just look up videos of him preaching hellfire to the infidels (everyone but him, basically) in a self-righteous robot tone, and any empathetic human being will be horrified about what's been done to him.

When I say it was something Dylan recognized (cynics say when he saw the sales figures for his "Christian albums"), something he waged a struggle to recover from, I say it with admiration. A courageous struggle, I believe. One he acknowledges in one of his late-period songs, "Mississippi"—a song he insisted on including in *three different versions* in his *Tell Tale Signs* CD (2008), and which indeed tells a tale:

> *You can always come back*
> *But you can't come back all the way*

That's fairly explicit, but I'd argue there was a more allusive metaphorical reference to what he'd lost in the refrain to that same song. The mournful lament:

> *Only one thing I did wrong*
> *Stayed in Mississippi a day too long*

Mississippi was, of course, a slave state, a legacy of bodies in shackles, corpses hanging on trees. For Dylan it was his mind that was shackled, virtually enslaved in a Mississippi of the soul, in bondage to a dogma. Such a sad fate for a man who rejected exactly that in his beautiful, rueful, self-critical examination of "My Back Pages," in which he declares he became his "enemy in the instant that I preached."

He stayed a day (a three-year-long day) too long in that Mississippi to ever come back "all the way." He knows he lost something—the gift of speaking in tongues—that he may never get back. But the lost language was still there, and he found it again.

EXCEPTIONALISM

And Dylan has come back in his own way, if not "all the way" (if "all the way" means regaining the impact, the cultural capital he once had).

Maybe not all the way but—and this was something it took me a long time to realize and acknowledge—he managed to recover from the theft of his soul and slowly began, in a manner often obscured by a plentitude of mediocre product, to craft some shimmeringly beautiful post-Jesus songs that almost transcend the planet-bumping past. And, when I finally brought myself to return to listening to him after the Jesus period, he earned my respect "on a whole other level." Seriously, for many years after the 1978 "conversion" and the self-righteous songs about how there's only one way, he knows it and you don't, I could barely pay attention to him. But now, attention must be paid.

In fact, my change of heart on this question was almost as much a conversion as was his to Jesus. A re-conversion. And one mission of this book, one I only discovered when I began to watch YouTube videos of his later songs, such as "Things Have Changed" and "When the Night Comes Falling from the Sky," is a desire to document just how many beautiful songs gleam amid the dross, how much the ever-present "crazy sorrow" is so often transmuted to other kinds of loss. The inexplicability of his relationship to God is not unlike the inexplicability of his relationship to a lost loved one in his songs.

I want to make people like myself, non-Bobolators, recovering Bobolators, and those outside the Jesus freaks who have written off the post-Jesus period pay attention to Dylan again. And not just because the Swedish Academy told you to. I told you, too. The conventional wisdom is wrong. The conventional wisdom has it that Dylan lost it all to Jesus. One almost feels—and this has no evidentiary basis—that he was ashamed by what happened. But has he ever admitted to shame?

Now, to return to the question of why this book is different from other Dylan books. I would argue that we already have enough formal comprehensive biographies and memoirs of Dylan.

Herculean efforts by the likes of the magisterial Michael Gray and the combative Clinton Heylin make another such one really unnecessary. In fact, we probably know too *much* biography by this time, anyway. Dylan's fabled reclusiveness, his charisma, his cult following has drawn like a magnet a legion of obsessive biographers and fanatic fans, the self-styled pro-am Dylanologists or, as I've called the particularly devoted sort, the Bobolators (after Shakespeare's bardolators). The pitch of their urgent passion was heralded when one of the very first, a gifted writer named Toby Thompson, went so far as to sleep with Dylan's high school girlfriend—whose impossibly resonant name was Echo—ostensibly in order to glean something more about young Bobby Zimmerman's days at good old Hibbing High. (She's since had to change her name.) I have not sought to follow in his, er, footsteps—although I have had long acquaintance with more than one of Echo's successors (Echo's echoes?).

The only additional biographical material would require mind-reading skills, since Dylan's own words about his work, as he has often conceded, are frequently evasions and put-ons. And—as indefatigable researcher Scott Warmuth has discovered—strange incidents of virtual plagiarism. (Such as the hilariously inscrutable possible put-down that transpired when Dylan was first introduced to Norman Mailer, which I described in chapter two. It is an especially resonant moment, I'd suggest, since both these Jewish geniuses offer unorthodox but incompatible visions of God, and a hallmark of this book is a comparison of these Jewish cultural avatars' visions of theodicy.)

Was it *that* element, that unspoken, unsung essence—the Jewish mysticism—that seemed so profound to Daniel Matt in some uncanny way, as it did to many, many others? What *was* the dog whistle, the bat signal that drew so many like a magnet?

What was it, then? I argue that it was in the music, in the sound, in the "crazy sorrow" beneath it all. More than anything, my exchange with Matt helped me define what this book would be about, what made Dylan different, and where that difference came from. His response was especially meaningful to me because, when it came to Dylan, Matt was—and still is—an exceptionalist.

You know the word, or in any case those who have read my previous books know I'm drawn to the exceptionalist question as a way of asking how distinctive a phenomenon is. The argument over exceptionalism is a philosophic, historical cultural debate about the uniqueness of certain figures. For instance, in the arguments among the Hitler explainers, which I write about in *Explaining Hitler*, there is the abiding divide between the normalizers and the exceptionalists. The normalizers argued that Hitler was on the continuum of evildoers in history—at the far, far end of that continuum, the edge of the spectrum, however you want to visualize it, but still explicable in theory at least by the same modes of inquiry into iniquity that we use to explain others on the continuum: psychological, historical, ideological, etc.

The exceptionalists argue, by contrast, that Hitler is off the grid, beyond the continuum in a realm of "radical evil" all his own. ("Radical evil" was Hannah Arendt's initial term before she bequeathed us "the banality of evil.") I don't pretend to have resolved the argument, just examined its consequences for how "normal" we think the world is.

And in my Shakespeare book (*The Shakespeare Wars*), a similar question emerged: Was Shakespeare on the continuum of other great writers, a very, very, very great writer but a greatness of a sort shared and recognizable in the likes of Tolstoy and Goethe, say? Or was he an exceptional phenomenon, did he create a realm beyond the rest, if the players knew how to conjure it? It's an intuition I had ever since I was fortunate enough to see the legendary Peter Brook/Royal Shakespeare Company *Midsummer's Night Dream* when it opened at Stratford-upon-Avon. I've spent a lifetime seeking and rarely finding Shakespearean experiences that exceptional but knowing they were *there*, waiting to be conjured up, glimpsed even in reading certain passages that transported one to such a realm beyond the continuum. It's an experience that is hard to express intellectually but one I found suggestively recalled when I read Matt speaking of a "gateway" that "penetrated to the core of everything."

Similarly, in writing a book that dealt with the way nuclear weapons affected centuries-old "just war" morality precepts (*How the End Begins*), my argument depended on what degree of exceptionalism you accorded radioactive weapons; what made nuclear weapons fascinating intellectually beyond their obvious terror was how one had to rethink the entire idea that there could be a "just war" because such weapons were more than merely exponentially more powerful per gram than conventional weapons. They demanded that our calculations include the question of *time*, as was argued by a little noticed or little regarded advisory opinion issued by the World Court in 1995. The half-life persistence of radioactive poisoning convinced the World Court to join the Catholic Bishops who declared (in 1983) that even the threat of using nuclear weapons for retaliatory purposes is in itself a war crime to be considered genocidal.

It is worth noting how utterly obsessed the young Bob Dylan was with a nuclear holocaust in his early topical songs. Caught in the vise of two holocausts, is the way I think of the way he thought. There was Hitler's, the ashes still warm after only fifteen years when Dylan first appeared on the scene, the smell of burned flesh Salinger inhaled still lingering in the air. And then there was the nuclear holocaust that seemed ever more imminent, especially at the time of the Cuban Missile Crisis of 1962, the year Dylan first entered the recording studio, the year he wrote "Let Me Die in My Footsteps" renouncing nuclear fallout shelters in favor of going out in a radioactive shimmer. The next year he wrote "A Hard Rain's A-Gonna Fall," which never mentioned nuclear war but never had to.

Now, in speaking of Shakespearean exceptionalism, I do not mean to imply Dylan is a Shakespeare (and please don't tax me with that stupid argument over whether he is "a poet." He is not a poet, he is a songwriter).

But there *was* something I took away from my talk with Peter Brook about Shakespeare and what makes Shakespeare Shakespearean, something that in some way applies to Dylan's exceptionalism. "One of the few things we can say about Shakespeare that is beyond dispute is that he was *alive*," Brook began, seemingly simplistically, in a theater talk. "But to say someone is alive is not enough! You can be one percent alive, you can be twenty percent alive. With Shakespeare you have something very extraordinary, a man who was not only one hundred percent alive, but perhaps a thousand [or] even ten thousand—a million percent alive. Now what is the difference between being one percent, ten percent, [or] a thousand percent alive?"

He didn't have to say anything beyond gesturing at an all-encompassing comprehensiveness that expressed the compounded "aliveness" of a million souls. But, I think, if you insist on being quantitative, if you want to talk in terms of the Brookian scale, you would not say Dylan is a million percent alive, you would not say that he channeled a million souls. But you might say a million (or more) souls channeled *him* in some very "live" way. Give the minstrel boy ten thousand percent.

So, yes, I've long had a fascination with people who provoke exceptionalist debates. There are not many. In literature, Nabokov comes to mind, which is not to say that any number of Nobel Prize winners living and dead were not exceptionally talented. But I can think of few who would provoke an exceptionalist claim.

ENTANGLEMENT

What do Nabokov and Shakespeare share? More than a northern lights shimmering radiance, though there's certainly that, especially in Nabokov's novel of that "northern land," Zembla, *Pale Fire*. But it's more than radiance. I've thought about this a lot, and I keep returning to a metaphor from quantum physics. Dangerous, I know, but thinking about Dylan can provoke risky speculation, so bear with me because it relates to something I've felt about his music. The metaphor from quantum paradoxes is that of entanglement. I'm not an adept, but I've discussed it with Harvard cosmologist Lisa Randall, I've discussed it with physicists and philosophers at Cambridge in the U.K., and I've discussed it with my favorite mathematician/philosopher, Jim Holt, so I feel I'm in the ballpark here. If it's a mystery to all of them, then it's a mystery worth speaking of as best an amateur can.

Entanglement is the name given to one of the central paradoxes of quantum/subatomic theory. It posits the notion that in some cases information—relationship information—can be transmitted between two particles *simultaneously*, even faster than the speed of light.

For instance, if subatomic particle A splits into particles B and C, and if B and C fly off in opposite directions, it is still possible that a change in a property of B—say, its spin direction—will be reflected in an instantaneous corresponding opposite change in particle C even though B and C are light-years apart—beyond the speed of light. They remain connected somehow, or entangled, so that a change in one is reciprocally reflected in the other.

Einstein called this "spooky action at a distance" and was never fully convinced it could be possible, but most contemporary quantum adepts accept it. The analog I'm making to certain song lyrics is that words and phrases that seem on the surface not to have any connection—they might as well be light-years apart in signification—have some kind of connection on some "whole other level," as if entangled they somehow resonate with each other, though the relationship is not readily apparent. Like lovers separated in distance and time.

Take, for example, the opening lines of one of Dylan's challenging, enigmatic, Late Period songs, "Things Have Changed":

> *A worried man with a worried mind*
> *No one in front of me and nothing behind*

See—he's alone, no one exists before him. *He* doesn't exist before then, and obviously he doesn't exist, as far as he knows, after that. There's no obvious relationship between the well-dressed guy waiting on the last train and the fellow "standing on the gallows." And yet, as I shall expatiate upon in a close reading of the great Late Dylan songs, one somehow sees a connection, and entanglement.

I know I've gone a long way to make a point, but that is precisely the feeling one gets when reading Shakespeare and Nabokov, that each particle, each word or phrase, seems somehow "spookily" aware of—and reflects—all the others. More, almost seems *conscious* of them.

I recall speaking about this to my friend the filmmaker Errol Morris (who was kicked out of two distinguished graduate philosophy programs—at Princeton and Berkeley—which I think speaks well for him). Errol told me that entanglement theory reminded him of Leibniz's monads: the seventeenth-century German philosopher envisioned individual building blocks of Being, each of which contains the whole of Being within them. Every infinitesimal monad is a hologram of the Universe.

Something strangely similar came up in a conversation I had with Virginia Heffernan, the former *Times* culture columnist who also has a Harvard doctorate in literature. She casually tossed off the phrase "the one consciousness in Dickens." Yes! This is something I felt when I read all of Charles Dickens in my late twenties and had a kind of spiritual experience, a sense that somehow the whole body of Dickens's work was a monad, entirely self-aware in a holographic way of every element that composed it. "One consciousness" *not* meaning it was all the product of one mind, but one consciousness meaning the work was somehow *conscious of itself*, that it *was* a consciousness of some sort: the late work can be found in the early work, and the early in the late, a snake swallowing its tail. This is a singularity to be found in some (but not all) of the greatest writers. I felt this with Dickens, in the presence of Shakespeare shot through his prose. I feel this with Dylan, a unity given in the early work by music and rhyme, but in the later work by the constant surprise each fragment of phrase offered. The *obscure entanglement*, I'd call it.

That notion of one consciousness is *exciting*, in a way; it's a thrill I get from Melville and Nabokov as well, and to a lesser extent Emily Dickinson, I. B. Singer, and Thomas Pynchon. The idea that a body of work is, in effect, a *new life-form* is an element of what I found exciting about Dylan. And exceptional. I think this was what Daniel Matt sensed, too. Phil Ochs was a great folk singer, and he intuited what made Dylan beyond great when he said that listening to Dylan is LSD set to music. But I think Ochs buried a sharp critique of Dylan in that compliment—that it was all about drugs, that the source of inspiration was an external chemical rather than the internal genius Ochs lacked.

In other words, the songs were psychedelic visions, and Ochs was saying that Dylan was a stenographer of the ergotized cortex and somehow didn't have *real* agency in terms of creating his songs.

It was Ochs's uncharitable way of saying he, Phil, was more original. This troubled Ochs to the end of his life, as I can testify from a dinner we had near the end of his life (in the weeks before his suicide—we dined in a depressing hotel restaurant in LA). More depressing was that Ochs wanted me to go to a boxing match with him, which I declined, but it left me wondering about the man who was writing these songs that were screeds against violence. "I ain't marching anymore"—so why did he want or need to watch one-on-one combat?

This may sound far-fetched, but it's another indication of what Dylan did; the closer a songwriter got to him—and Ochs did get close—the more *angry* he felt at being denied what Dylan had. The violence in the ring was, perhaps, an externalization of the inner rage.

It was plain Ochs was depressed, but I didn't think he was suicidal at the time. Maybe it was a mistake to talk about Dylan, but I got the feeling with Ochs that it was hard to avoid the subject of Dylan's exceptionalism. He was depressed because he would always be a would-be Dylan, hugely talented but not enough, though revered by many. Deservedly so. But to be close was even more a source of torment.

SONGWRITING

I find the subject of Dylan's songwriting particularly fascinating. And nothing more so than the different stories he has told about his songwriting methods and their evolution. They sound a bit crazy, but Dylan is more than a bit unique.

In my talks with him, I remember him alluding to three different modes of creation. First there was unconscious creation—a method in which he just opened up his mind and heart and words poured out. This served him well until about the time of the alleged motorcycle accident (which I've found to be just as likely a temporary retirement ploy).

When I spoke to him, he was already proselytizing for a second way of writing a song, one he imbibed from a gentleman named Norman Raeben, a visual artist guru type with whom Dylan studied and from whom, in an obscure way, he evolved an entanglement—of the sort you hear in "Tangled Up in Blue" and other fractured stories in *Blood on the Tracks*. Student of songwriting Andy Gill's *Bob Dylan: Stories Behind the Songs 1962–1969* relates Dylan's own account of his shift:

"'It wasn't art or painting,' [Dylan] learned from Raeben who claimed to be a son of Scholem Aleichem, 'it was a course in something else,' Dylan said. 'I had met magicians but this guy is more powerful than any I've ever met . . . [H]e looked into you and told you who you were. And he didn't play games . . .'"

According to one former classmate, Raeben was particularly fond of berating students, including Dylan, as idiots for their inability to understand forms in terms of shadow and light, which he tested by demanding they draw an object after viewing it for only a minute or so. Real perception, he believed, was not just a matter of looking but seeing.

It's been my experience that when talented people describe super inner-secret advice or exercises, they often seem vapid or mundane to us plebes, but this somehow gives them something to answer when people ask where their genius comes from. It's something to hang on to, a hook for them to explain themselves to themselves.

The effect on Dylan, according to Gill, was most pronounced in his songwriting, "which he had been struggling with about the time of the motorcycle accident, finding it took him 'a long time to get to consciously what I used to get unconsciously.'"

That was almost exactly what he said to me in our talk.

Dylan told Jonathan Cott that Raeben had taught him how to "see" again: "He put my mind and my hand and my eye together."

According to Gill, "Raeben had brought Dylan to a more fruitful understanding of time, enabling [him] to view narrative not in such strictly linear terms but to telescope past, present and future together to attain a more powerful version of the matter at hand." The immediate effect of this can be heard on *Blood on the Tracks* in songs such as "Tangled Up in Blue," Gill writes, "[w]here temporarily location and viewpoint shift back and forth from verse to verse rather in the manner of merged jump cuts in movies or the fictions of Don DeLillo or

Thomas Pynchon, allowing him to reveal underlying truths about the characters while letting them remain shadowy secret figures."

I don't know. Is this true? Or is Dylan's Raeben rhapsody a put-on to give critics intellectual fodder to chew on? I think the considerable appeal of "Tangled Up in Blue" is that overwhelming sense of *lostness*, of the fragments of innocence and experience calling out to each other. Discovering entanglements. But that's just me.

But wait, there's one more—a third—grand theory or mean-spirited put-on, Dylan's new way of dealing with the critics, which can be found if one reads closely some pages in the Grateful Dead chapter of *Chronicles*.

I say "Grateful Dead chapter" because it's the one (aka the Louisiana chapter, "Oh Mercy") where Dylan both (1) thinks he's come up with a radical new way—post-Raeben—of structuring his performance onstage, and (2) suspects that the Dead—whom he was touring with—dosed his drink with a psychedelic.

Are they related?

It was 1987, and he was feeling that his music was reflecting "too many distractions," he tells us in chapter four ("Oh Mercy") of *Chronicles*, when he says something transformative happened:

> It's like parts of my psyche were being
> communicated to by angels . . . the veil had lifted . . .
> The previous ten years had left me washed out and
> wasted out professionally . . . I felt done for, an
> empty burned-out wreck. I'm a '60s troubadour, a
> folk-rock relic, a wordsmith from bygone days, a
> fictitious head of state from a place nobody knows
> in the bottom of cultural oblivion.

And then, one night after he finished touring with Tom Petty and got ready to tour with the Grateful Dead, rehearsing in San Rafael, something happened.

He says he felt there might have been a psychedelic intervention by the Dead—what he describes next is, well, trippy. And they may have thought they were doing the depressed Dylan a favor.

This was the magical turning point (if it wasn't a put-on). He tells of leaving The Dead to walk into a smoky bar, and feeling "suddenly and without warning" the jazz singer on the bandstand "had an open window to my soul."

> I knew where the power was coming from and it wasn't his voice . . . I used to do this thing, I'm thinking. It was a long time ago and it was automatic. No man had ever taught me. The technique was so elemental, so simple and I'd forgotten. It was like I'd forgotten to button my own pants. I wondered if I could still do it.

It's great, listening to him explaining himself to himself.

He goes back to the Dead's rehearsal studio and decides to give the new method a try:

> At first it was hard going like drilling through a brick wall. All I did was taste the dust but then miraculously something internal came uncaged . . . [I]t blasted up from the bottom of my lower self but it bypassed my brain . . . I had to concentrate real hard . . . but now I knew I could perform any of these songs without them having to be restricted to the world of words. This was revelatory.

And then the closer: "Maybe they just dropped something in my drink. I can't say, but anything they wanted to do was fine with me. I had that old jazz singer to thank."

Could this be real? Is he scattering breadcrumbs to lead us astray?

At this point I would like to loop back around to my perhaps enigmatic, esoteric disquisition on quantum theory physics because of the way it fits what I would call the final solution to songwriting: the cigar box coherence. I know it sounds like a Bourne sequel, or perhaps Dan Brown. I believe the initial story came from a period when Dylan apparently did feel burned out, dried out, whatever, but got himself a movie deal of some sort with a big studio that gave him an office on the lot.

Aspirant writers and producers came in to talk about a possible story with him. To Dylan!

In response, Dylan would take out a cigar box. It was an ordinary-size cigar box stuffed full of what looked like scraps of paper from the gutter press to more distinguished outlets. Supermarket flyers, *Vanity Fair*, you name it. Torn out and stuffed into the cigar box.

And what he said to at least one producing team was "I have a lot of ideas," and then he turned the cigar box upside down and watched the snowstorm of graying pieces of paper drift to the desktop.

"The story's here," he'd say.

And they'd all go home with a "crazy Dylan" experience they could dine out on. But I would contend there *was* a story there, precisely in the entanglement of particles of information on superficially unrelated scraps of paper that the gravity field of Dylan's mind held tenuously in suspension. In fact, I tend to believe all of these "this is my method" stories; they are, at the very least, disguises for the artist's unknowable, unreproducible process of genius. Something extraordinary is already there but hard to articulate—to crystallize verbally—for those not experiencing it.

CHAPTER 5

THADDEUS STEVENS AND ELLEN WILLIS

I have made it a point to seek out discrete episodes, revealing themes and obsessions in Dylan's sixty-five-year career rather than attempt yet another comprehensive biography of someone who chooses (it's his prerogative) to tell tall tales in his autobiography. And even, as we've seen, in his account of the turning point, the initiation moment in his life. There are those like Scott Warmuth who spend considerable time and investigative acumen separating the truths from the tall tales and the lifted passages from others. I feel it's good to know as much as possible, even though with Dylan you can never be sure you know what you know. As he said, "Don't look back." Inevitably this means leaving out close study of my favorite aspects of his work. I'm thinking of Dylan's *Theme Time Radio Hour*, that voluminous late-night DJ of your dreams, that perfect husky, encyclopedically knowledgeable FM DJ Delta Blues cool-cat voice on that show, which ran once a week for almost three years. And again the Steve Buscemi *Ghost World* side of him—Dylan's own

Dylanologist emerges and creates a convincing persona that may indeed be the inner Dylan.

I could write a book about his offhand observations in between the obscure songs he digs out for us. But the book would probably consist of me quoting him and telling you "Isn't that great? How did he know that?" It's just too voluminous, though I recommend listening to more than one and making up your mind whether or not this is the *real* Dylan.

The other not-quite omission is his autobiography *Chronicles: Volume One.* I've devoted considerable attention to just one episode within one chapter—the Sun Pie encounter in the back bayou in the "Oh Mercy" chapter.

But I don't want to omit the exhilaration I felt when I first picked up *Chronicles* and read the opening, coming to New York—tales of the cold-water flats he couch surfed in Greenwich Village and the eccentric characters and oddball autodidacts who occupied them. Musicians aren't always magicians when they turn to prose, but Dylan was, at least in that magical chapter.

Back when it was published in 2004, I felt compelled to write a tribute to Dylan's account of his arrival in New York that snowy winter of January 1961, the culture of geniuses and weirdos he found who, I believe, formed the groundwork for his imagery forever after. (And his wide-eyed wonder at that disappearing scene. It reminded me of the time almost ten years later when I first caught a break and got a staff writer job for *The Village Voice.* I used to stay up all night in the Sheridan Square office—before I found a girlfriend with an apartment—and take calls from crazy and entertaining people from all over the nation who believed someone at the *Voice* would understand them.)

In this chapter, I'm excerpting part of that previously published memoir/appreciation of Dylan—the part about Thaddeus Stevens, the abolitionist, who, like Ahab, had one leg and one mission: to drive a stake through the heart of human slavery. He was the leading pre–Civil War senatorial abolitionist. I don't think I could write it any better than I did then. It conveyed what Dylan also tried and was overwhelmed by in the film *Renaldo and Clara* because it's important, because I want people to discover it who haven't.

The story of Dylan's sudden rise is so improbable. His repertoire had mainly been copying other folk singers' carefully curated array of sea chanteys and Child Ballads. He got a record contract, as we all know, after a rave review of a coffeehouse performance by a *New York Times* music critic. But that first album—you could throw it in the trash. It's all copycat stuff. Except for that one transcendent song to Woody Guthrie.

Woody was a bridge to Greenwich Village for Dylan, whether or not you buy that his ostensible reason for going to New York City was to sit at Woody's feet at the hospital for chronic diseases. Certainly, while all the Village people were playing Woody's songs for the people, Dylan earned a lot of street cred for actually going and tending to one of the most suffering of people.

But in the privacy of his own mind, the Civil War and the heroism of one Thaddeus Stevens on behalf of the antislavery cause took precedence.

Thaddeus Stevens? Who knew? One of the least understood of Dylan mysteries has to do with influences: His music seems to come from everywhere and yet from nowhere but him. You can listen to endless droning folk balladeers, and you can listen to Buddy Holly, Robert Johnson, Hank Williams. You can read Milton and Keats, as Christopher Ricks does, though we don't know if Dylan did.

So where does it come from, the whole Dylan carnival: the comic surreal characters, the recurring cryptic femme fatales, the ecstatic ironies, the declamatory cadences, and the insinuating sneers? The unmistakable Dylan voice. Yes, he invented himself, but not out of nothing.

That's where chapter one of *Chronicles, Volume One*, is most illuminating. He makes it clear that what made Dylan Dylan was New York, New York. Specifically, the New York of the Village—and, more explicitly, the Village when it was still The Village, not a theme park for bohemia. The Village and all that talk, all those hopped-up riffs, epic espresso-fueled denunciations and appreciations. He found a way to distill the attitude, transcend the bullshit, and turn New York talk into song.

Dylan writes that he came to New York from Hibbing, Minnesota, searching for something, for a "template," he calls it—a template for the raw gift buried inside him like the iron ore buried beneath the Mesabi Range that brooded magnetically over Hibbing. The story he tells is of the time before he became an instant seer in 1961, the time before his first record came out, when he was, for all anyone knew, just another struggling Village character on the folk scene.

At its best, in the New York chapters, *Chronicles* is a kind of prose ballad or a kind of hymn to the Village, to Village characters, to bohemian goddesses, and to the peculiarly skewed Village state of mind.

It was only years later, when I arrived in the Village and landed a staff writing job at *The Village Voice* and became by default their Dylan correspondent, that much of this had disappeared, leaving only some traces of that fertile critical mass of coffeehouse sensibility. The fervor for folk music had largely been engulfed by the antiwar movement's moral exigencies, but one could still feel the awe walking the crooked streets.

The cold-water-flat Village of the early 1960s, when it was still home to a stew of autodidact geniuses, mad seers, and obsessed oddballs, was the crazy attic of America. It was filled with the sailors and ex-cons-turned-hopped-up-philosophers who stacked their shelves with Byron, Thucydides, and obscure tomes on Thaddeus Stevens and lived with pre-Raphaelite bohemian goddesses like the one Dylan calls Chloe.

Could I pause for a moment, before I get to Thaddeus Stevens, to pay respect to Chloe? She seems to be the first in a long line of wised-up, sad-eyed ladies, the bohemian goddesses, Beat Angels, visionary Johannas, who splendidly, irrevocably, ruin lives in Dylan's best heartbreak songs. The obvious choice is "Sad Eyed Lady of the

Lowlands," but I'd go for "Queen Jane Approximately" from *Highway 61 Revisited* or "If You See Her, Say Hello" from *Blood on the Tracks*.

"Chloe had red gold hair, hazel eyes, an illegible smile," Dylan tells us, and "illegible smile" tells you all you need to know. He met her at some Village crash pad where she was living with a guy named Ray. "She worked as a hat-check girl at the Egyptian Gardens, a belly-dancing dinner place on 8th Avenue; also posed as a model for *Cavalier* magazine. 'I've always worked,' she said."

At another point, Dylan tells us: "She was cool as pie, hip from head to toe, a Maltese kitten, a solid viper—always hit the nail on the head." Case closed. (Although I can't help thinking about "cool as pie" and wondering if it's a reference or a foreshadowing to the figure of Sun Pie in the later "Oh Mercy" chapter.)

This archetypal Village angel seems to have been an influence on his verbal style as well as his emotions. Chloe is given to uttering cryptic, gnomic, bohemian-goddess-type aphorisms: "She also had her own ideas about the nature of things," Dylan writes, "told me that death was an impersonator, that birth is an invasion of privacy." Could have been that philosophe Sun Pie decades later.

In other words, in her idiosyncratically "illegible" way of talking about "the nature of things," she uttered a certain kind of cryptic, Dylanesque rhetoric before Dylan did.

"Death is an impersonator / Birth is an invasion of privacy" could be a couplet from *Street Legal* or *Blood* itself. Sort of a parody of less-than-great Dylan, but some of Dylan is a parody of less-than-great Dylan.

So Chloe was a dangerous *Blonde on Blonde* when Dylan was still a folkie singing sea chanteys and the like. "What could you say?" Dylan asks of her riffs on "the nature of things." "It's not like you could prove her wrong."

That last rueful, bemused remark is the tone of Dylan's voice in the book: sometimes capable of rhapsodic ecstasies (usually when talking about other music and other musicians), but more often the sharp, sardonic, deadpan observer you hear in his songs at their best.

Consider the way he describes Billy the Butcher, the kind of Village character who gave the place what Dylan calls its "carnie vitality." A would-be singer who hung out around the Cafe Wha? folk scene, Billy "looked like he came out of nightmare alley. He only played one song—'Hi-Heel Sneakers'—and he was addicted to it like a drug . . . Billy would always preface his song by saying, 'This is for all you chicks.' The Butcher wore an overcoat that was too small for him, buttoned tight across the chest. He was jittery and sometime in the past he'd been in a straitjacket in Bellevue, also had burned a mattress in a jail cell . . . all kinds of bad things had happened to Billy. There was a fire between him and everybody else. He sang that one song pretty good, though."

You have to love that last line, the perfect deadpan Dylan twist, comic but affectionate, too. One can't help but think it comes from a wry recognition of the Billy the Butcher inside himself, the part of himself capable of being knocked silly by a song, the part that can love a song to death.

In fact, some of the best moments in *Chronicles* are when Dylan describes the way certain songs, certain singers, became his "Hi-Heel Sneakers," the way that upon hearing certain singers he is recurrently knocked out, paralyzed, mesmerized, devastated. There are the obvious ones—Hank Williams, Woody Guthrie, Robert Johnson—but some obscure and unexpected ones too: Lonnie Johnson(?), Johnny Rivers(!), Harold Arlen . . . Dylan is the best kind of music critic: he really reacts. He's a kind of Geiger counter dialed up to eleven; music is radioactive to him. I think some people are born with a gene for song obsession, even those who can't play a note, like myself. I'll admit it: I was once obsessed with "Hi-Heel Sneakers," too.

By the way, I don't use the Geiger-counter metaphor idly: another weird detail we learn from *Chronicles* about Dylan's Village days is that, at one point, he actually owned a Geiger counter. It seemed there were a lot of them in Village pads. It's a detail that reminds us of the shadow of nuclear terror that hung over America and impressed itself even more forcefully on the seismic souls of the Village, whose seize-the-day (or seize-the-cappuccino) mentality owes much, it seems in retrospect, to an apprehension of an onrushing nuclear Holocaust so soon after the horror of Hitler's came to light. Norman Mailer, a Village contemporary of Dylan's, talks about it most memorably in "The White Negro," in which he contends (among many other things) that the madness of Mutual Assured Destruction (MAD) as a nuclear doctrine made "secret psychopaths" of us all.

I've argued elsewhere that Dylan's best work has an affinity with the black humor genre of 1960s American literature, such as Joseph Heller's *Catch-22* and Ken Kesey's *One Flew Over the Cuckoo's Nest*. Underlying both is that awareness of MAD-ness. (Can you believe we only had a dozen years between the [apparent] end of nuclear terror and the onset of the post-9/11 kind? I wish someone had told me.)

So there he is, Dylan, little older than a high school graduate, toting his Geiger counter and his guitar around from one Village crash pad to another, when he comes on one crash pad in particular, the one inhabited by Chloe, whose nominal live-in boyfriend, Ray, has the crammed bookshelves with which Dylan distracted himself from Chloe.

In fact, I think it is to his crush on Chloe that we owe his discovery of Thaddeus Stevens.

Dylan makes the "library" in Ray and Chloe's place sound like the Old Curiosity Shop of literature: "books on typography, epigraphy, philosophy . . . Books like Foxe's *Book of Martyrs*, *The Twelve Caesars*, Tacitus lectures and letters to Brutus . . . Thucydides' *The Athenian General*—a narrative which would give you chills . . . talks about how human nature is always the enemy of anything superior . . . Sometimes I'd open a book and see a handwritten note scribbled in the front, like in Machiavelli's *The Prince*, there was written, 'The spirit of the hustler.'"

(Later, in a line that is one of my favorites in *Chronicles*, Dylan takes issue with Machiavelli on the question of love: "Machiavelli said . . .

that it's better to be feared than loved—but sometimes in life," Dylan says, "someone who is loved can inspire more fear than Machiavelli ever dreamed of.")

Along with this profusion of the classical and the contemporary—*The Temptation of St. Anthony* and Ovid's *Metamorphoses* next to the autobiography of Davy Crockett, Milton's "On the Late Massacre in Piedmont" (his "protest poem," Dylan calls it: point for Christopher Ricks)—Dylan finds some old tome about Thaddeus Stevens, and his Geiger counter reacts to the presence of the fiery-tempered antislavery crusader.

"He's from Gettysburg and he's got a club foot like Byron," Dylan tells us. (He later drops the fact that he's read the entire sixteen-thousand-line Byron epic *Don Juan* "and concentrated fully from start to finish," and you can hear it in his sense of humor, his romantic posturings, and his feminine endings.) Anyway, Dylan tells us, Stevens "grew up poor, made a fortune and from then on championed the weak and any other group who wasn't able to fight equally. Stevens had a grim sense of humor, a sharp tongue and a white-hot hatred for the bloated aristocrats of his day . . . once referred to a colleague on the floor of the [Capitol] chamber as 'slinking in his own slime' . . . denounced his foes as those whose mouths reeked from human blood . . . [and] called his enemies a 'feeble band of lowly reptiles who shun the light and who lurk in their own dens.'"

Needless to say, one hears the prophetic anger of the early Dylan jeremiads like "Masters of War" and "The Times They Are A-Changin'" in this appreciation of Stevens's wrathful eloquence. Later, Dylan tells us—evidently following up on his Stevens reading—he spent an intense period in the 42nd Street library reading old newspapers and pamphlets from the Civil War era.

And then he says a fairly remarkable thing about the power of his Civil War reading: "Back there America was put on the cross, died and was resurrected. There was nothing synthetic about it. The godawful truth of that would be the all-encompassing template behind everything that I would write."

The template at last! Thanks to Thaddeus Stevens (and Chloe and Village autodidact Ray).

The template behind everything? Well, when you think about it, love is a kind of Civil War in Dylan songs, sometimes between two people, sometimes within one; sometimes it's a Civil War where the slaves don't always want to be free.

I don't want to give the impression that *Chronicles* is all about New York, although it begins and then circles back and ends in the Village of the early 1960s. It's a strangely structured patchwork first volume of a memoir, one that jumps forward from the time before Dylan cut his first record.

THE MYSTICAL TRANSITION

Something happened. Something changed shortly after Dylan's shift from the Village to Chelsea. Something emerged, a new kind of songwriting, a new kind of lyric, that would come to define a new kind of Dylan. One who was more elusive, some would say difficult or merely mystical, but often in need of decoding.

You can hear it in three key songs, transitional songs between the often-aching sincerity or raging anger of the Village folkie, acoustic-protest period, and the frequent absurdist black humor exemplars of what might be called the Chelsea Hotel / *Highway 61 / Blonde on Blonde* era. The songs I mean are "She Belongs to Me," "Love Minus Zero / No Limit," and "Love Is Just a Four-Letter Word."

I believe the shift in songwriting was a division that emerged from his idiosyncratic immersion in the obscure that characterized Dylan's Thaddeus Stevens period, the product of being the kind of autodidact who just happened to *know* little-known things that mystified those who knew only the folkie Child Ballads and the snoozy "American Songbook." Someone who swerved away from the easily understandable.

Each of those three songs (from the album *Bringing It All Back Home*) bore the fingerprints of an elusive occult sensibility, an absorption that often defied explanation, making them, for a certain cohort, all the more appealing—the signature of a new changing, or changed, Dylan.

A Dylan who in some way drew on the strangeness and resistance to interpretation he found in the idiosyncratic character—and characters—of the Thaddeus Stevens period. A continuity could be found, but only if you searched hard for it.

I can't help thinking the songs that emerged in some way echoed the absurdist chaos that was the world of the Village from Thaddeus Stevens to Billy the Butcher Boy and his "Hi-Heel Sneakers." It was the crazy eye-opening world of postwar downtown Bohemia when all aesthetic rules were being broken by poets like John Ashbery and abstract expressionists like Jackson Pollock and Robert Rauschenberg, a whole new Warholian sensibility. New rules, or non-rules, were being broken and nurtured in their brokenness, all of which prepared Dylan to leave behind the "walking antiques" of the music world.

There's no doubt that there's a gap, a lacuna, an aporia between the Village Dylan and the Chelsea Dylan. A shift in his songwriting to "a whole other level." This began sometime in 1964, I'd estimate, two years after he arrived in New York and began absorbing what was going on. It was as if he'd burned through the folk zeitgeist and began writing songs that would define a new Dylan, songs that would mystify his previous followers with their often enigmatic, esoteric lyrics.

You can see it—hear it, that is—if you compare his undoubtedly beautiful Village regret and remorse trilogy—"One Too Many Mornings," "Don't Think Twice," and the incomparably heartbreaking "Boots of Spanish Leather"—with what I call his transitional trilogy. Those transitional songs, by comparison with the other three, are somewhat mystifying and "difficult"; they didn't give up their treasures easily. And they seemed to be written with a different kind of woman in mind. Two women in particular: a singer (Joan Baez), and a critic (Ellen Willis).

The first of the key songs I'll discuss, in order of composition, is "She Belongs to Me." It opens with a tribute to a witchy woman:

> *She's got everything she needs, she's an artist*
> *She don't look back*
> *She can take the dark out of the nighttime*
> *And paint the daytime black.*

It's the kind of woman—like Chloe in *Chronicles*—that a small-town kid just turned twenty could be dazzled by. Certain women in the Village, proto-feminists in their defiance of the rules, seemed to have mystical powers that weren't to be found in the soda-fountain girls of his hometown.

After all, the artist in "She Belongs to Me" wears "an Egyptian ring that sparkles before she speaks." Something supernatural, something "on a whole other level."

And what does it mean to "take the dark out of the nighttime and paint the daytime black" anyway? He would address this question several decades later in "When the Night Comes Falling from the Sky."

And then there is "Love Minus Zero / No Limit," a song whose title alone is defiantly difficult to deconstruct. Its lyrics have one of the best and most difficult of what I call Dylan koans: "She knows there's no success like failure / And that failure's no success at all." I'm still trying to figure that out; it's like a snake swallowing its tail, isn't? A DNA verbal double helix.

And finally, "Love Is Just a Four-Letter Word." Is he being superficially snarky or profoundly ironic?

These are questions/riddles/enigmas of the sort he had not seemed preoccupied with when he was Village Dylan. Our image of him had been the one on the cover of his second album, *The Freewheelin' Bob Dylan*, which showed him and his first serious New York girlfriend, Suze Rutolo, striding arm-in-arm on a snowy Village street (Jones Street—not Great Jones Street) looking like All-American young lovers. But then the cover of *Bringing It All Back Home* offered the lush, louche, sinful Chelsea Dylan, featuring a beautiful but indifferent, unreachable, sophisticated fashion-model type in the background. And not much later, after the breakup with Rutolo and the Village regret trilogy, the songs from the *Bringing It Back Home* album suggested entanglement with Warhol muses such as the beautiful, doomed socialite Edie Sedgwick and the exotic German chanteuse one-name Nico.

Much later, Dylan would write a song for his estranged wife, Sara (who was said to have mystical tarot reading and other psychic powers), about how he recalled "stayin' up for days at the Chelsea Hotel / Writing 'Sad Eyed Lady of the Lowlands' for you." Whether or not this was just a ploy—I knew a couple of sad-eyed ladies who implied that it was written for them—it was a Chelsea Dylan ploy.

But whomever the song was for, the Chelsea Hotel—that rusty pile on 7th Avenue off 23rd Street—had become the new locus of Bohemian glamor and goddesses, Bohemia 2.0, though it seemed to carry a curse, cast a malign spell. When it was newly built, the Chelsea was a house of sorrow: it served as a refuge for relatives and survivors of the victims of the *Titanic* disaster. I myself once stayed up all night at the Chelsea Hotel, but it was in the course of investigating a murder (or possibly suicide).

A dark romance had ended tragically with the death of Nancy Spungen, the girlfriend of Sex Pistols bass player "Sid Vicious" (the quotes are because it was an ironic, made-up name for a gentle junkie whose friends couldn't believe he was capable of murder). She died of a knife wound in the stomach, and it's unclear whether the blade was wielded by Sid, as the cops thought when he fled, or by Nancy, who could have stabbed herself to death. (Sid died of an overdose before he stood trial.)

It wasn't all tragedy. The Chelsea was the place where Leonard Cohen wrote his infamous ballad about Janis Joplin giving him oral sex while her limo waited outside. Although there's a heroin overdose in that story, too.

But that hotel was a brooding symbolic presence in Dylan's life, the sharp edges of which (like Sid's knife) could be felt in the edgy lyrics. Lyrics that changed and mystified and won the approval of the widely respected critic Ellen Willis, who seemed to *get* Dylan early on and wrote eloquently about him when she became the first full-time music critic for *The New Yorker.*

Willis's approval was, I believe, key to Dylan's adoption by a certain kind of brilliant, intelligent second-wave feminist.

I knew a couple of them (in addition to the one I lived with for three years), and they were adventurers. There was Faye, who, after graduating summa cum laude from Harvard, took off to travel in the Himalayas (like Daniel Matt) but found herself in the midst of a dangerous war at the top of the world, the one between India and China. Her response: turn herself into a war correspondent and garner news-magazine cover stories and awards for her courageous reporting before coming home to spend time on the exegesis of Dylan songs. And Jane, my colleague at the *Voice,* who was fascinated by the internal civil war involving communist China's Gang of Four and decided to spend a year there checking it out.

I can't help thinking that women like this inspired Dylan to be more adventurous in his songwriting. I know they inspired me.

It's often true that a great artist needs or feeds off a great critic. And Willis did that for Dylan. She seemed to step in between the folkie Village Dylan and the decadent Chelsea Hotel Dylan and find the intelligent thrill at the heart of both of them. Here's an example of the appreciation of Dylan that Willis wrote—and that helped make him a cult figure for both genders:

Rock-and-roll, which was already in the midst of
a creative flowering dominated by British rock and
Motown, has been transformed. Songwriters have
raided folk music as never before for new sounds,
new images, new subject matter. Dylan's innovative
lyrics have been enthusiastically imitated. The folk
music lovers who managed to evolve with him,
the connoisseurs of pop, the bohemian fringe of
the literary community, hippies, and teen-agers
consider him a genius, a prophet. Folk purists
and political radicals, who were inspired by his
earlier material, cry betrayal with a vehemence that
acknowledges his gifts.

Willis lived a divided, adventuresome life herself, which I think may
well be what brought her to Dylan.

I remember a remarkable story she wrote for *Rolling Stone* about
spending a year in a Jerusalem commune for women thinking of
becoming Orthodox Jews, and she had a difficult time deciding if
she wanted a convent-like life or the wild ride of rock and roll. Ultimately, somewhat like Dylan leaving his born-again "fellowship,"
she decided that she couldn't abandon writing about Dylan and his
ilk. I remember reading her spiritually suspenseful account of the
indecision—between rock and religion—in an Air Force hangar
somewhere in the badlands of North Dakota. I had just come out
of a nearby subterranean missile-launch silo, and I wrote her a letter
then and there, telling her how glad I was she wasn't abandoning the
world. And how much I liked the final line of her story, after she's
made her decision to leave the Orthodox confinement and come back
to America and Dylan.

The final line was from a Lou Reed Velvet Underground song:
"You know her life was saved by rock and roll."

It was for a lot of us.

CHAPTER 6   # "THAT THIN, THAT WILD MERCURY SOUND"

L et us now praise famous sounds.

Who remembers what tunes Homer sung the Odyssey to? What melody was Shakespeare's "full fathom five" sung to? In no way do I mean to disparage Dylan's melodies. Dylan's tunes will not be subjected to analysis by me. But it's worth noting that, when he most eloquently strove to describe his music, he described not a melody but a *sound*. It's a sound that's become almost as famous as Dylan himself. It's "that thin, that wild mercury sound."

It was perhaps the most memorable thing said to me during our week of face-to-face talks on the Burbank back lot.

He went on to call it "metallic and bright gold" and "you can hear it on *Highway 61* and *Blonde on Blonde*."

"Is it the sound you hear in 'I Want You'?" I asked.

"Yeah, it was in 'I Want You.' It was in the album before that too."

"*Highway 61 Revisited*"?

"Yeah, also in *Bringing It All Back Home*."

He went further than specific albums, which is what made the quote so resonant. "That's the sound I've always heard" and "I've got to get back to the sound."

Clearly that sound and the way he talked about it made an impression. One of the earliest bootleg albums—those unauthorized pressings of alternate takes, unreleased versions of songs that often would become underground classics (Like "Up to Me" and "I'll Keep It with Mine")—was given the name *Thin Wild Mercury*.

Yes, it was unofficial, unauthorized, but Dylan had the generosity and the genius not to go after the flowering of this bootleg culture legally. He let it thrive, and it has been claimed, accurately I think, that that particular bootleg and the ones that followed were responsible for creating, giving birth to, what would be the entire worldwide culture of bootleg enthusiasts, probably making Dylan an even more important cultural figure, if a little less rich in the short term. It was a brilliant democratic gesture: bootleg music that allowed the masses to co-create in a way with the celebs, like a glowing penumbra around the official releases.

The phrase "that thin, that wild mercury sound" is used in almost every single Dylan book I've ever read, sometimes without the quotes that indicate it came from an interview—and yes, I have a proprietary feeling about the phrase, almost as if *I* said it to *him* rather than him to me.

"That thin, that wild mercury sound." Any discussion of Dylan and his sound requires a preliminary inquiry into that strange verbal anomaly: synesthesia.

Not the same kind of synesthesia one can find throughout Vladimir Nabokov, who famously described (in *Speak, Memory*) how, as a child, he discovered he could experience letters as colors and even tastes. When, for instance, he heard the letter K, he *experienced* the taste of blueberries. Yes, he tasted words, and in a way we can taste them through him. There is something ineffably *delicious* to the ear about Nabokovian prose. One can find this convergence of the senses in other greats and other art forms.

Here's the final couplet of Shakespeare's Sonnet 23: "O learn to read what silent love hath writ / To hear with eyes belongs to love's fine wit."

To hear with eyes! Synesthesia.

In Dylan, this is found in peak moments. Perhaps *the* peak moment, to my mind, of early pre-Jesus Dylan, is in "Chimes of Freedom." This is an ode, an anthem, reportedly written on a Kerouacian cross-country road trip with Dylan typing away in the back seat, having visions and somehow conflating them with the civil rights freedom movement moments he'd experienced. In simplest terms, it's a description of finding shelter from the storm (I needn't mention a title of one of his most beautiful pre-Jesus odes) in a church with a bell tower, wildly ringing out its chimes as a thunderstorm thrashes the bells:

> *We ducked inside the doorway as thunder went crashing*
> *As majestic bells of bolts struck shadows in the sounds*
> *Seeming to be the chimes of freedom flashing.*

A concatenation of synesthesia images: bells of bolts, shadows in sounds, chimes flashing. Chimes transmuted from sound waves to light waves. An *aurora borealis* of sound (and one can't help thinking of the "flashing" that is the eeriest thing about the northern lights and their sheets of light).

There's a beautiful essay in Michael Gray's enormously erudite *The Bob Dylan Encyclopedia* in which he explores the synesthesia within another less well known but undeniably peak period Dylan song, "Lay Down Your Weary Tune." Gray calls it "a kind of pantheism of the senses."

This synesthesia is something to remember when we try to understand what makes Dylan exceptional. It has something to do with sound—his quest for the precise sound that would take his work to "a whole other level." It's interesting because of its emphasis on the whole sound of a Dylan song: not just his voice, not just his words, but the whole aurora borealis of sound.

It's notable as well for the way a single phrase seems to strike a gleaming nerve in so many Dylan fans, Dylanologists, and Dylan biographers. A popular bootleg was named *Thin Wild Mercury*, and one can find websites and social media accounts named after it. (Clinton Heylin has used the phrase incessantly without attribution, as do many other Dylanologists, including *The New Yorker*'s David Remnick.) It is my claim to fame in the Dylan realm, even though all I did was elicit it.

All of which suggests that, when Dylan gets going, even riffing eloquently without music he can come up with that dog whistle appeal, striking just the right nerve.

In fact, that "wild mercury sound" has become a central descriptor, the perfect compressed shorthand for the sound of Dylan's music at its peak, and the essence of the Dylanesque sound—in many ways, the essence of Dylan himself—I'll try to place it in context.

During our lunch at that Burbank back lot greasy-spoon lunch counter, I had asked him—since so many seemed to care—if there was a moment when he made a conscious decision to leave behind acoustic folk in order to work with an electric-guitar-based band. He must have been infinitely tired of the question, but he'd never really answered it, to the dismay of Dylanologists. But that day, he did.

"Well, it had to get there," he said. "It had to go that way for me. Because that's where I started and eventually it just got back to that."

When he says "that's where I started," he's talking about staying up late in his early teens listening to the first "clear channel" rock-and-roll stations sending Chuck Berry and Little Richard and the like through the night sky from below the Mexican border bouncing off the ionosphere to reach the howling winds of the North Country. It's often forgotten he was a rock-and-roll soul before he became a folkie. It's often forgotten his first professional gig was when, at about age fifteen, he talked his way into playing piano at a Bobby Vee ("Take Good

Care of My Baby" and other hits) concert. It's often forgotten that the high school band he formed, the Golden Chords, was anchored by Bob on the electric guitar. Which meant he was always thinking in terms of a sound larger than himself, larger than folk music could contain. He wanted something larger than himself. The Golden Chords has a mystical, Pythagorean ring to it, doesn't it? The golden ratio and all that. He was always playing Golden Chords.

"I couldn't go on being the lone folkie out there, you know, strumming 'Blowin' in the Wind' for three hours every night," he said. Now, "I hear my songs as part of the music, the musical background."

"When you hear your songs in your mind, it's not just you strumming alone, you mean?" I asked.

"Well, no, it is to begin with. But then I always hear other instruments, how they should sound. The closest I ever got to the sound I hear in my mind was on individual bands in the *Blonde on Blonde* album. *It's that thin, that wild mercury sound. It's metallic and bright gold, with whatever that conjures up.* That's my particular sound. I haven't been able to succeed in getting it all the time. Mostly, I've been driving at a combination of guitar, harmonica, and organ, but now I find myself going into territory that has more percussion in it and [pause] rhythms of the soul" (my italics).

("Whatever that conjures up." The Golden Chords, the northern lights.)

"Can't you just reassemble the same musicians?" I asked ploddingly.

"Not really. People change, you know, they scatter in all directions. People's lives get complicated. They tend to have more distractions, so they can't focus on that fine, singular purpose."

(Love "that fine, singular purpose." The guy was always focused.)

"You're searching for people?"

"No, not searching, the people are there. But I just haven't paid as much attention to it as I should have. I haven't felt comfortable in a studio since I worked with Tom Wilson. The next move for me is to have a permanent band. You know, usually I just record whatever's available at the time. That's my thing, you know, and it's—it's legiti-mate. I mean, I do it because I have to do it that way. I don't want to keep doing it, because I would like to get my life more in order. But until now, my recording sessions have tended to be last-minute affairs. I don't really use all the technical studio stuff. My songs are done live in the studio; they always have been and they always will be done that way. That's why they're alive. No matter what else you say about them, they are alive. You know, what Paul Simon does or Rod Stewart does or Crosby, Stills and Nash do—a record is not that monumental for me to make. It's just a record of songs."

I wanted to draw him out more about the "sound" he'd been speaking so eloquently about.

"Getting back to your transition from folk to rock, the period when you came out with *Highway 61* must have been exciting."

"Those were exciting times. We were doing it before anybody knew we would—or could. We didn't know what it was going to turn out to be. Nobody thought of it as folk-rock at the time. There were some people involved in it like the Byrds, and I remember Sonny and Cher and the Turtles and the early Rascals. It began coming out on the radio. I mean, I had a couple of hits in a row. That was the most I ever had in a row—two. The top ten was filled with that kind of sound—the Beatles, too—and it was exciting, those days were ex-citing. It was the sound of the streets. It still is. I symbolically hear that sound wherever I am."

At last: "You hear the sound of the streets?"

Note here how he describes the sound in terms of light. Synesthesia!

"That ethereal twilight light, you know. It's the sound of the street with the sunrays, the sun shining down at a particular time, on a par-ticular type of building. A particular type of people walking on a par-ticular type of street. It's an outdoor sound that drifts even into open windows that you can hear. The sound of bells and distant railroad trains and arguments in apartments and the clinking of silverware and knives and forks and beating with leather straps. It's all—it's all there. Just lack of a jackhammer, you know.

"All pretty natural sounds. It's water, you know water trickling down a brook. It's light flowing through the—"

Oh, why couldn't I have shut up! Light flowing through the— We'll never know. Nonetheless, I had an urgent question, and as it turned out, in seeking to clarify something about the nature of that flowing light, a minor revelation ensued:

"Late-afternoon light?"

"No, usually it's the crack of dawn. Music filters out to me in the crack of dawn."

"The 'jingle jangle morning'?"

"Right."

Bingo!

"After being up all night?"

"Sometimes. You get a little spacy when you've been up all night, so you don't really have the power to form it. But that's the sound I'm trying to get across. I'm not just up there re-creating old blues tunes or trying to invent some surrealistic rhapsody." (In fact, you could say that's exactly what he ended up doing.)

At the time, though, the critics got it all wrong, attempting as some do to trace every line, every note, every word of Dylan to some long-dead blues shouter or some Appalachian hillbillies from "that old weird America," or imagining he was imitating surrealists. Yes, Dylan had roots, but his roots don't entirely explain him, exhaust all interest, negate innovation.

"It's the sound that you want?" I said. It seemed like one of those rare occasions when he was willing to talk about his sound.

"Yeah, it's the sound and the words. Words don't interfere with it. They—they—punctuate it. You know, they give it purpose. [pause] And all the ideas for my songs, all the influences, all come out of that. All the influences, all the feelings, all the ideas come from that. I'm not doing it to see how good I can sound, or how perfect the melody can be, or how intricate the details can be woven or how perfectly written something can be. I don't care about those things."

"The sound is that compelling to you?"

"Mmm-hnh."

Note that he concludes his answer not with words but with a sound: "Mmm-hnh." A hum.

And then he said, almost wistfully, "I have to get back to the sound, to the sound that will bring it all through me . . ."

"Bring it all through me"—fascinating. What is "it" that he wants brought through him? Something that "brings it all back home," as the album is titled? Some numinous uber-sound beyond the ken of the note-by-note annotation, or more like a force, a cloud? Something from "a whole other level." The sound beneath the sound—the one Daniel Matt heard.

Mercury and Dylan. Let us dwell for a moment on *that* resonant connection. Mercury, of course, is the messenger god, quicksilver with an emphasis on *quick*. A mercurial temperament gleams and flashes, shifts shape unpredictably, can't be pinned down.

Mercury held a special place in Shakespeare's verse pantheon. In one of his earliest plays, but one saturated, intoxicated, with wordplay, at the very close of *Love's Labor's Lost* we find "The Song of Mercury," a song of winter following a song of spring, and it provides the very last line of the play after the song is done: "The words of Mercury are harsh after the songs of Apollo." Mercury: fleet-footed, sometimes light-footed, but not always lighthearted.

Shakespeare's Mercury, dear to Byron. In Canto IX of *Don Juan*:

> *Shakespeare talks of "the herald Mercury"*
> *New lighted on a "heaven-kissing hill"*

(It's actually Hamlet describing the picture of his father before he was murdered.)

And, of course, one of the great wild-talking and perhaps most Dylanesque characters in all Shakespeare is Mercutio (not an idly chosen name) in *Romeo and Juliet*.

I love Mercury, seen "new lighted" on that "heaven-kissing hill." New lighted as in gleaming. "Metallic and bright gold, with all that conjures up," as Dylan put it. To me it conjures up the gleaming, labile, liquefaction of gold, a heavy metal's solid mass transmuted to quickened, glittering rivulets of illumination. The poet Robert Herrick celebrates his mistress's clothes by conjuring up "the sweet liquefaction of her dress."

There's something alchemical about it. The element mercury was the symbol of transubstantiation in many alchemical texts, the key to the transformation of lead into gold. It "conjures up," as Dylan put it, something to do with liquid utterances, the liquefaction of language. Dylan's "sad eyed lady of the lowlands" with her "mercury mouth" uttering mysterious incantations.

So much is packed into that phrase, "conjures up." I felt that somehow this was a window into his sound, if not his soul. When I think about Dylan's mystical quest for a sound that incorporates and transcends individual voices and musicians, it brings me back to Daniel Matt's sense of Dylan and also to the fact that Jewish mysticism sees the universe as the creation of the utterance of sounds. The synesthesia of sounds: a voice that says (aloud), "Let there be light." Sound conjures up light. There is a mysticism of letters and a sonic aura that surrounds them.

CHAPTER 7

CHRIST / ANTICHRIST

Bob Dylan has been the cynosure of what we think of as charisma for all but one period of his long career. The one that begins with the hallucinatory appearance of Jesus in his Tucson motel room. Hallucination, breakdown, neurological lightning storm—we may never know, but one thing is certain: it initiated a crucial period in which he lost his charisma and became a lapdog of dogmatists, parroting scolding Bible phrases in ranting tones that turned off the followers once drawn to him.

Perhaps it's worthwhile to begin with a more precise definition of charisma.

As I was writing this book, I came upon a discussion in a *Times Literary Supplement* review essay, a discussion of the enigma of charisma in the work of Max Weber, the early-twentieth-century German sociologist who had endowed the Greek New Testament word "charisma" with its current distinctive omnipresent secular role—its own incantatory charisma, charisma's charisma—as a descriptor for the way we look at iconic figures in politics and culture.

The *TLS* reviewer, Miri I. Rubin, a professor of Medieval History at London's Queen Mary University, wrote that, for Max Weber, "the essence of charisma resides in a certain inscrutability—in gnomic sayings, in baffling gestures—also disciples are charged with the task of interpreting, enshrining and repeating for future generations, often ineffable experiences. To truly know a charismatic presence 'one has to be there.'"

Yes, I know others have "been there," within close range of Dylan's charisma. Many others have witnessed Dylan's "gnomic sayings," "the baffling gestures," the "inscrutability" that is part of the Dylan mystique, his charisma.

But I was *there* at an extraordinary pivotal point in his life, a time when his argument with God was coming to a head, a time when the first cracks of what can only be described (in Fitzgeraldian terms) as a crack-up began to open up under his feet. And though I didn't know the exact nature of what was to come—the way Jesus freaks would exploit his misery and steal his soul—the factors that put him at the breaking point were evident.

So you have to be careful with Dylan when, for instance, he told *60 Minutes*' Ed Bradley with a straight face that he met the Devil on his way from Minneapolis to New York, back in 1961, on Highway 61—and claimed to Bradley that the Devil offered him a deal. When Bradley, always a good reporter, asked for details of that deal, Dylan just smiled, as if to say, "What do you think?" And of course he put his finger on something that probably mystifies him to this day: What happened? How did it happen so fast, that within a year he was the secret icon of a small culture and within two years a national figure soon to be staring down Norman Mailer for the claim of reigning god of Hip culture? Who would have believed then that Dylan was more likely to win the Nobel than Mailer? Or did Dylan really *know* when he told Ron Radosh that "I'm gonna be bigger than Elvis"? Was that a put-on?

He does keep referring to the Devil. In "Highway 61," of course. He sings about making a deal with a devilish God to do some dirty work "out on Highway 61." Even Jesus before the Jesus freaks. In a beautifully enigmatic verse in another song ("It Takes a Lot to Laugh, It Takes a Train to Cry") on the same album, he gives us:

> *Oh the wintertime is comin', the windows are filled with frost*
> *I went to tell everybody but I could not get across.*

Could not get a cross! Both senses make sense. He finally got a cross in Tucson, but from whom? Was it really Jesus, as he'd been set up to believe by the mind-control Christian sect that ensnared him? Or was it the Antichrist? Or was he the Antichrist? He spends a lot of time warning us about *that* fellow. And besides—just what was the Antichrist doing at that motel? Taking advantage of the all-you-can-eat breakfast in the courtyard prior to unleashing the Four Horsemen of the Apocalypse? What do we know about how Dylan thought about Christ and the Antichrist? Was he baffled himself?

He certainly seemed to believe it was Christ who visited him; at least he seemed to believe it sincerely and grimly for two or more years.

And yet he also believed the Antichrist was capable of deception. Capable?

A master of it!

In one of Dylan's last religion-inflected albums—*Infidels*—one can find a shockingly overlooked stanza taking off from the New Testament claim that the Antichrist will come to us as—song title—"Man of Peace":

> *Well, first he's in the background, then he's in the front*
> *Both eyes are looking like they are on a rabbit hunt*
> *Nobody can see through him*
> *No, not even the Chief of Police*
> *You know that sometimes Satan comes as a man of peace.*

In other words: if you believe this, if you believe in this cosmic trickster at all, then you are compelled to believe Jesus himself (aka "the man of peace") could be the impostor. You are compelled to believe that ultimate good and ultimate evil are ultimately indistinguishable by words alone. That if there is a God who made the universe, it was a God capable of playing a practical joke on its inhabitants. A God capable, like Dylan, of relishing a put-on "man of peace."

It is far from simplistic, that stanza from "Man of Peace." It brings back an echo from "Just Like Tom Thumb's Blues" way back on *Highway 61 Revisited*: "You must pick one or the other though *neither of them are to be what they claim*" (my italics).

Truly it is a song of radically subversive wickedness. "Man of Peace" does the task of undermining the smug self-assurance of the born-again and the once-born: You can't *know*! You just can't know who is Satan and who is the Lord. The former is an adept at disguising himself as the latter. It could well be a kind of gnostic anthem—the gnostics of the first few centuries AD. entertained the heretical idea that the true ruler and creator of the material world could be the sort of supernatural being bent on ruin and chaos and content with the triumph of evil. Whereas, if there was a God, He or She presided above the realm of depredation on a lower sphere. On a sphere removed from the fate of good or bad men.

Still, I must admit that, cumulatively, listening to Dylan's scolding Jesus songs, I was deeply disheartened by what I saw and heard from the moment the news leaked out in mid-1978 that Dylan had "gone Christian" (the way he'd "gone electric"). I blamed myself for weighing him down with unanswerable Jewish questions; I blamed Jesus, too, I blamed Jesus freaks, and finally, yes, I blamed Dylan himself for bringing the intemperate wrath of some of his songwriting into angry attacks on those who loved his music. My new interpretation of his Jesus period is that Dylan turned his considerable self-criticism (if not self-hatred) on himself and on those who worshipped him, false prophet that he knew *he* was. And perhaps worst of all, I blamed him for being boring. More than anything, the sermonizing concert videos available on YouTube cast me into despair. And—thankfully, ultimately—the YouTube videos are what rescued me from it.

Below is a sample of the kind of lecture scolding Dylan delivered on his infamous Gospel Tour in 1979. Rather than singing, he *tells* us. As you read this, try to put yourself in Dylan's place, in his mind. Is he aware of how he sounds, does he have an awareness of the profound gulf between the one-time skeptic and the ranting scold he's become, this fellow who warned he'd become his "enemy in the instant I preached"? How does he sustain, how reconcile the contradiction? Or does he not even feel a change—like that Berkeley neuroscientist who had a revelation in the Judaean desert that he didn't seem to need to question (albeit Dylan's came in the somewhat more pedestrian confines of a Tucson motel room)?

I know I still find it a wonder: the epitome of cool, sarcastic charisma and discernment turning himself into a Bible-babbling scold. One is tempted to wonder if perhaps, prompted by unendurable family pain and stress, he decided to engage in, to stage, a prolonged Andy Kaufman–like put-on identity shift. Does he even recognize this robotic version of himself? One can't overestimate what a radical revision it is. And what about that hallucination that Jesus himself (or was it the Antichrist?) visited his motel room, placing his soul at the center of concern by the Lord of Creation? Can he be serious?

> You wanna know something, we're not worried
> at all, even though it is the last of the End times;
> because we see all these hostages being taken here
> and drugs being outlawed there. All these sad
> stories that are floating around. We're not worried
> about any of that. We don't care about the atom
> bomb, any of that, 'cause we know this world is
> going to be destroyed and Christ will set up His
> kingdom in Jerusalem for a thousand years, where

the lion will lie down with the lamb. Y'know the
lion will eat straw that day. Also, if a man doesn't
live to a hundred years old, he will be called
accursed. That's interesting, isn't it? And we don't
mind. We know that's coming, and if any man
have not the spirit of Christ in him, he is a slave to
bondage. I know you're all into bondage, so you
need something just a little bit tough to hang on
to. This song's called "Hanging on to a Solid Rock
Made Before the Foundation of the World." And if
you don't have that to hang on to, you better look
into it.[1]

There's a lot more where that came from, much from one-time bestselling
prophet of doom Hal Lindsey but plenty lifted from the most mean-spirited, doom-struck section of the New Testament: the Book of Revelation.

You really need to get the full flavor of one of the most shocking
instances of brainwashing in American popular culture. So, here, try
to digest this, from that same Gospel Tour (which records horrified
crowd reactions):

Well. What a rude bunch tonight, huh? You all
know how to be real rude. You know about the
spirit of the Antichrist? Does anybody here know
about that? Well, it's clear the Antichrist is loose
right now, let me give you an example . . . I'm
gonna give you a real good example . . . [lots of
heckling and others trying to shout the hecklers down]
Turn the lights on in here. I want to see these
people. Turn some lights on. Give them some light.
Let them in the light. [applause] . . . All right, so

---

1 Bob Dylan onstage, introducing the song "Solid Rock," on Nov. 19, 1979.

this guru, he made a film of himself. He had one of these big conventions. He does have a convention I think every so often, like once a month, he'll go to a big city. [*"Praise the lord with puke!" "Shut that guy up!" applause*] Now, so, I took a look at this tape, and sure enough he was having himself a big convention. He had, must have had five thousand to ten thousand people there. Eight thousand people. And what he was doing on the stage was, he was sitting on there with a lot of flowers and things. And he sure did look pretty, though. He'd sit up there, you know like kind of like on a throne, and you'd listen to him talk on the tape. And on the tape, he said, you know, what's life all about is life is to have fun. He said, "I'm gonna show you now how you all can have fun." And he had a big fire extinguisher there and he put colored water in this fire extinguisher, and he would spray it out on the people. And they all laughed and just had a good time. They took their clothes off. They were overjoyed to be sprayed by this man. [*Booooo!*] And a little while after that, he started talking about his philosophy. And he said that he was God—he did say that. He said that God's inside of him and he is God. And, you know, that those people could just think of themselves as God. I want to tell you this because there's many of these people walking around. They might not come right out and say they're God, but they're just waiting for the opportunity to. And there is only one God. And let me hear you say who that God is? [*mixed shouts*] Their God, he makes promises that he doesn't keep. There's only two kinds of people like the preacher

says—only two kinds of people. Color don't
separate them, neither does their clothes . . . ["*Rock
'n' roll!*"] . . . You still want to rock 'n' roll? I'll
tell you what the two kinds of people are. Don't
matter how much money you got, there's only
two kinds of people: There are saved people, and
there's lost people. [*applause*] Yeah. Now remember
that I told you that. You may never see me again.
I may not be through here again, you may not see
me, sometime down the line you'll remember you
heard it here. That Jesus is Lord. And every knee
shall bow to him.[2]

Not to be overly contemporary-bound, but this is Dylan clearly suffering from the same self-absorption as our current president, Donald
Trump. It makes one wonder if Dylan had a personality implant. The
fellow I spent time with in Burbank was a quiet, subdued, even shy
figure. No bombastic charisma in evidence.

He had a soft-spoken voice and a shy, sometimes sly smile, that was
it. He didn't need any more magnetism. The bombastic Bob of the
born-again period had nothing but—and sent people away from any
desire to follow him and his cruel messiah.

Yet the cowardly Dylanologists are afraid to call out what was done
to him. It's one of the great scandals of American cultural criticism,
the way this woeful Dylan has been elided from view or wrenched
into a false continuity with the Dylan of before and after.

There were really two stages of my initial abhorrent reaction to
Dylan's apostasy.

I can't deny I felt personally hurt. As a Jew. And I'm not even
religious, certainly not observant. But it just seemed so unnecessary

---

2 Dylan onstage, introducing the song "When You Gonna Wake Up," Nov. 26,
1979.

for a post-Holocaust Jew who didn't like Jahweh to announce his enslavement to Jesus.

I don't like being lectured to about the cosmic mysteries of the universe by anyone representing any deity. And the songs seemed to me so sterile, so scolding, so mean-spirited. Songs that were all about punishment for being human.

And so, at first, I simply, though shockingly—I never thought it would come to this—just refused to listen to any more of Dylan's postconversion music. Not just the three Jesus albums themselves, but everything that came after. This was my mistake.

I thought my Dylan days were over as soon as I saw the sermonizing tapes, which seemed like self-criticism sessions not unlike the dogmatic North Korean Marxism of *The Manchurian Candidate*. It was the Manchurian Dylan!

Okay, there were a couple of songs—maybe three—I'd feel tugging at the hair on the back of my neck the way Nabokov speaks of aesthetic experiences: "Slow Train," certainly, with its sinister, serpentine movement gathering speed. "Precious Angel," a genuine love song without dogma. And of course the nondenominational but emphatically spiritual "Every Grain of Sand."

But the question—what happened?—wasn't answered to my satisfaction. This cross he supposedly got in the motel room in Tucson—who was it from? Was it really Jesus, as he'd been set up to believe by the mind-controlling Christian sect he joined? Or was it the Antichrist? Dylan spends a lot of time warning us about this fellow, the Antichrist. God does he rant about him in the YouTube videos. He's here, he's there, he's you, he's the guy next to you. For a while Dylan seemed to believe the Antichrist was real—and what a brilliant ploy if he posed as Jesus in Tucson. Typical Antichrist trick. I found myself wondering: Did it ever *cross* Dylan's mind as well?

I wondered about this especially when I watched YouTube videos of a seemingly brainwashed Bob Dylan—once the sultan of sneering skepticism—mechanically, robotically mouthing apocalyptic New

Testament prophecies as if in some mind-control trance. This person who sang—in "My Back Pages"—about the heady days when he was "fearing not I became my enemy in the instant that I preached." I feared he *had* become his own enemy.

And there he was, preaching. When I finally *heard* those three songs—the exceptions—long after the "conversion," they recalled to me with horror the close of Ken Kesey's *One Flew Over the Cuckoo's Nest.* You know the terrifying moment when that rebellious spirit, McMurphy (played by Jack Nicholson), returns from a forced lobotomy to the psych ward, the one he's chosen over jail, the one where his refusal to obey Big Nurse has him hauled off for a brain needle.

When he comes back, hope is briefly raised among the downtrodden followers in the ward—like those three songs, heartbreaking reminders of what once was—when he seems at first to be his same old self. But it turns out to be an unsustainable mechanistic replication, a brief tragic simulacrum of that old self that soon lapses into a kind of zombified compliance. I've never gotten over that scene, and memories of it came rushing back to me in full force when I watched the YouTube videos of Dylan miming the most self-righteous, self-satisfied biblical dogma. I had read about his conversion. I had *written* about his conversion shortly thereafter in an essay called "Dylan's Conversion: Four Theories." (My fourth and final theory was based on the near-parodic Marin County coke-dealer Christ logo of the Vineyard Fellowship: "Blame it on California.")

But what I was watching was worse: a cultural crime. I thought I'd never forgive him—or, rather, them, the Jesus freaks who robbed him of his soul.

Highway robbery. *Highway 61* robbery.

It's interesting how many "conversions" and divides disrupt the chronology of Dylan's life: folk versus electric, Jew versus Christian, conscious versus unconscious songwriting, simplicity versus complexity, earnestness versus put-on, sincerity versus authenticity. This Jesus conversion was a much more important divide in Dylan's life and work than all the previous so-called conversions.

Far, far too much has been made of all of the other divides, at least compared to the divide between his pre-Jesus period and the post-Jesus period. The latter was itself divided into his robotic mind-control convert period and his slow courageous self-deprogramming, as I will argue is allegorized in the Sun Pie section in *Chronicles*.

I know I write harshly here, but when I say I was there, I say it as someone who was present at a crime scene or its inception. A cultural crime. The theft of Dylan's brain. I wish I had been able to see what was going on in that brain, but he was always wearing his dark shades when we talked, and he seemed both stoic and kind—at least, he seemed to take pity on me with my yellow legal pads full of nerdy questions and my half-pint flask of tequila, to which I resorted to calm my nervousness. It was me, not him, who seemed like a man on the verge of a nervous breakdown.

I suppose I shouldn't be so harsh in characterizing the conversion to Christianity as a nervous breakdown—a crack-up. I'm not blaming the Christian religion, I'm blaming the Jesus freaks who took advantage of him. So maybe it wasn't a nervous breakdown, but it was a divide that gives shape to his life and work. Because until I saw the YouTube clips (long story: my reconsideration involves abandonment of my 2004 MacBook, which had long lost its access to YouTube, and all this new thinking only emerged when I bought a new computer and got back on YouTube with a vengeance), until I saw Dylan preaching unto the multitude, the depth of his distress did not come home to me.

I had also not recognized the magnitude of the great schism. Among the better Dylan writers, there was only one—Tim Riley— who seemed to feel as strongly as I did about the Jesus period. Yes, there were the normalizers—it's just Dylan being Dylan contrarian and all that. They made a strenuous but unconvincing case that the songwriting during the Jesus period was executed at his customary high level. My friend the late Paul Williams made a strenuous effort to convince us that he was still there, still Dylan. And there were those who felt that nothing had been lost.

And then there was Dylan himself, who ultimately seemed divided against himself. This suspicion occurred to me when I wondered about the strange inclusion of no less than *three* versions of a single song in one of his compilation albums—three separate versions of a post-Jesus song called "Mississippi"—something I don't believe he'd done on any other disc.

Why? I think it was because there came a point (this was in the mid-1980s) when he may have been losing that sublime confidence in himself, felt he'd lost his cultural cache and commercial importance. Here's the stanza:

> *They say you can always come back*
> *But you can't come back all the way . . .*
> *One thing I know I did wrong:*
> *Stayed in Mississippi a day too long.*

In other words—as I read it—he felt he'd stayed in another kind of slave state, stayed in that mental slave state, that state of sinister dogma so long he knew he'd lost something, couldn't "come back all the way."

What a stunning reversal this was for me: being there for the onset of the crack-up followed by three decades of being unable to *forgive* Dylan. Once you are witness to the theft of the soul of a great artist, it takes time to recover. Then, I wondered if he was unable to forgive himself. I credit Greil Marcus, a brilliant writer, with giving Dylan a temporary escape route from his Jesus servitude by recasting him in the mold of that backcountry blues man—what Marcus called "that old weird America," made up of Black sharecropper blues hollerers and white hillbilly songsters. The problem was that, for quite some time, for several albums, he still wasn't Dylan; he was a different simulacrum, the rootsy choogling curator of centuries of old singers and ancient songs.

An American past, yes, but one that no longer offered the radical originality that made Dylan Dylan. It no longer measured up to the meteoric first planet-bumping sixteen years earlier. Who knows what he would have turned to without Marcus's sophisticated vision of unsophistication?

I admit I was too dogmatic myself. I still didn't want to listen to the simulacrum Dylan who replaced Christ with the all-blind banjo players Marcus dug up. But I was reacting against those who (to my mind still) think they can indiscriminately praise album after post-Jesus album and ingratiate themselves with the Dylan, Inc. types who hand out the liner notes and assignments to critics who still buy the notion that the album is the aesthetic unit to be twisted and turned and judged rather than the bearer of one or two unforgettable songs on each. (Such people even praise the atrocious Dylan film *Masked and Anonymous*—that's a test. Flee from anyone who pays homage to it.)

But eventually I began to open my ears to some thrilling new Dylan compositions among the rootsy sludge. I've named the songs, and I will devote part of this book to giving them their unjustly withheld due.

So I now place myself in a neo-anti camp—someone who believes album after album taken *as a whole* can be disappointments, nothing like the planet-bumping classics. But someone who *has* found something wondrous among the sludge of rootsy choogling. One or two tracks on each album deserve hosannas.

CHAPTER 8

DYLAN'S ESCAPE: THE BAYOU REVELATIONS OF SUN PIE

I'm not claiming that the magnetic force he exerted on the culture on some "whole other level" was entirely due to the repressed depth of the Jewish rage he felt. Or that his consequent cynicism about piety and conventionality was a thin mask for the murder embedded in Western culture. Though I wonder if that's *one* reason why so many Dylan obsessives turn out to be Jewish.

I would just argue that Dylan's argument with God often gives his songs and words otherwise inexplicable depths and edges. ("We'll meet on edges soon," he cries out in "My Back Pages.") The often-esoteric nature of his work issues an invitation for Talmudic exegesis as well. Perhaps this is not evident to everyone, this other dimension, this "whole other level," but it's *there*. Seek and ye shall find.

Certainly, his argument with God affected the arc, the trajectory, of his own life and art. He was preoccupied with God, particularly with God's responsibility not just for "every grain of sand" but also every drop of blood spilled in His name. His "License to Kill," as one song title has it.

Dylan can be seen to provoke in some sensitive souls at first anger and rebuke of Jehovah, then submission to Jesus. Perhaps payback to the Old Testament God is a flight to the New Testament Savior. That's the portion of the arc I seek to speculate about here, since its trajectory is not well explained by Dylan himself. After being prompted to look again at the New Orleans chapter of Dylan's *Chronicles*, I discovered a new way of thinking about a key extended passage, previously inexplicably esoteric, but one I now believe to be legibly allegorical.

In that passage, I believe Dylan has found a way of telling us about how lost he'd been—and how he found himself again. Telling us without telling it explicitly, it's an esoteric allegory to be found in a strange section of the New Orleans chapter of *Chronicles*. The chapter he calls "Oh Mercy."

It's a chapter that excavates the pit of despair he'd found himself in post-1981, after he allowed his total allegiance to Jesus to lapse. Cynics might say "follow the money" and take note of sales figures for the three Christian albums, *Saved* (1979), *Slow Train Coming* (1980), and *Shot of Love* (1981). But in fact the first album sold comparatively well—one million units the year it came out, which is equal to *Blood on the Tracks*. Cynical but sycophantic Dylan rock critics have found themselves incapable of saying a discouraging word when liner notes gigs are in the offing (Grammy nominations!). And some will seek to say there's a continuity between Dylan's songs before and after Jesus that attempts an aesthetic equivalence between what he wrote when his mind was not in shackles and when he was straitjacketed by dogma.

They don't pay much attention to the "Oh Mercy" chapter of *Chronicles* because they don't think the album of that name (1989) is as fully consequential as some other, more celebrated ones, and they've been taught by the record companies to write about music as if the album—not the song—was the aesthetic unit to be judged, since (up till recently) that was the unit for sale.

Dylan doesn't talk about what came immediately before New Orleans, the years when they stole his soul. No doubt about it, they turned him into a puppet for a New Age Christian group whose logo was a line drawing of Jesus resembling a benevolent Marin County coke dealer. It was embarrassing for those who believed in him (or Him), for those who had been faithful to Dylan for so long through so many wavelike ups and downs in his life. Until his Jesus period, it had still been ever onward and upward—whether electric or acoustic, thin wild mercury or spun gold. But then came the utterly unexpected plunge into dogma, and a good percentage of his fans stopped listening; a good portion of his cultural capital (the phrase coined by the French philosopher Pierre Bourdieu) lost interest and principal. It was dramatic; it was the real motorcycle crash of the spirit, one from which there seemed no prospect of recovery.

That Jesus freaks stole his soul and constricted it to painful, puppet-like replications of New Testament homilies in his new CDs. Constricted it to a dogmatic hostility to the pleasures of the world, whereby he prayed for apocalyptic punishment for those not purified like him. It was really tragically distasteful that few spoke up to urge him to snap out of it or to suggest an intervention, even deprogramming. However, the latter would probably have been counterproductive; he had to erase his own brainwashing, and more power to him for having crawled out from the dungeon, the lion's den they threw him in. (I'm not the forgiving type.)

And I just won't buy the rock-critic-sycophant obsession with false continuity. Imposing an arc—imposing continuity—is, I've found in my reading, often the biographer's downfall.

The mystery has always been how Dylan escaped from the trap, from becoming "my enemy in the instant that I preached." And what replaced it.

He heard the boos and jeers ("*rock and roll!*") at the concerts, but of course he'd faced hostile audiences before when he "went electric." But nothing like this. ("*Judas!*") And he never bothered to scourge the naysayers and scald them with biblical scolding the way he began to do in his Gospel Tour.

He never gives an explicit account of an escape in his partial autobiography, *Chronicles: Volume One*. But I believe one can find a disguised allegory of his spiritual exfiltration (as the spy trade calls it) in a little-remarked-on section of the "Oh Mercy" chapter of that book.

This allegory suggests that he found, in a strange, spooky corner of the bayou country, a new way of looking at things that allowed him to once again embrace the world. I'm speaking of the unexpected depths—the meditation on prayer and paganism one can find in the Sun Pie section of that New Orleans chapter, ostensibly about the struggle to make an album called, like the chapter, "Oh Mercy."

Sun Pie was "one of the most unique characters I've ever met," Dylan tells us. After a while, though, you wonder if he's making up this strange seer-like fellow—the carpenter proprietor of a weird backwoods bayou haunt called King Tut's Museum. After all, is it just happenstance that he went from celebrating the son of a carpenter (Jesus) to a carpenter named Sun? Or is he Dylan's artistic creation?

Dylan sets the stage for this story of regeneration with some of the most relentlessly despairing pages in the book. Where he'd been left by his escape from the invisible bonds of the born-again group and the hole in his soul it left.

Almost everyone who has read *Chronicles*, Dylan's partial autobiography, has noted, has wondered, has speculated, about the big gap in the chronicle of his career that he otherwise writes so eloquently about. He skips between fifteen and twenty years from the late 1960s to the mid-1980s. From a chapter on his unsuccessful collaboration with the writer Archibald MacLeish in the late 1960s, when Dylan had come off the riotous concert road that produced an early peak moment of his rock stage (now available on the *Manchester '66* CD, previously misidentified as the Royal Albert Hall concert bootleg; that's the one in which you can hear a distraught folkie fan crying out from the audience "*Judas!*"). He goes on to a chapter about the making of the *Oh Mercy* album in the late 1980s in New Orleans.

Back home in Woodstock, he was raising a family when we last see him in *Chronicles* before Jesus gets him. He was trying to hide from fame and fans with his hyped-up "motorcycle accident"—creating an aura of mystery akin to "the famous silence of God," as the writer Don DeLillo put these submergences. All the while, he was taping scores of songs with the group that would become the Band (the so-called *Basement Tapes*). Their quantity exceeds their quality. Only two of them, "I Shall Be Released" and "This Wheel's on Fire," belong in the pantheon.

Anyway, Dylan writes in a desultory way about being summoned to write the songs for MacLeish's would-be Broadway production called *Scratch*, a nickname for the Devil. Dylan abandoned the project, which ultimately closed after two performances. The songs instead ended up, he says, on the album *New Morning* (1970). An album that itself turned out to have a greater cultural/symbolic significance than the music within.

People talk about it, people write about it—Dylan's cultural capital. Not so much his charisma after a while but his "man of wisdom" persona, or the one attributed to him by the difficulty in deciphering his lyrics. People talk about how it (once) meant something, how he had generational power. It sounds mythic now. But I was there to witness it in action at street level. Beginning with a deadly bombing.

"New Morning" turned out to be the title of the turnaround peace-out manifesto issued by the fugitive underground radical bomb-making faction of SDS. They had adopted their very name, "Weatherman," from Dylan's young rebel troublemaker song, "Subterranean Homesick Blues"—specifically from the line "You don't need a weatherman to know which way the wind blows." As in the storm is coming, no, it's here. You ought to know by now.

It was a marker of the market value of Dylan's cultural capital one step *before* that arc peaked. (I believe that one of those stock market bond charts with *multiple* rising and falling lines would do more justice to Dylan than wrenching his career into one simple procrustean arc.) There would be an upward and downward curve of cultural capital that crossed the curve of his lyrical talent about the time in late 1974 when he recorded the first version of *Blood on the Tracks*.

But for the moment, back in 1970, his generational influence arc was peaking. The true measure of his cultural capital could be found in the wake of what became known as "the townhouse explosion": the May 5, 1970, blast that blew up the interior of a landmark Edith Wharton–style brownstone townhouse on West Eleventh Street just west of Fifth Avenue, a block from where I lived and a block from the *Village Voice* office where I then worked.

A young woman was seen fleeing naked from the scene, and two young people who—it turned out—were members of the Weatherman faction of SDS were blown to bits, left for dead. The others "went underground"—became fugitives, several for decades. They had been making bombs they intended to plant at the huge army base at Fort Dix, nearby in New Jersey. To kill soldiers bound for Vietnam, at a festivity they called "The Big Dance." (The war was awful and criminal, blowing up innocents; this was, too.)

I had recently covered a court-martial at Fort Dix for a soldier who'd gotten acquitted on a charge of setting the brig on fire. I thought the verdict was just but I also thought he did it—as did the rabble of radicals supporting him. There was violence in the air; it was the time of Kent State in Ohio (four dead) and the illegal bombing of Cambodia that led to the takeover by the genocidal Khmer Rouge Marxist death sect (four million dead).

Strangely, Dylan still had a power over the zeitgeist brewing, at least in America. A few months after the West Eleventh Street townhouse blast, a crudely printed pamphlet seemed to appear out of nowhere in Village haunts. On the cover was the title "New Morning" and a pictograph-like symbol for the sun rising with rays (lines) shooting out. It was "signed" by the Weather Underground.

The pamphlet's content was an argument that violence and bomb making was not going to stop the war in Vietnam. A mass movement, inclusive, radical but peaceful, was needed.

It didn't have any particularly brilliant political analysis. But it had that title, that Dylan title, though Dylan himself up in Woodstock had nothing to do with it and in fact refused when asked to state his position on the war. Everyone just assumed what it was. He would later say he refused to join the resistance because he didn't want to encourage any illusion among his followers that he had The Answer.

But he had a certain kind of credibility, an authenticity, a gravitas lacked by Abbie Hoffman, Mark Rudd, and the other Weathermen.

It was almost like night and day, the change that the Dylan-titled pamphlet "New Morning" had. It spread like wildfire (well, in certain circles), and it's only a slight exaggeration to say it changed the hearts and minds on the home front overnight.

This is ironic, because Dylan the person was so remote from the prophetic figure he'd become.

But in the bubble of the Village and Village-like enclaves all over America, it was as if Dylan, like Moses, had waved his hand at the frenzied worshippers of the Golden Calf of violent extremism and they fell silent. Boiling with rage one minute, suddenly quietly thoughtful.

He was the Man, he was the Prophet. They got him so wrong, so absurdly wrong it almost drove him crazy. But he may have changed a history that was heading for a real fiery crash. Why did he have that effect?

"You'd have to ask them," Dylan told an interviewer from *People* magazine in 1976. "Those people who are involved in that state of panic where my works seem to take them."

Panic? I'd never thought of that before I came upon that quote. He was doing the interview to promote the network TV concert documentary called *Hard Rain* coming up. That concert was no easy one-off, by the way. I thought it might be the death of him. It was pouring rain throughout the concert, thunder and lightning; it's amazing no one was electrocuted. It was also kind of beautiful: an Olympian struggle against the elements, lightning versus electricity. Or "the ghost of electricity" howling back at the howling *Lear*-like winds. Don't listen to the rock critics; this was Dylan and his fellow musicians at their best—magnetic to watch and electrifying to hear.

Panic. What a thing to say. And yet I remember watching this concert on TV and feeling that he was setting himself up for electrocution. Perhaps he wanted to go out in a flash that way, truly "going electric."

Is that the answer to Dylan's "you'd have to ask them" why they were so crazy for him? Panic? What an interesting choice for Dylan's view of the Dylan-besotted mind. I hadn't heard him use that word before.

"I'm not an activist. I'm not politically inclined," he told *People*. "I'm for people, people who are suffering."

Dylan didn't make it clear in whom the panic inhered—in him, or in his fanatical fans, or in the wide world over, the zeitgeist. It was the beginning of the era of the endless war (war itself on a Never Ending Tour): the war in Vietnam, the war at home, the struggle (far from won) for civil rights (here Dylan's commitment was early and real), the assassinations. Nuclear war lurked or was threatening, such as in the Cuban Missile Crisis. The 1962 panic over that trauma had more, I believe, to do with creating the '60s than anything else. There used to be a myth, long disproven, that Dylan wrote "A Hard Rain's A-Gonna Fall" because of the Cuban Missile Crisis, which we know now was one heroic Soviet submarine commander's *nyet* from erupting into nuclear war (by countermanding the order to fire a nuclear torpedo at a US destroyer). But you could say every moment thereafter was accompanied by a mild to acute subtextual sense of panic.

Was there a subterranean homesick panic Dylan fans were exhibiting or projecting onto him?

There *are* the songs of what I would call ominosity. Perhaps most of all I'm thinking of "All Along the Watchtower" ("two riders were approaching / The wind began to howl").

Those songs were a kind of prelude to panic. For example, the much underrated "Billy," about being hunted down by "the man who was [his] friend." "This Wheel's on Fire" was a prelude to a motorcycle accident. And Scarlet Rivera's unforgettable violin wailing on "Hurricane." No, sorry, I'm not here to argue about Hurricane Carter's guilt or innocence. Just to point out the eerie power of the song and the rancid racist atmosphere it evokes. The dread. Of course it was a sixth sense for many who are sensitive; the sense of dread colored everything.

Today, the bestselling mental-health drug in America is clonazepam, the generic name for Klonopin, the antianxiety drug recommended especially to forestall panic attacks. Are those who cleave to Dylan doing so because of panic? If the nation had been on Klonopin then as it is now, would Dylan have been the face of—or the refuge from—panic arising from the amygdala?

Of course, Dylan still made two strong albums in the 1970s, *Street-Legal* and *Desire*, in addition to the forever classic *Blood on the Tracks*, before Jesus stomped out the desire from his music. I have a special affection for *Desire*, which was written in a loft I once stayed in for a while, postdivorce, a place located over the once-fabulous, now-gone Bruno's Bakery whose cannoli made all the rest in Little Italy seem like graham crackers, so intensely, densely, creamily infused they were. I can see Dylan and his sometime collaborator on *Desire*, Jacques Levy, dizzy with them at times.

And there are two love songs on *Desire*, "Oh, Sister" and "One More Cup of Coffee," that are what one might call intensely infused with Dylan's emotion.

There followed the *Renaldo and Clara* period (1974–78), which I now think Dylan, Inc. was smart to withdraw from circulation at the time he did. I think it will age like fine wine, this pageant of Eminent Bohemians and Children of Bleecker Street.

It was a wildly ambitious attempt that probably had to fail commercially, but it failed grandly, if not grandiosely. Dylan misjudged the strength of his social capital with some of the target audience.

In the heart of Bohemia 2.0, to give you a sense of the fraught atmosphere of the time, I was living above the then-notorious Spring Street Bar—haunt of artists and actress-waitresses. Little did I know my landlord, the owner at the time, was a major smuggler of Thai hash, and it was only later I opened a secret compartment in my apartment and came upon artistic photo-nudes of one of the women wanted for a Weather Underground bombing in DC. (I think she was innocent—of the bombing, anyway.)

I understood the film's mystique, but my adorable ex-wife threw Larry Sloman's account of the making of *Renaldo and Clara* across the room before she got very far. I thought Sloman's book was personal, funny, the ultimate fan's notes. I won't try to persuade you. But when *Renaldo and Clara* is finally released in 2300 or whenever, at its rightful five-hour length, it will be a perfect portrait of the aspirations and pretensions of a genuine historic, creative community, something a dour joyless film like *Inside Llewyn Davis* entirely dismisses. Yes, with all the jealousies, but with all the friction causing artistic sparks to fly.

Renaldo and Clara asks a question Dylan was probably asking himself, at least at times: Why me? Why, out of this matrix, should Dylan alone rise to cosmic cultural heights? I think that's a question the film asks and doesn't fully answer.

But I know it took a lot out of him; I saw how thin he was, how pale from the editing room, scarfing down that grilled cheese sandwich so greedily and smoking for dear life.

He was ready for Jesus.

THE RIDE INTO THE BAYOU

*C*hronicles then skips fifteen years at least. From 1969—just about the time I was assigning Dylan lyrics to the freshman English seminar I was teaching at Yale (in addition to the usual suspects, Donne, Keats, and Eliot)—to the mid-1980s.

Dylan himself disappeared (the alleged motorcycle accident). *Chronicles* does not mention Jesus once. It's not like a lot wasn't going on. There was the moment in 1974 when Dylan suddenly emerged from his internal exile to do a full-blown concert tour. It's hard to re-capture the kind of excitement that elicited. And all the rumors! Some fans were expecting plastic surgery reconstruction from the overhyped motorcycle accident that some Dylan writers are still saying "almost killed him" and dire things like that.

From what I gather, having spoken to someone who spoke to one of his doctors, his bike tipped over at slow speed and there was minor cervical trauma that didn't interfere with any music-making activities for long. He just wanted to avoid the public eye, so yes, you could say it was a kind of Dylan put-on, eagerly bought into by mythmaking writers and fans because it made his alleged brush with death a dra-matic addition to the myth—a moment of peripeteia. (But his experi-ence in New Orleans—I'm getting to it—was more significant.)

But in early 1974 there was the announcement of a reappear-ance—a tour that would kick off with a concert in Chicago—and I recall shamelessly pulling what little rank I had to get the tickets allotted to the *Village Voice*. It's hard to recapture the anticipatory ex-citement because, yes, I too had been caught up in the mythic mystery of Dylan's brush with death. And in his mystic journey to commune with Tibetan monks (another popular theory). I was still a Bobolator. I'm not sure how, but I recall rolling up to the old indoor Chicago hockey stadium venue in a smoke-filled VW van driven by a Dylan fanatic named Adam.

What, I wonder, became of him? Of Adam? He—like many of his kind—seemed to have little else in his life. That's how Dylan affected the vulnerable.

I'll never forget the mixture of awe and shock at hearing Dylan open that concert with a couldn't-be-more-obvious kiss-off song to his shivering fans: "Most Likely You'll Go Your Way, I'll Go Mine." It was a pure statement of distaste for those who loved him—or at least the lack of any desire to meet and mingle and share soulful insights with his fans (who mostly didn't care, being just happy he was there, alive).

But then there was a strange ending to the concert that Dylan only reveals later in *Chronicles* and that I still find hard to believe. He claims *he* was in a state of panic at the end. Yes, panic.

After the final encore, most of the fifteen thousand or so people held up lit BIC lighters, like votive candles saluting him. It was beautiful to watch the little flames spread throughout the crowd in the darkness. I don't know if this was the first instance of what became a standard practice at rock concerts, but I remember the light-dappled darkness and I remember being surrounded by people, some of them with tears streaming down their faces in gratitude that he was alive and could give so much to them.

But Dylan claims, not entirely convincingly, that the mass Bic display put him in a state of panic. He thought these votive-bearing devotees hated him so much (the old distaste for electricity) they were *planning to burn down the stadium* with him—and them—in it.

Now, it's true he'd faced hostile crowds of folkies on his last tour (which led him to the memorably mean-spirited revisionist aperçu about folk-music fans: "Folk music is a bunch of fat people"). Seriously, though, if he was being sincere in *Chronicles*, then it's a measure of how much his withdrawal from the world had left him prone to delusion at moments like this. Regardless of how trivial the motorcycle accident was, the retreat that followed left him radically perpendicular to the consciousness of the culture and his fans.

The panicky vision of the performer was a perception so far off. Those people in the stands with tears streaming from their eyes, those were tears of joy and gratitude. And yet Dylan could only see things through the lens of his grudge: "I was sick of the way my lyrics had been extrapolated," he wrote in *Chronicles* of his self-exile. "Their meanings subverted into polemics and that I had been anointed as the Big Bubba of Rebellion, High Priest of Protest, Czar of Dissent, the Duke of Disobedience, Leader of the Freeloaders, Kaiser of Apostasy, Archduke of Anarchy, the Big Cheese." He's still fighting that misperception—fighting it in 1974, when most had got the point and gotten past it, and fighting it in 2004, when *Chronicles* came out.

Actually, Dylan's rant could make a great "Subterranean Homesick Blues"–type rap song. He claims the titles enumerated are "all code words for *outlaw*." But let's be real: at the very least he adopted the *persona* of an outlaw in many of his songs, especially from the *Highway 61* period. "When you live outside the law, you must be honest" is just one gem (from "Absolutely Sweet Marie" on *Blonde on Blonde*).

So I suppose it's possible Dylan thought they were expressing fiery wrath that he'd abandoned his outlaw ethos and therefore wanted to burn the place down with him and them in it. Or maybe not.

Still, he went on to an amazingly productive year in 1974: he continued a long, sold-out tour, produced an album based on live concert recordings of him and the Band (*Before the Flood*) and produced what I would call his "Dad-rock" album (*Planet Waves*), of which more later. He was still planet bumping. And then he reached what many (I am among them) believed was his songwriting peak with *Blood on the Tracks* at the very end of the year. It's an album that deserves a separate chapter on Dylan and love. (See the "Love and Other Variants" chapter in this volume.)

Perhaps that was the peak of his charisma in America. The guy I met from Ecuador told me he was surprised him when he got to America in the 1970s and discovered that Dylan wasn't so big, "not as big as he was in Ecuador!" I think that's the transformation that has happened. Dylan cults have sprung up all over the world as he's continued his global touring, and his international star has grown bigger. I think in part that's what made him Nobel-worthy, despite the fact his albums only sell moderately well, if that, here in the United States.

By the way, the Ecuadorian guy was struggling to explain Dylan's appeal—since English was not his first language—and he arrived at something like "he gets into you really deep and even if you don't understand all the words you understand *him*." Few have said it better.

Still, somehow Dylan also found the time in the early '70s to spend months in Mexico filming a small role in Sam Peckinpah's surprisingly moving film, *Pat Garrett and Billy the Kid*. Dylan played a store clerk named Alias. We know Dylan always thought of himself as an alias to be shrugged on or off. "Someone else." "I'm not there." "I'm not him." "It's not me." Aside from the symbolism, it wasn't much of a part; I think he'd been promised more, but he played it for all it was worth. His big scene was when he was forced at gunpoint to read the names on the labels of a wall of canned goods during a robbery. There is a Warholian reference here, but even without him it's emblematic of the sameness, the canned-ness, the hermetically sealed-up personae he saw all around him. Or the way he had hermetically sealed himself in.

But he did the soundtrack to Peckinpah's movie, and the album released thereafter (*Pat Garrett and Billy the Kid*) contained not only the surefire popular "Knocking on Heaven's Door" but, I think more significantly, *three versions* of a Billy the Kid composition that for many fans may have been the best or most idiosyncratic Dylan effort since *Blonde on Blonde*, returning to the outlaw spirit that made him once so magnetic. Of the three versions of the "Billy" theme on the album, one is purely instrumental; the one I found myself attached to, the one that found a place deep in my heart, was called "Billy 4," and I think its haunted, hunted, achingly plaintive theme is one of those you can play on repeat 24/7 and never tire. In part, this is because you feel it's from the heart: he's a family man and a national treasure, but there's a skinny rattlesnake outlaw inside him that spits venom at propriety—and knows he'll pay for it sooner or later.

Perhaps this is why I have always found myself almost allergic to the Dad-rock Dylan you find on *Planet Waves*. Yes, there is at least one good song, half cribbed from George Harrison's "Something There Is About You," but it's a swoony delusion of a song, pushing its piety to the point of inauthenticity. It's too ostentatiously virtuous, as "Wedding Song"—also on that album—is, albeit in a different way.

"Wedding Song" is one of those universally popular Dylan ritual anthems like "Forever Young" and "Every Grain of Sand." For all too many, it's all the Dylan they know. Except when naming their child after him.

In fact, retrospectively, I think the Dad-rock years were as artistically sterile as the Christian years. Secular piety, not Testamental piety, but piety all the same. It's blasphemy to say, but Bruce Springsteen was better during those years. Dylan is almost always more entertaining when he lets his impiety loose. Less so when he gets into holier-than-thou mode, so perhaps there's more of a bridge to the Jesus years in the Dad-rock era than I'd imagined.

For all his respectability, now Nobelized, Dylan always was a kind of outlaw. In any case, he loved the outlaw myth. Loved it and lived it to the max when he and the Band took on the world with their electric guitar laser sabers. If the serpent isn't there, *he's* not there. It's not him.

After that 1974 tour—and the live album *Before the Flood*—that resulted, there were three years in which he gathered the elements for what was to be *Renaldo and Clara*, such as a grand tour (Rolling Thunder) plus the grandiose reincarnation of the Bohemian characters and Village folkie sensibility that gave his fame birth, with the original Village players he seems to have felt indebted to or conflicted about it. In addition, of course, he gave his ex-wife and his ex-lover (Joan Baez) star billing. Whatever happened to that motto, "don't look back"?

Perhaps it was only because of his Borgesian mental trick of separating himself from his past that he was able to attempt the folly of recreating it. Because—aside from the music, which was at its absolute peak (the *Rolling Thunder* and *Hard Rain* albums capture it)—the ambition of *Renaldo and Clara* to refute time (and offer us the formative characters of his oeuvre two decades after their formation) could be said to have a somewhat limited appeal. There's me. And there was the French girl in SoHo and similarly besotted Bobolators. But Dylan was unwilling to frame or explain to outsiders what to him was obvious: the anthropology of a vanished culture whose effects still saturate the world.

And then, in late 1977, as he was looking back over the footage from *Renaldo and Clara*, he met me. Just about the fulcrum, if not the apex, of the arc of his career, I like to think. Before *Renaldo and Clara* was released to almost unanimously irritated reviews (in January 1978)—the four-hour length a particular target—before his marriage was irrevocably broken (a backup singer was allegedly involved), and before Jesus entered the picture in the Tucson motel (August 1978).

All that is skipped over in *Chronicles* as he jumps from Archibald MacLeish to Daniel Lanois—and more importantly to Sun Pie—in New Orleans.

The chapter "Oh Mercy" is ostensibly about the making of that album with producer Lanois in New Orleans. Among other things, it's an extended granular look at songwriting and record making, two very different disciplines and their difficulties. Both of which Dylan says leave him unsatisfied, although it is apparent in these sessions that he produces a couple of masterpieces that he just inexplicably *leaves off the album.* He wants to let us know what *hard work* producing a Dylan album had become, when it used to be just being Dylan, being himself. But I think he wants to tell us more in his own elliptical way. The "Oh Mercy" chapter contains, I believe, a remarkable, esoteric subtext: an allegory of Dylan explaining—without alluding specifically to the Jesus period—how he escaped that dark time and learned again to embrace life and music.

It's all there in an amazing, ecstatic motorcycle trip he takes with his wife to the back bayou country of New Orleans and his meeting with a fabulous character I think he could well have made up: Sun Pie. Although it seems like *some* strange figure—perhaps not with that allegorical name—did play a part.

The structure of the chapter is unusual. Tripartite. In the way that *Chronicles* itself is tripartite. He begins where he ends. It begins with Dylan at what seems to be the absolute zero, lowest ebb of his life. His hand, the one he uses to strum his guitar strings, is in a cast ("a freak accident . . . ripped and mangled to the bone . . . severe nerve damage, still acute," he says, though he gives no description of how this trauma happened).

The accident to his hand has infected not just his physical but also his metaphysical outlook on life, he says. When the chapter opens, he's in "a state of regeneration." This is the secret theme of the "Oh Mercy" chapter: regeneration. Without speaking Jesus aloud, he's telling us how he, Dylan, rose from the virtual death, the artistic death, of being a born-again puppet and how he "regenerated" his love of art and life—and of the things of the world, however temporary and contingent. This is the time (late 1980s), he says, when he learns a new secret of music and songwriting. A time when the inability to play guitar causes him to turn to songwriting (and singing) instead of guitar playing—to performance as his focus. And a time when he finds himself "on a whole other level" in New Orleans and meets a character called Sun Pie.

But you could interpret the next few anguished pages about his state of mind at the time as a prose song of woe beyond woe.

This is Dylan in the late 1980s. In his late forties. No longer with Jesus. Left with a shrinking cadre of acolytes. Bored with performing, the intrinsic inauthenticity of faked sincerity, aware of his diminished cultural capital.

Here are some of the despairing things he says about himself at that time in *Chronicles*:

"I wasn't keeping my word with myself. What that word was I couldn't exactly remember."

"I had single-handedly shot myself in the foot too many times."

"There was a missing person inside me and I needed to find him."

"My own songs had become strangers to me. I didn't have the skill to touch their raw nerves. I couldn't penetrate the surfaces."

"I was always making some lame excuse. Actually I don't know who was making the excuse, I had closed the door on my own self."

"After depending so long on instinct and intuition both were ladies who had turned into vultures and were making me dry. Even spontaneity had become a blind goat."

What an unimaginably terrible state of mind. And yet such an eloquent way of expressing it.

"I hadn't planned to take it any further," he concludes. "Hadn't talked myself out of that."

Out of *that* that! Out of taking it further. Meaning stopping writing songs or stopping existing (suicide).

Whoa. I suddenly realized these epigrammatic expostulations of despair could be joined together—or loosely aligned—to make a fantastic Late Dylan song of despair. Or perhaps they were—as Shakespeare had it—"ripped untimely from the womb" of a song we'll never get to hear. Never came together. Was too terrifying for the singer to complete. Too dangerous for a listener to hear. A song just so powerfully bleak that Dylan had to bury all but a few traces of it in his prose. I wonder if he realized he had gotten to the bottom—or *a* bottom of his arc at this point, or feared there would *be* no bottom.

It seemed like he had.

He projects that fear even unto the Devil, claiming the Devil himself fears Hell. "The Devil comes here and sighs" when he reaches New Orleans. The Devil sighs. In all recorded literature this may be the first instance I've come upon in which the Devil is humanized enough to sigh. Not quite the Stones' "Sympathy for the Devil." But empathy for the Devil. Something one has never quite thought about:

What lies beneath Hell that would cause the Devil to sigh in despair? The Devil knows. And maybe Dylan now, too.

He was in a bad way.

But then the scene abruptly shifts. Part two of the tripartite structure. With no transitional words, Dylan takes us from the Devil in New Orleans to his encounter with the Dead, a name given additional sinister context by his previous meditations. But like the Joseph Campbellesque hero of epics, like Odysseus, Aeneas, and of course Dante, a hero seeking to complete a quest, a mission, must visit the underworld and commune with the dead in order to fulfill his destiny. Dylan's problem was that he had lost contact with whatever mission or destiny he was supposed to fulfill by those childhood "projections."

Then suddenly, perhaps from a magic potion, the serum of regeneration—one thinks of James Joyce's "moly"—he seems to find himself, musically at least. Apparently having imbibed, without at first knowing it, the Dead's acid—undoubtedly the finest, dropped in his drink—he discovers a mysterious new secretive musical trick. That "odd numerical system" that is the key to regenerating his performance persona. It reenergizes and regenerates him. Frankly, I don't know what to make of this, nor do musicians I've talked to. He writes:

> If you're using the [diatonic] scale, there are eight
> notes. In a pentatonic scale there are five. If you're
> using the first scale, and you hit 2, 5 and 7 to the
> phrase and then repeat it, a melody forms. Or you
> use it three times. Or you can use it once and 7
> twice. It's infinite what you can do and each time
> would create a different melody. The possibilities
> are endless. A song executes itself on several fronts.

On whole other levels. Still, "a song executes itself." Is that good?

Whatever you say Bob, if it works for you. But wait, is this a put-on?

"It's not a heavy theorized thing," he asserts unconvincingly, "it's geometrical. I know the universe was formed from mathematical principles and I was going to let that guide me."

He goes on in this sort of vein. At last, due to Bono, who also worked with Lanois (they did the superb U2 *Joshua Tree* album together), Dylan decides to take up temporary residence in New Orleans and begins to work on an album.

It is there in New Orleans that he takes up the story (in *Chronicles*) of his creative rebirth, the motorcycle trip, and his communion with Sun Pie.

Sun Pie owns a broken-down Old Curiosity Shop out in the bayou country where Dylan, riding a borrowed Harley with his wife on back, makes a stop.

It's the mid-1980s, and Dylan has been drifting away from hardline Christianity, though he still seems to love the promise of the apocalypse and the battle of Good and Evil, God and the Devil, Christ and Antichrist, it offered. But he knows his social capital—and his personal soul—has suffered for it. "I wanted to be a kinder person," he tells this fellow Sun Pie, a carpenter. When asked what he prayed for. Most likely in reference to the unkind scorching, scalding he had been subjecting his listeners to.

That it should be on a motorcycle ride is of course, as they say, karmic. Dylan and motorcycles. Someone could write a book. His love of them, the fake motorcycle crash. The title of the album *Street Legal* (which refers to the kind of overmuscled cycle fitted out to meet the restrictions permitting superpowered bikes to ride the highways) and the song "This Wheel's on Fire" in *The Basement Tapes* album. The Marlon Brando *Wild One* leather jacket. And of course the song (not one of my favorites) "Motorpsycho Nightmare," a weird combination of a traveling salesman joke and Hitchcock's *Psycho*.

Dylan is—in a (good) way—a motor psycho. And I have to admire the death-defying courage it takes to ride them big hogs. They seemed to be essential to his self-image.

It turns out that, in New Orleans, Dylan discovers a large number of cycles right to hand. "Lanois and his crew [had them] parked out back in the courtyard of the studio."

Dylan knows them all. "Mostly panheads with Hydra-glide front forks, chrome driving lamps, tombstone taillights . . . I had to have one of these."

Of course: "tombstone taillights."

So he starts cruising around New Orleans. And he starts to hear songs in his head, "the kind of songs when you're wide awake in your head and see and feel things and the rest of you is asleep."

But I want to tell you about this one particular motorcycle ride he describes in *Chronicles* and how it seems to suggest the "regeneration" of his arc.

He tells us that one morning he wakes his wife up (he never names her or tells us which one; it's not Sara, though) and they get on the Harley and head out into the bayou country. What follows is some of the most beautiful kinetic cinematic writing in all of Dylan's songs and prose.

Way out in the barely inhabited bayou country, he spies "[a]cross a vacant field stood an obscure roadside place, a gaunt shack called King Tut's Museum."

The subsequent five pages Dylan wrote about his encounter with Sun Pie and the King Tut hut may be the most resonant prose and perhaps the most resonant—and least well-known—language he has produced. What's more, I believe he is using the encounter with Sun Pie—whether fictional or not—to display how he escaped from the Christian straitjacket to a kind of pagan pantheist vison. Not a necessarily upbeat one. The key line might well be when Sun Pie wonders whether "all the good in the world has already been done." Have you ever heard anything bleaker? Or more like a memorable Dylan lyric?

> Across a vacant field stood an obscure roadside
> place, a gaunt shack called King Tut's Museum and
> it caught my eye. After filling the gas tank . . . We

went up the short steps and I walked in. My wife
stayed outside on a wooden swing bench.

Okay, need I call further attention to the exoticism of a King Tut museum in the outer swampland of the bayou? Tut conjures up an allusion
to still-hidden esoteric pyramidal secrets. Will any be disclosed here?

> The place sold trinkets, newspapers, sweets,
> handcraft items, baskets made of swamp cane that
> were woven in the area's elaborate patterns. There
> were figurines and sham jewels, some items in
> display cases, umbrellas, slippers, blue voodoo
> beads and votive candles . . . [T]he place was also
> a crawfish joint with a small counter on one side
> of the room. There were hog parts hanging from
> hooks on walls—hog jowls, hog ears, make you
> wanna squeal.

It's a celebration of *objects* for their very objectness, their varied objectness. It reminds me a bit of J. D. Salinger's description of the
Glass family medicine cabinet in "Zooey." Of flesh for the sake of
flesh—no holy ghostly, supernatural transubstantiation figures here. A
carnival of the manmade and the carnal. It made me think as well of
Harvard philosopher Elaine Scarry and her contrarian celebration of
materialism—well, of the material objects woven and crafted by men
and women—as the "glory" of consciousness.

And then the proprietor.

> It was run by an old-timer named Sun Pie, one of
> the most singular characters you'd ever want to
> meet. The man was short and wiry like a panther,
> dark face but with Slavic features, wore a narrow
> brimmed, flat topped straw hat . . . Sun Pie was

> working on a high loft chair. It looked like it
> came out of a cathedral. It was disassembled in
> pieces, clamped up on the sides and glued. He was
> sandpapering an edge of a six-planed leg.

The chair "came out of a cathedral"—a "disassembled" cathedral. Like Dylan, the chair is a refugee from a religious framework. And is the name Pie an accident? In the first section of *Chronicles*, the bohemian goddess Chloe is "cool as pie." But the referent here, I believe, is pi, as in pi r squared—the sacred ratio by which one can calculate the area of a circle (for instance, the face of the sun) if you know the diameter and thus the radius. We've seen Dylan playing with the mystical significance of musical numbers just above, so is the pi reference a figment of his mystical mathematical disposition at the time? Dylan seems attracted to the subtle potential mystical side of things that are not explicitly so categorized . . . as am I. As the song from that period "I and I." One of his "twice" songs.

> There were posters displayed, one of Bruce Lee,
> another of Chairman Mao. Behind the counter
> taped to the mirror was a wide, framed photograph
> showing the Great Wall of China. On the other
> brick wall was a jumbo sized American flag.

> The radio was on from beyond a wall and the
> sound was coming through in static. The Beatles
> were singing, "Do You Want to Know a Secret."

This evocation of secrecy causes Dylan to say to us readers, "Okay, do you believe me now something esoteric is going on?" And then make a rare comment about his friendly rivals, the Beatles. "Secret" (the song) is a perfectly sappy '50s love ballad, but nobody does it like them. They offered intimacy and companionship like no other group.

Okay, do you believe me *now*—that something esoteric is going on, something secretive? Or do you think it was just a cosmic accident that that particular Beatles song happened to be playing on the radio at that exact moment? A cosmic accident or an artistic contrivance by Dylan in case we need the nudge?

Dylan goes into a brief reverie about the Beatles, who were, after all, his coevals and his putative rivals, though close friends. The two, particularly Dylan and Lennon, bestrode the world for a time influencing each other, challenging each other, making each other better. The Beatles were flabbergasted by Dylan's *Another Side* album; Dylan was jump-started again creatively by *Rubber Soul* and *Revolver*, which reflected his inspiration and in part were influenced by Dylan's getting them high. (Have I mentioned Dylan pal Al Aronowitz, who was the intermediary in getting them the grass that turned them on for the first time with Dylan? I knew Al and he told me the story, and I believe it.)

"They were so easy to accept," says Dylan of the Beatles, and you think he's going to put them down for being easy, considering the raucous reception his changes got. But no, he goes on, they were "so solid. I remembered when they first came out. They offered intimacy and companionship like no other group. Their songs would create an empire. It seemed like a long time ago. A perfect '50s sappy love ballad ["Do You Want to Know a Secret"] and nobody but them could do it. Somehow there was nothing wussy about it. The Beatles blasted away."

I'll mention here the touching moment I saw Dylan and Lennon actually work together. Perhaps the only time, sadly. They were behind the mixing console at Electric Lady Studio on West Eighth Street in New York, where they collaborated on producing an album for the dodgy street singer David Peel featuring his signature song, "The Pope Smokes Dope." A billion dollars of musical talent behind that console. Silly as it seems, I found it oddly touching; Dylan and Lennon were extremely serious about their task, except when they'd occasionally exchange glances with a hint of a smile. I suppose you must have heard Dylan's very late song "Roll on, John," a beautiful tribute to the murdered Beatle that always brings me to tears.

But to return to King Tut's hut, the question of prayer now emerges in full.

Looking at Dylan's wife, Sun Pie asks Dylan if he is a "praying man." I find this quite amusing, a comment on her attractiveness and the problems beauty can cause, enough to call for prayer. But prayer is a loaded question for Dylan. We don't know (from Dylan) where he was on his journey in and out of straitjacketed Christian conversion.

This was followed in *Chronicles* by a long, mad disquisition from Sun Pie about how the American Indians were originally Chinese:

> You know, the Chinese were here at the beginning.
> They were the Indians. You know, the red man.
> The Comanche, the Sioux, the Arapaho, the
> Cheyenne—all them people—they were all
> Chinese. Came over here about the time when
> Christ was healing the sick. All the squaws and
> chiefs came from China—walked across from Asia,
> came down through Alaska and discovered this
> place. They became Indians a lot later.

And, Sun Pie says, "The Chinese nightingale will sing in the land."

This, of course, is crazy as history but not as a kind of evocation of identity change, conversion. The Chinese going Indian like Dylan going electric.

And then it takes a biblical "ten lost tribes" turn, when Sun Pie tells Dylan, "Trouble was that they split up into parties and tribes and started wearing feathers and forgot they were Chinese." ("That's not me." "I'm not there.")

I love that line, "The Chinese nightingale will sing in the land." Where does this all come from, though? The bayou or the thickets of Dylan's mind? You feel there's a Dylan song lost or being born in Sun

Pie's monologues ("he who's not busy being born is busy dying"—from "Gates of Eden").

And then we get to the really religious or spiritual part, where Sun Pie asks Dylan what he prays for, whether he prays for the world. Dylan replies that he never thought about praying for the world. Instead, he says, "I pray that I can be a kinder person."

Fascinating: An important concept; it took me a long time to learn, as I always thought prayer was a selfish thing. Asking God to "pull strings for you," as Dylan had characterized it in my interview with him a decade or so earlier. But one finds praying for *others* is a powerful thing. One doesn't have to believe in God to pray! A revelation to me and perhaps to Dylan.

"'Sea of Love' came on the radio," Dylan continues. "It felt like I must have been cast off somewhere and it was time to go back and that if I had come out of New Orleans with any bitterness or hostility, it ought to be dead by now."

Is that a clue? Is it too much to believe that Sun Pie's disquisition on prayer would be capped by that song? Do you know it, "Sea of Love"? It's not the hippie anthem the name suggests. It's an extremely mournful—ominous—sounding tune: "Come with me, my love / To the sea, the sea of love." The singer makes the sea of love sound like a place of reunion after communion—or death.

In any case, it's almost all too pat, isn't it? The capstone of a spiritual journey from an abandoned dogma to a Sun Pie paganism. And yet, "It felt like I must have been cast off somewhere and it was time to go back and that if I had come out of New Orleans with any bitterness or hostility, it ought to be dead by now."

Clearly, in telling this story, truth or fiction, Dylan is announcing in his own idiosyncratic way a different kind of spirituality that doesn't need the Ten Commandments of the Abrahamic religions. But it does need prayer.

I can't help thinking of one of Dylan's beautiful though ominous songs—one of the gems of the 1980s—that rock critics disparage.

"(Who's Gonna Take Away His) License to Kill" comes directly from this riff. I'd always thought it was another Dylan song that came out of his argument with God and *His* "license to kill" arbitrarily, uncaringly.

And then, curiously, Sun Pie says this: "Does your conscience bother you? It doesn't matter; a man's conscience is useless clear or guilty, a live man's is anyway."

"That conscience stuff would stick in my mind," Dylan muses. After all, he'd been taxed all his life with being the "conscience of his generation."

"Sun Pie was inspiring. He didn't play kids' games. He was the right guy to run into at the right time."

Exactly the time the arc began to shift upward again. But why? What do we make of this?

First and foremost, one can't read this without feeling the renewed love of the world. Of objects in their radiant strangeness. I remember Mario Cuomo, politician and spiritual thinker, telling me once that the achievement of Teilhard de Chardin's theology was to allow one to simultaneously love the things of the world and the unseen things of the Spirit and that the things of the world all contained a germ of Spirit growing toward God. I wouldn't go that far.

Dylan had run afoul, run aground, run away in his unmediated love of the alleged things of the Spirit that his Christian group demanded. One can now feel his secret joy at the carnivalesque pageant of objects, oddballs, and their esoteric truths—and how they lead one upward toward prayer.

And so, as the Clancy Brother asked of the Holden Caulfield–Dylan way back when: "What have we here?"

One thing we have here is a fellow named Dylan who not long ago threw it all away, all earthly material substance (including love and respect for worldly things) to worship the son of a carpenter, Jesus. And here we have Dylan encountering Sun, a carpenter who puts things together for him in a new way.

Nails it, you might say.

CHAPTER 9

GOD AND WILLY LOMAN

I was only dimly aware of the drama behind the scenes when I met Dylan. I knew that there was a bitter postmarital breakup, a custody battle going on between him and Sara Lownds, the woman who had been his "mystical wife," the one he wrote "Sara" for. You know "Sara," a beautiful ode in which he makes a *very* special point of claiming to have "stay[ed] up all night in the Chelsea Hotel writing 'Sad Eyed Lady of the Lowlands' for you." (A somewhat defensive-sounding, even doth-protest-too-much gesture, knowing how many self-proclaimed sad-eyed ladies in the Village claimed to have been the ones he wrote "Sad Eyed Lady" for.) There had been a marital reconciliation—purportedly when Sara walked into Dylan's studio just as he "happened" to be playing a take of "Sara" (I always had my doubts about the accidental nature of that). But then the split became even more bitter.

And then there was the movie. Someone very close to him, one of the sad-eyed-lady candidates (who actually had and still has—if I may say so—dark sparkling eyes that dance with mischief, so you can believe it), told me just how important the three-year-long effort to create *Renaldo and Clara* had been to him. How its success would mean a quantum leap from folk and rock icon to movie star and movie maker.

It was not to be. It could have and maybe *should* have, but it just wasn't. And perhaps that, as much as the divorce, was the reality that made it all come crashing down in a way that surrendering to Jesus ("spiritual self-medication," as I once wrote of J. D. Salinger) was the only way to keep on keeping on in the face of shattering disappointments.

Indeed, it may be that, for those looking for the real divide in Dylan's career, it shouldn't be folk to rock or Jewish to Jesus but hope to despair over *Renaldo and Clara*. It could have changed everything, lastingly.

It was *Renaldo and Clara* that led me to the lunch-counter grilled cheese question about God. Which I'm getting to. But that week I spent with Dylan might be said to have been the week that decided the movie's fate. It was the week in which Dylan made the final push to cut the hundreds of hours of footage down to what was a "slender" four-hours-plus release print.

He couldn't cut it any further. Believe me, I understand the feeling. But in refusing to cut he almost inevitably doomed it, cut its own throat. Which is a tragedy because, among the other great Dylan Studies schisms, I'm on the side of those who believe *Renaldo and Clara* was a flawed masterpiece. Still is, even though it's been withdrawn from circulation. Indeed, as I've indicated earlier, one of the higher purposes I hope to serve with this book is to convince Dylan, Inc. (and Dylan himself, of course) to make it available again.

It may have its problems (I'll get into my problem with the lamentable influence of Allen Ginsberg on it), but for one thing it contains the very peak of live Dylan music—and a peek at the culture that helped create that phenomenon.

Its generosity and historical perspective in that respect is impressive. It's a great document that might be called—in homage to Lytton

Strachey's famous *Eminent Victorians*—"Eminent Bohemians." It just so happens that, the night before I wrote this paragraph, one of the proliferating Dylan websites published all the fragments of lost or unreleased footage from *Renaldo and Clara* that could be found. I got chills watching Joan Baez sing "Diamonds and Rust," one of the many beautifully framed and deeply colored patches of film. I want to see it all again—perhaps in conjunction with the release of this book. One can hope.

I don't know what to think about the risk of releasing it at four-hours-plus back then. In hindsight, it could have been hailed for its daring, but to most, it seems like a terrible miscalculation or a brave bit of defiance. Not that the four-plus-hours version didn't have its fans.

There are those who have made erudite cinematic cases for it. Here is one of the more articulate reviews, an excerpt of which I found online:

> The movie is a masterpiece in its original 4 hrs.
> version. But you need to watch it several times to
> understand the system that was used to construct
> the film. According to Allen Ginsberg the movie
> was edited based on a system Dylan had laid out on
> index cards. There are recurring themes and motifs
> (the rose, the lady in white, the use of certain colors,
> the use of masks, "reality" vs. stage etc. etc.). Each
> scene was assigned one of those themes/motifs
> and the movie was constructed along those lines.
> Furthermore one interpretation sees the whole
> movie as Renaldo's dream. Check the scene of
> Dylan as Renaldo "waking up" near the end of the
> movie. The dream interpretation would explain the
> dream-like flow of the film.

Indeed, during talks, Dylan would bang on about Renaldo's dream—Ginsberg's influence, I'd wager.

In order to get into the film it helps to study the movie that inspired it: the French movie "Les Enfants du Paradis/Children Of Paradise" (1945). A movie that also uses stage performances to comment on the relationships between the protagonists, just like "R & C." "Les Enfants du Paradis/Children Of Paradise" also is a very long movie (approx. 200 mins). The [once] famous "Rolling Thunder Revue" logotype was inspired by the opening title card of "Les Enfants du Paradis/Children Of Paradise." Both films feature one of the leading characters in whiteface, both have a "woman in white," both repeatedly use flowers as a prominent symbol, both alternate between on-stage, back-stage and "real life" scenes, the dialogue in "R & C" shares similarities with the dialogue in "Les Enfants du Paradis/Children Of Paradise" and both films use a cubist approach in that they present the main characters from the differing perspectives of the other characters.[3]

All of which makes clear that Dylan wanted *Renaldo and Clara* to be his *Children of Paradise* for all those achingly hopeful fellow players in the early '60s Village folk scene when he was "a complete unknown." You can see what I mean about the influence of Ginsberg's schematizing. And scheming. According to several insiders, Ginsberg had a pathetically unrealistic dream of becoming a big rock star like Dylan and hoped that *Renaldo and Clara*—in which he's an annoying intrusive presence as a wandering interlocutor—would catapult him to fame. Sadly (sort of), no.

---

3 Anonymous commentator on the blog *Music Ruined My Life*, http://musicruinedmylife.blogspot.com/2013/03/dylans-fiascoes-renaldo-and-clara-1978.html

But the music! The music represented what I believe is a now-unassailable peak of a great artist's work. Almost every song crackles with energy, pulses with passion.

It took me a while to come to this view. I had to take the *Renaldo and Clara* test first.

Let me put this pivotal moment in the context of the arc of Dylan's career. It was after he had become a rock star of "the struggle"—the civil rights, antinuke, antiwar struggle (even if his views on Vietnam are hard to decode—everyone assumed he was on their side). It was after he turned down Joan Baez's pleas to join the anti–Vietnam War protesters—a refusal that turned a large segment of lefty/folkies off. He then turned off another large segment by going electric in 1965 and 1966, and by "reinventing rock and roll," as more than one commentator has put it (something I most recently heard in a documentary featuring critic Clinton Heylin). In any case, by all accounts (including what Dylan told me), this attempt at the cinematic heights was the very peak of all he'd been seeking—then, like karma, like retribution, like a prophet being stoned (as St. Stephen was), he suddenly stopped "tearing through these quarters" like the fiery St. Augustine. At that point he was burned-out Bob.

Then, in early 1975, arguably the greatest Dylan album of all was released: *Blood on the Tracks*, with its polysemous title—train tracks, the tracks of a wounded animal escaping from a trap, the tracks on a junkie's arm, the tracks on a vinyl album. It contains a string of masterpieces and two near misses. I'll have a lot more to say about it, especially about the shocking, radical revision and dumbed-down lyrics that have been substituted for one of the greatest Dylan lines of all: "she still lives inside of me / we've never been apart."

In 1975–76, he arranged the filming of his electrifying tour, the Rolling Thunder Revue, to supply the visuals and musical soundtrack for *Renaldo and Clara*; it was a masterpiece of performance art in motion and perhaps the peak of all rock and roll up to that time. The film was designed to be a record of a tour, an Origins Myth of Dylan and the bohemian culture, the folk and rock matrix from which he emerged.

The Rolling Thunder Revue was an agglomeration of musicians from Dylan's coffeehouse beginnings (Ramblin' Jack Elliott, Joan Baez) to his rock-and-roll notoriety, traveling across the land and pausing for an overly pious Ginsberg-orchestrated visit to Jack Kerouac's grave (designed to make it more about him, Ginsberg—no, he gets no quarter from me) and other landmarks of alternate, Gnostic American, culture. The tour was Dylan's summa of his romantic life, as well, with his wife and Joan Baez playing mysterious roles.

Nevertheless, the tour and film to follow were not exactly mainstream fare, though he and those around him wanted it to reach and be embraced not just by Dylanologists and his cult followers but by all America.

This is where I came in.

This is where my *Renaldo and Clara* test comes in. Dylan's people had embarked on a major attempt to expand his base in order for this film to break out and make its auteur a star of a higher magnitude, "on a whole other level."

They had contacted *Playboy* (circulation then five million or so), asking if the magazine would like Dylan to engage in one of its notoriously long and sometimes notoriously controversial interviews. (This was shortly after Jimmy Carter had almost derailed his presidential campaign by admitting in a *Playboy* interview—in what seems like an attempt to ingratiate himself with what he regarded as its sex-crazed readers—that he had "lust in his heart.")

As it happened, the interview editor there, Barry Golson, had, about a year before, asked me if there was anyone I'd be interested in interviewing, and—without thinking too much about it—I'd said, "Howard Hughes or Bob Dylan." I forget the order, but they both seemed fascinating because of their famous secretiveness, and Dylan had not given an interview since he suffered some unspecified trauma—the rumors were rife of brain damage—from an alleged motorcycle accident.

In any case, a year or so later Golson called and told me that Dylan would be available and that Golson had struck a tough bargain with his people granting me a week's worth of access—unprecedented, they said. They also promised that the fiasco (or, depending how you looked on it, accidental triumph) of Dylan's last *Playboy* interview— with Nat Hentoff in 1967—would not be repeated. (Dylan had largely taken the interview transcript from Hentoff and rewritten it, mostly in put-on form.)

But it didn't turn out to be as easy as promised. I arrived in Los Angeles and checked into the *Playboy* suite in the Sunset Marquis, that small boutique hotel tucked cavern-like under the slope that ran south from Sunset Boulevard and which was the haunt of touring rock stars and glam groupies who graced the pool.

The next morning, I packed up my tape recorder and several large yellow legal pads I'd already filled with exegetical, not to say Talmudic, questions, and I drove to the Burbank studio where Dylan was engaged in the mind-numbing, painstaking process of "looping" dialogue and synching sound in a cavernous editing room.

But I learned, to my dismay, that I would not be allowed to speak to him yet. Possibly not at all. "Bob wants you to see the rough cut [of *Renaldo and Clara*] just to get a sense of what he's up to."

It was not unreasonable, though what I got a sense of was a test: Was I worthy? Would I understand the grand ambition, the profundity, packed into the slender four hours?

Nonetheless, I was fortunate on two counts. As soon as I sat myself down in the deeply cushioned screening room armchair and the lights dimmed and the sound came up, I knew I'd be able to pass the test. First, the music: much of the onstage footage shot on the Rolling Thunder Revue was Dylan at his most crisp, committed, and passionate in his delivery of his best work. If it was modeled on *Children of Paradise*, I felt like a child of paradise hearing it and seeing it (remember I was still a Bobolator; the looming shadow of the Jesus brainwashing tragedy was as yet invisible to me).

As for the actual *Children of Paradise* aspect, there was much for those who were into marital and romantic gossip; the scenes between Joan Baez and Sara Dylan were nerve-racking and cringe-worthy. But the film itself suffered from the heavy hand of Allen Ginsberg and his schematic overlay of color-coded symbolism and all-too-obvious allegorical metaphors and "moments" like the uncomfortable visit to Kerouac's grave, which Ginsberg designed to show that Ginsberg and Kerouac were the real progenitors of Bob Dylan.

Whereas *Children of Paradise* had a kind of graceful, heartfelt, light touch, here there was a heavy-handed overlay of schematic symbolism that was evident in the very first image: Dylan onstage singing, his face painted white as if he were a (*Children of Paradise*) mime, and on top of that a *transparent mask*. Get it: It's a mask but it really doesn't *conceal*, it *reveals*! But reveals only *another* mask, the whiteface paint. I found myself relaxing: As an English major, this was right in my exegetical wheelhouse, you might say. Everything fell into place, fortunately for me, less fortunately for the strained obviousness of its avant-garde pretensions: A Woman in White, someone playing "Bob Dylan" who wasn't really Bob Dylan, that kind of Child's Garden of Surrealism thing.

Did I mention that I have always felt Ginsberg was a kind of aesthetic con man/parasite in relation to Dylan? A groupie who clothed himself in Buddhist gravitas in order to insinuate himself into Dylan's graces? One of the things I've always wondered is how Dylan fell for it.

But among the Eminent Bohemians, Ginsberg was a certified Eminence, the real "Pope of Greenwich Village," and Dylan fell for it. Still, it made things easy for me.

I took copious notes, went back to the Sunset Marquis, and repaired to the great old-school diner just above it, on Sunset—Ben Franks—for their signature green chili cheese omelets, and I prepped for my test the next morning.

I was so confident that I walked into Dylan's office, shook hands with him, and said, "You know, Bob, I just don't think we should do this unless we're on the same page about this film," or something like that. Then I proceeded to deconstruct all four-plus-hours in four-and-a-half minutes like the good little English major I was. Not that I was so good, it was that the pretensions to complexity were as see-through as that transparent mask.

Dylan looked at me quizzically. I could tell he was a little *hurt*. I had perhaps overplayed my hand. Was I saying it was too easy to decode? Then he found a way to respond that was signature Dylan: turning the whole moment into a way of insulting me.

"You been talkin' to *Ginsberg*?" he half sneered. As if I'd *cribbed* my entire painstaking analysis from Ginsberg. Which confirmed my suspicion that the overrated, over-weighted poet had been responsible for the over-freighted symbology that bogged the film down.

To me, in retrospect, it was a badge of honor that Dylan had thought enough of me to insult me!

Nonetheless, my exegesis had gained me a ticket to ride, and over the course of the next week I could see how the explosive pressure cooker Dylan was in led to the crack-up and the Jesus-freak soul theft.

For one thing, Dylan had unwisely posed an impossible problem in his film: woven throughout was a plotline that involved Renaldo (played by Dylan) being torn between the Woman in White (played by his "mystical wife," Sara) and the girlfriend in black (played by his former lover Joan Baez). He made the risky choice to feature this real-life triangle as the centerpiece of the movie, even after he and Sara had broken up and gotten back together—shakily—again. Pro tip: don't make a movie about your wife and the one-time love of your life as-suming your marriage is going to last.

What a profound Hell that must have been for Dylan. And yet he was very decent to me, as I've said, almost like a workman doing his job, a chore for the film. I didn't care. He said a *lot* of revealing things, more of which I'll get to.

WHAT DR. DEATH'S LAWYER SAID

L et me preface the next section—a plunge again into the theodicy question—by describing the strangest rumor, legend, myth that I've never seen reported anywhere else in Dylan lore. It may be a fantasy, but it speaks to the seriousness of the post-Jesus aftershocks that Dylan—and his fans—had to overcome, how much it took to come back from the conversion. It reveals how much self-knowledge there is in that line from "Mississippi"—"They say you can always come back / But you can't come back all the way." (And, by the way, who exactly was a certain Judaean who promised He'd "come back"—all the way?)

It's a story I first heard from one of Dr. Death's lawyer's. That's the late Dr. Jack Kevorkian, whose first trial for his first assisted suicide I'd been covering. It turns out that the lawyer had a close connection in Los Angeles who had a close connection to someone closely connected to the production of Dylan's absolutely worst low-point post-Jesus album (*Under the Red Sky*), the one that raised the question if he *could* rise from the dead, if he'd ever come back at all. (Try listening to "Wiggle Wiggle" without feeling profound sorrow and the pain from which it emerged.)

That's as specific I'm going to get about the source, but it's actually closer than I've made it sound. Very close, otherwise I wouldn't repeat it at all. In any case, the word from this source was that, about this time (in the late 1980s), Dylan had to be hospitalized for a hushed-up nervous breakdown. One that took the form in which, it was said, he had come to believe he *was* Jesus Christ. Incarnate.

If not precisely true, it makes sense "on a whole other level." Look, I was a Bobolator; it shouldn't be entirely surprising that at a certain point *Bob* became a Bobolator, too.

At least bardolators focus on idolizing the divinity of Shakespeare's *language*, not necessarily on the divinity of the *man*. Bobolators, on the other hand, very often have some feeling that there was something about the man himself that partook of "a whole other level" than mere humanity.

Of course, some have carried it to ridiculous lengths, as a sort of secular religion—Dylanism—in which every one of his words is parsed and searched as if from an oracle, a seer, a messenger, a demi-god, or more.

GOD AND THE HOLOCAUST

But I want to go back to that last day at the greasy spoon in Burbank when I asked Dylan about God over grilled cheese sandwiches. Because it was the beginning of my thinking about Dylan and theodicy, his argument with God, and the "crazy sorrow" that drove it.

Here's how we got to it.

"Did you grow up thinking about the fact that you were Jewish?" I asked him.

"No, I didn't. I've never felt Jewish. I don't really consider myself Jewish or non-Jewish. I don't have much of a Jewish background. I'm not a patriot to any creed. I believe in all of them and none of them. A devout Christian or Moslem can be just as effective as a devout Jew."

"You say you don't feel Jewish. But what about your sense of God?"

"I feel a heartfelt God. I don't particularly think that God *wants* me thinking about Him all the time. I think that would be a tremendous *burden* on Him, you know. He's got enough people asking Him for favors. He's got enough people asking Him to pull strings. I'll pull my own strings, you know."

Which was a great answer itself. But then he goes on to say something that still cracks me up every time I read it, it's so *echt* Dylan. We had been talking earlier about the "spiritual crisis" that seemed to beset the world and create discord, wars, suffering. Without using the word "theodicy," Dylan had an answer. I'm still not sure how serious he was—was it a put-on, and even if it was, did it express something real?

"I remember seeing a *Time* magazine on an airplane a few years back," he said, "and it had a big cover headline, 'IS GOD DEAD?' I mean, that was—would *you* think that was a responsible thing to do? What does *God* think of that? I mean, if you were God, how would you like to see that written about yourself? You know, I think the country's gone downhill since that day."

"Really?" I said, trying to assess his seriousness.

"Uh-huh."

"Since that particular question was asked?"

"Yeah; I think at that point, some very irresponsible people got hold of too much power to put such an irrelevant thing like that on a magazine when they could be talking about real issues. Since that day, you've had to kind of make your own way."

"If you were God . . . ?" What a great image! God as Willy Loman dragging his carry-on baggage to the rear of economy class, passing an aisle seat where someone is reading *Time*'s (real) "Is God Dead" cover.

What was also remarkable was the exchange of souls/exchange of personae with God. He was putting himself in God's place, looking at the *Time* cover through the eyes of God.

That exchange of personae thing always reminded me of what is perhaps the single-most vicious put-down line in any Dylan song. Not put-on, put-down. The one in "Positively 4th Street" where he runs into some old Village hanger-on or folkie rival (on the Bohemian Boulevard of Broken Dreams, Fourth Street), a guy clearly jealous of his success but not wanting to admit it; instead, he expresses it in an undermining way by not acknowledging it, conspicuously.

Which prompts Dylan, in a cascading string of brilliant and cruel put-downs, to write derisive but incredibly melodic lines capped by his all-time best insult, I believe:

I wish that for just one time
You could stand inside my shoes
You'd know what a drag it is to see you.

Harsh. But funny. And I see a parallel between the standing inside his shoes and *his* standing inside God's shoes and getting a glimpse of pathetic human arrogance à la *Time.*

Clearly he was undergoing some shift in his relation to God. The shoes were on the other feet.

And something he said earlier about Jesus made me wonder (in retrospect) whether he was beginning to think of making a shift from the Jewish God to His Son:

"You talked earlier about a spiritual crisis. Do you think Christ is the answer?"

"What is it that attracts people to Christ?" he asked rhetorically. "The fact that it was such a tragedy, is what. Who does Christ become when he lives inside a certain person? Many people say that Christ lives inside them: Well, what does that mean? I've talked to many people whom Christ lives inside; I haven't met one who would want to trade places with Christ. Not one of his people put himself on the line when it came down to the final hour. What would Christ be in this day and age if he came back? What would he be? What would he be to fulfill his function and purpose? He would have to be a leader, I suppose."

Very ambiguous. Who would Christ be? "A leader, I suppose." Or maybe a folk singer with a miraculous career. I know this is somewhat indiscreet (and probably untrue), but this is not primarily an investigative biography—it's a biography of the impact of Dylan on the consciousness of culture, the outsized effect he had, even after he'd stayed in Mississippi just a day too long. And so an analysis of the form the mythology took is not inappropriate, I believe, and this may be the ultimate myth.

But to return to God as Willy Loman. When I came upon that passage and reread it recently, I couldn't help thinking of Dylan's God as Willy Loman. And of the amazing theodicy passage in Joseph Heller's *Catch-22*. I had written an essay on the occasion of the reissue of that novel and made the case that it was not so much an antiwar novel as an *anti-God* novel. A theodicy novel.

And I focused on the thematic centrality of the following passage, which begins with rage and then dismisses God as a bumbler.

Not a Willy Loman but "a country bumpkin" (or Arthur Miller's condescending simulacrum of a country bumpkin).

It grows out of an argument Yossarian recounts having with the wife of his commanding officer, Lieutenant Scheisskopf. (Occasionally, subtlety isn't Heller's strong suit.) It's Thanksgiving day, and she's reproving Yossarian for not being thankful, and Yossarian says, "I bet I can name two things to be miserable about for every one you can name to be thankful for."

Among her responses: "Be thankful you're healthy."

"Be bitter you're not going to stay that way," he says.

"Be glad you're even alive," she says.

"Be furious you're going to die," he counters.

They continue until Yossarian launches into a page-long denunciation of God that I think is the blasphemous heart of the book—and of the black humor culture that Dylan played an important part of:

> "And don't tell me God works in mysterious
> ways," Yossarian continued, hurtling over her
> objections. "There's nothing so mysterious about
> it. He's not working at all. He's playing or else He's
> forgotten all about us. That's the kind of God you
> people talk about—a country bumpkin, a clumsy,
> bungling, brainless, conceited, uncouth hayseed.
> Good God, how much reverence can you have for
> a Supreme Being who finds it necessary to include
> such phenomena as phlegm and tooth decay in His
> divine system of creation? . . . when He robbed

old people of the power to control their bowel
movements? Why in the world did he ever create
pain? . . . Oh, He was really being charitable to
us when He gave us pain! [to warn us of danger]
Why couldn't He have used a doorbell instead to
notify us, or one of His celestial choirs? Or a system
of blue-and-red neon tubes right in the middle of
each person's forehead. Any jukebox manufacturer
worth his salt could have done that. Why couldn't
He? . . . What a colossal, immortal blunderer! . . .
His sheer incompetence is almost staggering."

Wow! Welcome to the world of black humor. It's a tour de force of comic theodicy. People speak too narrowly when they talk of *Catch-22* as a satire of humanity. Or mainly an antiwar novel. It's that, yes, and there are few better. But it's really a vicious satiric attack on God as much as on his poorly made creatures. This denunciation of God comes from the heart—Yossarian's, anyway—and transcends any denunciation of the evil of war. It's about the evil of existence itself and the creator of that existence and that evil.

I actually think that the importance of this passage in *Catch-22* dwarfs the obviousness of the passage about Snowden's death, which critics tirelessly tell us is the supreme moment of the novel. Yossarian's supposedly shocking discovery of mortality just does not live up to the metaphysical venom of this novel. Okay, it's horrible to have someone's guts spill into your hands, but give me a break, he's been through war, he's seen death.

A passage in the "I see everything twice" chapter is far more caustic, scathing, and deeply shocking and disturbing. Because it's not saying death is bad. It's saying life is bad, existence is horrible. Why, in fact, get all upset about leaving the shambles of existence that this deranged "country bumpkin" Creator has bequeathed us?

In conjunction with that "I see everything twice" passage, I would mention "Don't Think Twice" and the cry at the close of Dylan's most manic, frantic, and funny song from his peak black humor tragic–absurdist period, "Stuck Inside of Mobile with the Memphis Blues Again." The one that ends on "twice":

> *And here I sit so patiently*
> *Waiting to find out what price*
> *You have to pay to get out of*
> *Going through all these things twice.*

Which things twice? (Don't think twice.) Well, since I'm approaching a far deeper look at Dylan and theodicy, I'll tell you: two Holocausts. Hitler's and the nuclear one to come. And the feeling of existence being trapped between them and what one is really compelled to think of God. No Willy Loman, no country bumpkin. Not even the "nebbish," as Yehuda Bauer, the greatest Israeli historian of the Holocaust, would put it to me in Jerusalem not far from the place at Hebrew University where Gershom Scholem had his study.

That encounter with Bauer was a landmark one for me in terms of thinking about theodicy. In addition to being a legendary historian, Bauer was at the time editor of the not-exactly-cheerful-sounding scholarly quarterly *Holocaust and Genocide Studies*.

I was there to talk to him for the book that would eventually become *Explaining Hitler*. I had just come from an exhausting discussion of post-Holocaust theodicy with Emil Fackenheim, who wrestled to the end of his life with how to reconcile the God he wanted to continue to believe in with the God who was silent, absent from the death camps. Fackenheim conceded he did not have a good answer but referred to what has come to be known as his 614th Commandment (after the 613 that the Orthodox believe are to be found in the Bible about how to live all aspects of life). His 614th Commandment is: "Thou shalt give to Hitler no posthumous victories." One such posthumous victory would be to reject God because of Hitler.

That directive is noble but, to many, unsatisfying. It was certainly unsatisfying to Bauer. We had been discussing various post-Holocaust theodicies, including the noxious one proposed by the ultra-Orthodox Sephardic Shas rabbi in Israel who construed the Holocaust as just punishment for European Jews who had fallen away from strict observance of the Commandments with their modernism.

Bauer called this "obscene," and he launched into one of the most unforgettably caustic post-Holocaust formulations I have heard:

"There's no way that there can be an all-powerful and just God. He can be all-powerful *or* just. Because if He's all-powerful, he's Satan [in that an all-powerful God could have spared the lives at least of the million and a half children whom even the Shas rabbi would agree had no time to sin]."

And then he added: "If He's not all-powerful He's just a nebbish."

Nebbish is, of course, the Yiddish word for "hopeless bumbler"—Heller's country bumpkin, Dylan's bumbling Willy Loman!

I asked Bauer to expand on his "nebbish" view of God.

"Well, you know, a poor chap who has to be *supported*, a God who needs to draw his strength from us. This is [theologian] Irving Greenberg's idea."

Greenberg, not well-known outside Jewish scholarly circles, is in fact a foundational figure in the post-Holocaust attempt to reconcile God and the Holocaust. His essay "Pillar of Smoke" suggested that God is in *combat* with evil and it is the responsibility of human beings by acts of reverence and mercy to "support" God in His struggle. It has been quite influential, though often unacknowledged. It is—as Norman Mailer once conceded to me—the source of the single recurrent powerful idea that animates Mailer's entire oeuvre: that every act of human courage or cowardice (Mailer's formulation) either helps or hurts God in His struggle with the Devil.

Greenberg's theodicy can be found in the enormously successful but entirely unpersuasive book by Rabbi Harold Kushner, *When Bad Things Happen to Good People.*

Bauer was having none of it: "I don't need a God like that. What kind of God *is* that, you know he's not all powerful, he's all *present?*" Bauer's argument with God was not dissimilar to Dylan's. Kushner seeks to explain God's absence from the death camps as inaction, yes, but we must celebrate God's presence.

Bauer's phrase *all present* is a direct reference to Fackenheim's theodicy, his tortured rationale for the absence of what Fackenheim called "The Commanding Voice of God" at Auschwitz. That is, Fackenheim wanted to find *some* presence of God at Auschwitz, even a silent witnessing presence. But supposedly he was *there* in the acts of love and generosity, however futile.

Bauer had no patience for a God who merely suffers silently with the victims: "When He's there He cries," he says, mocking Fackenheim. "That's very nice of him, but it doesn't help me much. He's totally superfluous. There's no one to pray to in that concept."

God as Satan. Or as an impotent nebbish. These are the alternatives we're left with in the bleak post-Holocaust landscape, according to Bauer. Or perhaps Dylan's implicit indictment: "Hitler WAS history."

But Bauer and Dylan were not alone. Indeed, this bleak view was essentially the core of an influential cultural movement among post-Holocaust American Jewish artists: the black humor movement. It translated the absolute bleakness into absurdist black comedy. Not haha comedy but caustic, Beckett-like comedy.

When I reread Bauer's dismissal of Fackenheim's concession about God's recusal of "The Commanding Voice" recently, I could not help recalling the invocation of a failed "commanding voice" in a central Dylan song, on the same album in which he mocks the Abraham/Isaac "kill me a son" command. It's in the aptly named "Tombstone Blues," and it offers a scabrous New Testament–era story about the alleged Son of God:

> *Well John the Baptist after torturing a thief*
> *Looks upon his hero the Commander-in-Chief*

Saying, "Tell me great hero, but please make it brief
Is there a hole for me to get sick in?"

This is strong stuff, however humorously it's phrased. Now we're moving from Old to New Testament and leaving no stone unturned or unthrown. Everybody must get stoned. Even every divine figure— God, Jesus, John the Baptist—"must get stoned." Those who write about *that* song trace it to the New Testament stoning of St. Stephen. Saints, too. There is anger here, such as John the Baptist vomiting his disgust for the torturer God (he was "just following orders"). The responsibility is "on a whole other level."

I'm not sure why no one has put this together. I think it forces one to think the unthinkable: God is Satan or a nebbish.

Nobody wants to hear that. I recall when I gave a lecture at Stanford under the auspices of the Jewish Studies department, and I presented a kind of unvarnished version of Dylan's antitheodicy position—I called it "Bob Dylan's God Problem—and Mine." And I quoted Bauer on the post-Holocaust theodicy in regard to "Satan or a nebbish." At the end of the question period, an aged rabbi in the department (as I later learned) approached the stage shaking with rage, virtually shaking his fist at me. I eventually wrote and published an apology to him, expressing understanding for his anger, an anger I shared, although it led to different conclusions. You can imagine he would like Fackenheim's or Greenberg's rationales for not questioning God, rather than respond to what I regarded as a more stringent theodicy.

But perhaps I was not taking into account what might be the man's personal history. Interestingly, following that moment, a woman who worked in the Jewish Studies department, a person of very stern mien and a heavy European accent who looked of an age to have lived through it all and who I feared would be another chastiser, told me how because of *her* personal history she much appreciated what I said, "in every respect." I still feel bad about hurting anyone's feelings, but I feel as a Jew (even a nonobservant Jew, but someone who loves the

Jewish people as my extended family) that I owe it to the dead to be as honest as possible in ascribing blame for their murder. Yes, Hitler, but Hitler was God's minion.

THE DARK HEART OF COOL

But to return to the question of Dylan's impact, which is one thing that this book is about: the reason I've dwelt on Dylan's theodicy is because, in a study of Dylan's wider impact on the culture, there is no more powerful evidence of his influence than that which we can hear in the way we speak, in the default attitude of deadpan sarcasm that undermines all conventional piety in popular culture, calling into question what were once proprieties in a world afflicted by the absurdist horror of the two Holocausts hovering about it all—Hitler's and the hydrogen bomb—and reverberating in the rasp of Dylan's voice and the subterranean edginess of his lyrics.

I'm not asserting that Dylan was the only one who broadcast this default deadpan reaction to conventional propriety. He was part of the largely Jewish cohort of writers and entertainers who came out of the 1960s and whose work responded with clear, horrified eyes to the state of the world and the silence of God, the ludicrousness of pretending He was not a nebbish or even Satan. But Dylan exemplified that attitude, which first infiltrated the youthful cohort he appealed to and then spread as they became culture makers for generations. He exemplified it and he made it *sing* and thus more unforgettable, more unable to be ignored, than the black humor novelists. It was the dark heart of Cool. It may be his lasting legacy.

The default attitude of sarcasm and disdain perpetuated by pop culture, by Salinger, by *Saturday Night Live*, by punk, by hackers, even by Valley Girl upspeak—it all can be traced back, I will argue, to the default deadpan sarcasm that has been the new, ingrained, standard mode of response in the American vernacular, an attitudinal sarcasm, a virtually hardwired irony.

In this way, Dylan has remade American speech, American thought, American *attitude*. All of which can be traced back in large measure to the validation of sarcasm "on a whole other level"—a much more than lighthearted (in fact, definitely dark-hearted) vision of existence. One in which Dylan's songs and attitude are embedded in rock and roll, in film (Jack Nicholson), and in literature (Joseph Heller, Don DeLillo, Thomas Pynchon, Jonathan Lethem), a kind of antinomian counter-establishment of culture that has become mainstream. (Lethem has long been a Dylanophile and introduced me to such secret Dylan in-cunabula as the legendary—to some—Little Red Notebook, an item that containing some apparently discarded—or alternate—drafts of songs from the *Blood on the Tracks* period.)

CHAPTER 10

LOVE AND OTHER VARIANTS

I've spoken of the Dylan experience earlier as a communal, generational immersion in his music, especially when played loud in a fast car with fast company. A shared ecstatic experience.

That kind of Dylan experience offers a wild, openhearted, open-road, thrill-seeking fusion of mutual romantic exhilaration. The Byronic Dylanesque.

But there is another form of Dylan experience—more intimate, inward looking, intense. An emotional maze that the love songs, in particular, can lead one into.

I made an interesting discovery on social media worth noting. Ted Gioia, the author of a purported comprehensive book about love songs, declares in it that Dylan didn't write love songs. When I registered my astonishment, Gioia bombarded me with a stream of direct messages on my social media, attempting to defend this misapprehension. And he was not alone: an NYU professor chimed in with the view that the locus of Dylan's greatness was his more political songs, "big hits" like "Blowin' in the Wind" and "The Times They Are A-Changin'," and he claimed that a count of the number of love songs per album would back him up. As if the quantity or the percentage is what made Dylan—or anyone—a love poet, not the quality. Not, for instance, the number of children conceived and named after him.

It may be lack of the Dylan receptor; in any case, this was a failure on their part to recognize that others might have a different response, no matter how many songs were involved. I just found Gioia's lack of emotional receptivity a bit shocking. It suggests that there is something almost frightening about the kind of intensity whose extremes constitute, I would argue, a realm of their own, a different kind of experience. I have experienced the extremes, and I feel a book about Dylan would not be complete without an account of them, even though it may sound mad to some not susceptible to Dylan's influence.

I've found that certain Dylan love songs—especially the ones that evoke regret, remorse, and the remembrance of things past (and lost forever)—mesmerize and somehow fuse one's memories to the music in a way that creates a kind of trance state. Somewhere between Edmund Spenser's allegorical "Garden of Adonis" and his softly imprisoning "Bower of Bliss."

Playing one song over and over and over again, on any device, can induce a trance state, a kind of stasis of melancholic self-absorption. This is the story of what I can only call a freak-out when something like that happened to me.

First, the larger question: What is it about Dylan's songs that gives some of them distinctive powers like that?

Yes, Dylan's argument with God gives his works, his voice, a kind of depth and resonance that's not always immediately apparent on the surface but is there on "a whole other"—ungraspable—"level." A spirituality with a shadow of the tragic. His love songs, for instance, are often indistinguishable from despairing prayers, devoted with laser-like focus to a single aspect of love: they are hymns to loss and regret (with some exceptions, but even the brazen, "thin wild mercury" song "I

Want You," ostensibly joyful, evokes the gap between the desire and fulfillment that is somehow sad; "the lonesome organ grinder plays" is line two in the song).

It is that other level that distinguishes him from Phil Ochs, from Bruce Springsteen. I'll never forget a proud—self-congratulatory— quote from Springsteen's bandmate Little Steven, who said Bruce's achievement could be explained by "forty years without drugs."

This is *possibly* true in some metaphorical sense of Springsteen being clean-cut, collegial, an all-round good guy. (One has to believe Little Steven was making this pronouncement as a kind of subtweet of Dylan, the Bad Boy.) But it limns Springsteen's limitations as well, his final conventionality. The difference between Springsteen and Dylan is not that Dylan did his share of mind alteration but that Springsteen never strayed off the straight and narrow and Dylan never strayed onto it. His Highway 61 wasn't on any map.

Dylan is nothing *but* straying—in a way beyond Little Stevie's minuscule comprehension. Often weird but never—with the exception of what I call the Three Affirmations ("Forever Young," "Wedding Song," and "Every Grain of Sand")—adaptable to weddings and bar mitzvahs.

But I want to discuss the scandal of the variants in Dylan's greatest love song. And before getting to that scandal, I want to put the problem of Dylan variants in perspective by talking about the climax of Shakespeare's *King Lear* and the problem of the stark variants between the 1608 Quarto and the 1623 (posthumous) Folio version. The close study of word variants—of one in particular—is not something to be left to pedants. Not when the variants can shift an entire mighty work's impact.

At the close of *King Lear*—at least of every *King Lear* you're likely to see onstage in your lifetime (the posthumously published 1623 Folio version)—Lear comes in howling with grief as he carries his daughter Cordelia's apparently lifeless body for all to see. But just before the curtain comes down on this grief-maddened tableau, Lear thinks he sees something. He thinks he sees a feather move—the feather he has placed on Cordelia's lips. It was an age-old way of registering if any breath of life was left in a body. In the 1608 Quarto, the feather does not move, and Lear is forced to conclude that his dear daughter is dead.

But in the Folio version, the feather moves! Or so it seems to Lear, who exults, "Look there! Look there!" at a purported fluttering of life. But we don't know whether it's a hallucinatory vision. We don't know what—if anything—he sees when he cries out "Look there! Look there!" because "Look there! Look there!" does not exist in the earlier 1608 Quarto version, the one scholarly consensus has recently taken to calling authorial—in other words, directly written by Shakespeare or directly copied from his manuscript. The one without "Look there! Look there!" instead ends the play in a moment of maximum tragic bleakness.

What then of "Look there" and the dialectical drama of hope and delusion that is compressed in those two words twice said in the 1623 version? Did Shakespeare himself at some point decide to add these touches, to make the feather seem to move for Lear in order to . . . to what? Perhaps to give him a last look at his daughter, one that allowed him to believe her alive even as he died. Or was it added to make Lear seem even *more* deluded—out of his mind at the bleak end, mistaking death for life—and to give us, the audience, something to hang on to in the otherwise relentless grip of *Lear's* tragedy? Or to deepen that tragedy beyond measure with sad delusion, so that there is only a grief-stricken landscape, like those reconstructions of no-man's-land on the Somme, or alternately the bleak landscape of Beckett?

Who made the "Look there!" addition? Was it Shakespeare himself, because he could see he was leaving his audience in a state of hopelessness, abandoning future plans to go to the theater in favor of staying home and slitting their wrists? Giving them the gift of ambiguity? Or was it because the company's lead actor, Richard Burbage, wanted to extend his closing lines so he could endow them with his mighty talent for conveying emotion? A stage manager with playwright ambitions? A jumped-up printer's shop buttinski?

This is not trivial philological pedantry. It goes to the question of how we can describe Shakespeare's outlook on the way the universe works.

The problem is: Nobody knows. Nobody *can* know. For a time in the 1980s, there emerged a scholarly consensus that we knew. Enough erudite philological polemics had convinced publishers to issue at least two versions of *Lear* on the theory that the 1608 Quarto was an authorial text and the 1623 Folio an authorial revision.

But then a riptide of counterargument disrupted this consensus. By 2016, the *Lear* controversy reawakened once more as the British scholar Brian Vickers argued that there were not two versions but, as his book title had it, *The One King Lear.* This drew a rebuttal from Stephen Greenblatt (among others), who had actually published *three* versions of *Lear* in his Norton complete works of Shakespeare edition, the third being a traditional "best bits from both" that *conflated* the two seventeenth-century versions. Now, though, it seemed Greenblatt had abandoned the binary—or tripartite—approach and was arguing (in *The New York Review of Books*) that we will never know "the real *Lear,*" never know the answer to the origin story of each *Lear* text, but rather—in my interpretation of his interpretation— they were both different *snapshots* of a play that was constantly, fluidly evolving as it was played onstage over the years. In other words, there was a *spectrum* of potential *Lears,* not "the daydream of a Master text," as Greenblatt disparaged it.

These are some of the questions that textual variants provoke, and they led me to spend a couple hundred pages in my Shakespeare book and subsequent reflections on the Bad Quarto of *Hamlet* (was it a botched original or an early draft?) in *The Chronicle of Higher Education.*

It may seem I'm taking a long way around to get to a consideration of the variants in what I believe is Dylan's greatest love song, "If You See Her, Say Hello." Variations that I initially thought—and still believe—are scandalous desecrations of a beautiful work of art. A mustache on the *Mona Lisa.*

All of which sensitized me to the depth of the problem presented by the Dylan variations, a problem compounded by the release in November 2018 of an entire multirecord treasure of "If You See Her" studio variations. (Obligatory disclaimer: I do not *equate* Dylan with Shakespeare. Yet he is an author worthy of such study. As the Nobel Prize Committee adjudged, it is "literature.") The questions go to who Dylan is, what he believed, and how we should take the potential meanings of his songs, when they are so scandalously mutilated.

Yes, scandalized; that's how I felt when I made the belated discovery, hiding in plain sight, of the Bad Quarto–like version of Dylan's signature love song, "If You See Her, Say Hello." It's astonishing to me that, of all the millions of words written about Dylan, none of the Dylanologists or, more recently, the academics who have moved in like ants at a picnic have taken note of this fundamental fissure in the interpretation of the reality of that song.

We must ask ourselves why we'd consider one version on the spectrum more authoritative than any other, or, if not authoritative, then more expressive of an imagined essence of love in Dylan's work than another. Which means we'd need a confident sense of the author's attitude, which I don't think Dylan will ever give us.

But I think a focus on this memorable love song and its variants opens up the questions of Dylan and love in a more probing way than a superficial survey.

Christopher Ricks, the erudite former Oxford Professor of Poetry and illuminating writer on Milton, Keats, and Eliot, is known for writing about Dylan through the lens of sin (*Dylan's Vision of Sin*). I choose to write about Dylan through the lens of love. And if you seek to write about Dylan through his love songs, you either start or end with *Blood on the Tracks*. I'm not saying this is some outré idea. I was present when the novelist Rick Moody floridly proclaimed his love of *Blood on the Tracks* at a *New Yorker* birthday celebration of Dylan's fortieth year of performing at New York's Town Hall.

"Of thee I sing," Moody sang, "best album ever made, or that's my hypothesis, best rock-and-roll record ever—more heroic than *The Sun Sessions*, more consistent than *Exile on Main St.*, more serious than *Never Mind the Bollocks*, better than *Revolver* because there's no 'Good Day Sunshine' on it, more discerning in its rage than *Never Mind*, more accepting than *What's Going On*, less desperate than *Pet Sounds*, and more adult than *Blonde on Blonde* and *Highway 61 Revisited*." While I don't entirely agree with every comparative point, I can't help but admire his willingness to proclaim his love so openly.

And if you want to write about *Blood on the Tracks*, as far as I'm concerned you start and end with one song, "If You See Her, Say Hello." No, not the supposedly avant-garde "Tangled Up in Blue" or "Simple Twist of Fate" from that record, those overpraised, Norman Raeben–inspired fractured compositions. Not the all-too-embittered "Idiot Wind" or the genuinely generous "Shelter from the Storm." Maybe the song he left off the album, "Up to Me," but probably not even that. Perhaps a preliminary immersion in the earlier "I'll Keep It with Mine" might help.

But the compressed lyric of regret/remorse/remembrance in "If You See Her" is at the heart of the heart of it all.

Dylan owns regret. "Girl from the North Country," "Don't Think Twice, It's All Right," "Boots of Spanish Leather," "One Too Many Mornings," "It's All Over Now, Baby Blue," "Visions of Johanna," "I Threw It All Away"—he's painted in every color on the spectrum of remorse, leading up to *Blood on the Tracks*, which is one amazing hymn to regret.

In the spectrum of love songs, regret has its own color: the violet of a bruise. It's not a celebration of being in love, it's not an anticipation of being in love, it's the mourning and commemoration of what was once love. Is it true for Dylan what I've come to believe for myself, that the more one leaves one's youth behind, the more one yearns for what has been lost, the love that has been left behind that defined it?

Dylan owns regret. (Have I mentioned that more than once?) I remember in one of our conversations he referred to some song of his as having been written in D minor, which he called "the key of regret." The key *to* regret, it seems, is the inability to put the person in question out of one's mind. Which is why "Girl from the North Country" and "If You See Her" are structured around real and imagined reports of an encounter by *others*, spiking the regret with the admixture of jealousy. Of wanted but unwanted presence in absence. But no stalking here. She's no longer contained in a sealed compartment in one's mind; she has an existence of her own that persists. An enduring reproof to someone who has tried to deny it.

I don't know whether Dylan was putting me on with the key of D minor business. I did love the *Spinal Tap* parody of that moment (featuring Nigel Tufnel)—and consider it to be a badge of honor in music culture history to have fed their comic genius. In the movie, Nigel holds forth on the mysteries of B minor: "It's part of a trilogy, a musical trilogy I'm working on in B minor, which is the saddest of all keys, I find. People weep instantly when they hear it, and I don't know why."

But more than its melancholy key, "If You See Her" is the setting for perhaps the single most beautiful line about love and loss in all of Dylan. It's the final quatrain in the second verse:

> *We had a falling-out, like lovers often will*
> *And to think of how she left that night, it still brings me a*
> *   chill*
> *And though our separation, it pierced me to the heart*
> *She still lives inside of me, we've never been apart*

That line: "She still lives inside of me, we've never been apart." He hits "never" with a slightly quavering urgency, and some people have been brought to the verge of tears by the memory and hope the line stirs up. Others relate to "still brings me a chill."

You'd have to have a heart as cold as stone not to be melted—or chilled—by "she still lives inside of me, we've never been apart." Or, for that matter, by the dizzying death spiral of negativity in the closing line of the song: "She might think that I've forgotten her. Don't tell her it isn't so." This line could be said to encapsulate "Girl from the North Country," his early regret ode. Every time I try to wrap my head around that line, I lose track of its essential import. He wants her to think what?

But wait. That's the way the song reads now on the official Bob Dylan website, accessed February 18, 2017. That's the way he sings it on the official release of *Blood on the Tracks* (1975), now known as "the Minneapolis revision session." It's one of the bloodiest tracks, if you ask me.

But there's another version, which was first proffered in the 2002 volume *Bob Dylan: Lyrics 1962–2001*, and reappeared in the 2016 update of that book. However, the later edition differs from the version on the original CD, and from the BobDylan.com website version, which closely follows the CD version, which seems to me (implicitly) to be the new official version. As you can see, the confusion of versions can be dizzying, but trying to decide whether, as Michael Gray suggests, the differences reflect emotional changes may, at least in some cases, be the explanation.

In any case, I can barely bring myself to utter it. This is the way that second verse—"she still lives inside of me"—reads in the 2016 volume:

> We had a falling-out, like lovers sometimes do
> But to think of how she left that night, it hurts me through
>   and through
> And though our separation pierced me to the bone,
> I got to find someone to take her place. I don't like to be
>   alone.

This, *this*, is a Bob Dylan lyric? Forget how cosmically, comically clunky it is now. It also changes the entire tenor of the relationship evoked. The girl he lost is now just a replaceable part. A trip to Costco will do. Do I need to say it? Not liking to be alone is not the same as loving to be in love in a once-in-a-lifetime way.

But it gets worse.

In the next verse, the lyrics were, originally,

> *But I've never gotten used to it, I've just learned to turn it off*
> *Either I'm too sensitive or else I'm gettin' soft*

Put your hand over your eyes, because this is how that last line reads now, in *Lyrics: 1962–2012:*

> *And I've never gotten used to it, I've just learned to turn it*
> *off*
> *Her eyes were blue, her hair was too, her skin so sweet and soft.*

I'm not making this up; this horror has been perpetrated by someone deliberately. Someone human, despite the blue hair (years before the post-punk blue-hair fad), which suggests an inhabitant of the planet Zondar. I call it a crime; it's almost like a mad dog has ripped the song apart with its yellowing teeth. And left a dog's breakfast behind.

It seems almost as if the changes are designed to hurt. Perhaps to hurt himself. Who else would have done it, though? It makes the song a kind of meta-mystery layered on top of a love song. Self-harm has rarely been the subject of a love song—though, come to think of it, why not? Or perhaps it's an act of revenge on listeners or readers. A test, perhaps? Or last-minute sabotage by a Dylan hater at the printer's? But whom did they want to hurt? The woman? The reader? Was Dylan ashamed by the sexual resonance of "or else I'm gettin' soft"? Was he "too sensitive" to allow an unwelcome connotation here?

By the time you get to the final verse, you feel you're almost being physically assaulted, hurt by the awfulness.

Original:

> *If she's passing this way again I'm not that hard to find*
> *Tell her she can look me up if she's got the time.*

New edition, page 242 (now beginning to seem like Room 217 in *The Shining*):

> *If she's passing this way again and I sure hope she don't*
> *Tell her she can look me up. I'll either be here or I won't.*

Someone make it stop. Make it stop hurting, give me the *Eternal Sunshine of the Spotless Mind* treatment so I will never think of this again.

Did Dylan lose a bet? Worse, did he win a bet?

This is serious. The song is already difficult, possessing one of Dylan's intractable paradoxes, which also include "She knows there's no success like failure / And failure's no success at all."

Instead we have "I'll either be here or I won't."

This is felonious desecration in the first degree. How do we know such botched surgery hasn't been performed on other songs? I haven't yet found any. Maybe it's just that this song was, as I've thought all along, just too strong. Certainly for me, who can go on a play/repeat jag for hours. Perhaps for Dylan, too. I often wonder if Dylan can still feel the emotion of a song his listeners may have heard a hundred or so times but that he's often sung even more, sometimes thousands. How does it feel, indeed.

Yes, I suppose it's possible the line was too strong for Dylan himself to sing anymore, and he wanted to make it impossible for others. I could understand that. Dylan, broken up by his own words, banishes those words. Or perhaps this was his way of calling attention to them? Did he think no one would notice? Did he think *I* wouldn't notice?

Or, less likely, perhaps the object of the song's affection asked him not to sing it, no longer wanting to be reminded of it. And, in a fit of pique and angry despair that the loss had come back to haunt him further, he disfigured its sublime beauty. You don't want to be in it honey, here, take this then.

But there is something more to be said about this song.

THE LAKELAND VERSION

Something terrible—or perhaps wonderful—happened: I had a change of heart. Here's how it came about. I consulted Dylan encyclopedist Michael Gray, ever the gold standard in such matters. He argued that the changes in the lyric books and Dylan's performances of "If You See Her" are not some external intervention or error in transcription but reflect Dylan's own internal changes of heart on revisiting a searingly memorable climactic romantic episode. Gray recommended a webpage[4] to hear the version he sang for his first live performance of the song in April 1976.

I guess one of the perils of being a Bobolator is to be unreasonably attached to the first experience of hearing certain songs, especially if it's with someone you've loved, lost, and (maybe) never want to see again, versus the more ambiguous "maybe look me up" album version.

Here's the Lakeland version of those two tortured final lines of the song:

> *Well I know she'll be back someday, of that there is no
> doubt*
> *And when that moment comes Lord, give me the strength
> to keep her out.*

And here's a comment on it from the late Paul Williams, generally recognized as the first (and perhaps the best) of the breed of writers known as rock critics with his magazine, *Crawdaddy*. He had a particular empathy with Dylan, a mind meld that I was privileged to tap into for several hours sitting on the floor of the *Village Voice* office one afternoon.

---

4 http://alldylan.com/bob-dylan-if-you-see-her-say-hello-lakeland-april-
    18th-1976

> "If You See Her, Say Hello," in the shocking
> Lakeland version, becomes a song spoken from that
> deep sudden urgent place where pain and anger
> are indistinguishable and their expression seems
> a violent necessity. Dylan's 90% new words are
> humorously contemptuous . . . and yet the honest,
> even humble, pain of the earlier versions is also
> here, and as affecting as ever. No one listening can
> doubt this is a man talking about his own wife and
> something that's going on between the two of them
> at this very moment.[5]

I don't see this as a communiqué between married people. Or as an evocation of "something going on at that very moment." I see them still separated. She's in North Saigon, after all. But he's not doing that almost standard Dylan ambivalent shrug—"Tell her she can look me up if she's got the time."

He wants her to look him up. Badly. He wants to keep her out to avoid a repetition of the pain he's already gone through, is going through. Badly.

The shift from the January 1975 lyrics and the April 1976 performance debut offers a unique window into Dylan's soul as he struggles with an impossible love, impossible loss. A self-disclosure we never get to see before or after.

---

5 From *Bob Dylan: Performing Artist, Vol 2: The Middle Years 1974–1986.*

CHAPTER 11

WOODY VERSUS BUDDY: THE GREAT TRANSMITTAL

Woody or Buddy. Woody Guthrie or Buddy Holly. It wasn't a question. You didn't have to choose, not until April 2017. You didn't have to choose because there was no question Dylan liked them both; there was no question each was influential. But Woody, Woody was *foundational*, wasn't he? Now we'll have to question that foundation—a bizarre consequence of the Nobel Prize.

Dylan can barely contain himself in *Chronicles* when he describes first hearing Woody. Back in Hibbing, the year after his bar mitzvah (1954), he tells us, he met a girl in the drugstore and it turned out she had a brother who played Woody Guthrie records. And from the first moment the needle hits the grooves, Dylan tells us, he became maniacally addicted to Woody. All he wanted to do was play Woody Guthrie songs.

His description of exactly how he felt when he first heard Woody is memorable:

*My head spun, it made me want to gasp. It was like the
land parted. It was like the record player had flung me
across the room . . . Woody Guthrie tore everything in his
path to pieces. Woody Guthrie was the starting place for
my identity and my destiny. My life has never been the
same since I first heard Woody on the record player. When
I first heard him it was like a million megaton bomb had
dropped on my head.*

Maybe there's a clue here. Dylan is a master of praise, especially for
musicians he loves. But this—"million megaton bomb," a record player
flinging him "across the room"—has the feel of enforced hyperbole,
childishly clunky. Maybe he was trying to recapture his prepubescent
(or adolescent) rhetoric, but it almost feels too dutiful, as if the scores
and scores of Dylan biographies that make him out to be a virtual
creature, a puppet, of Woody are being sent up; he's feeling slightly
resentful that he has to have the burden of being an avatar of Woody
rather than something unique unto himself.

Still, his first great song, one that stood out in its almost mystical
gravity and aspirational identification, was "Song to Woody." The
1962 song has none of the strained hyperbole of the 2004 description
in *Chronicles*. It has some subtle mesmeric magnetic aura of the sort
that the writer Mikal Gilmore (in writing about "Girl from the North
Country") called "American transcendentalism."

I must admit. Dylan's raptures over Woody are a bit of a puzzle to
me. I just don't think he was *that good*. The dustbowl rasp and whine,
good-hearted, sure; affection for the oppressed, the wretched of the
earth, check. But really, "This Land Is Your Land"? Once you've
heard it, it can seem a bit rah-rah. And "Union Maid" (source of the
great line, "You can't scare me, I'm sticking to the union."), "1913
Massacre" (source of the melody of "Song to Woody.")? Dutiful, yes,
genius, no. However, I do like "Pretty Boy Floyd" (the template for
Dylan's *John Wesley Harding* album).

Woody's book—his modestly titled autobiography, *Bound for Glory*—celebrates life with the dispossessed, the tramps, and the wanderers, who lived like rolling stones. I loved it as a teenager, with its Tom Joad triumphant vibe. Dylan took its title as a fulfillment of his own "projections." The book, nearly seventy years old, shows signs of lasting, of becoming what Dylan and what Holden Caulfield are for some. (Though I would argue that Holden was at least as important for Dylan as Woody.)

And yet, is there anything left to say about Woody that Dylan hasn't said—and said so hyperbolically that his words about Woody begin to defy or diminish belief? Woody was the figure who made Dylan Dylan, at least at first, at least that's what he says when he isn't saying it was Odetta or someone else.

Woody was, as Dylan tells us, the reason he went east to New York: because he vaguely knew that Greenwich Village had lots of Woody fans and imitators and that Woody himself was there but not there, suffering from a degenerative disease in a New Jersey charity hospital. There is something fundamental about Dylan we can learn from this.

And he visited Woody and eventually began to write songs like Woody and finally—finally!—he wrote his first great song, a song on a level with the very best he's ever done: "Song to Woody."

Would Dylan have become Dylan without Woody? Would he? He might just as well have fixated on some other transformational figure. Buddy Holly, perhaps? And yet, yes, Woody was great in his way, but Dylan was far greater in *his* way. "Song to Woody" soared above the tedious though occasionally amusing "topical" songs that fill Dylan's early repertoire.

Do Woody's songs fling anyone across the room? Move them physically beyond a little toe tapping? But Dylan says, "Woody Guthrie tore everything in his path to pieces." Did he *really*? I know one is supposed to pay obeisance to Woody—Dylan biographers are all reverent, willing to accept Dylan's heroic mythologizing. I'm sure they're outraged at the April 2017 disclosure.

There's more, much more, where that came from. It's generous to a fault, to a flaw. "A million megaton bomb"?

Oh, come on, Bob! He's not *that* good! Woody's droning, saccharine, but eminently serviceable ballads of protest are so stolidly *square*, as they used to say, that I find them to be more than politically correct avant la lettre. Sure, they sent signals to the small circle of fellow travelers, particularly in Village folk circles. Cisco Houston, Pete Seeger, the Weavers, the Almanac Singers—all of whose appeal was their ability to fuse popular front patriotism with Marxist-oriented criticism of the inequities of America. Good job, but, as musical creations, I find them lacking.

And a "million megaton bomb" for a few dustbowl ballads? It is clear that Dylan lifted a lot in the early days from Woody. But Dylan, as I have suggested, was passionately over the top in his praise. You could almost say he made a new genre out of the colloquial dithyramb. He tells us that he wore out his welcome in Minnesota because he refused to play anything but Woody Guthrie songs, over and over again, in coffeehouse after coffeehouse. His Woody Guthrie almost became a Woody Allen parody of a politically committed folk singer. Or worse, the Coen brothers' *Llewyn Davis*. (Not a favorite film of mine because it's so harsh and joyless about a community of people who deserved better. But the conceit—a film about the forgotten guy who preceded Dylan onstage at Gerde's Folk City the night Dylan was "discovered" by the *New York Times* music reviewer—is, well, neat if nothing more.)

Dylan started out that way in New York, too—nothing but Woody, Woody, Woody, until he finally found some others to imitate, like Ramblin' Jack Elliott, whose haunting version of the traditional whorehouse ballad "The House of the Rising Sun" became a major hit in the hands of the British invasion group the Animals and helped introduce Dylan to the U.K. (which is inhabited by more folk purists and Dylanologists per capita than anywhere else but possibly Sweden).

Still, it was a long time before he actually wrote original songs, and we must give Woody credit because the first original song Dylan wrote and recorded on his very first album was one of his everlasting best, "Song to Woody." That first album, the self-titled *Bob Dylan*, can be such a disappointment when you return to it. But if you're patient, you'll find "Song to Woody." It just leaps out at you in its lovely, quiet beauty.

It's one of those songs that bring together "praise" and "prays." And one might say that's the reason "Song to Woody" rises above all the folk mediocrity: it's a kind of prayer to live life hard, like Woody did.

> *Hey, hey, Woody Guthrie, I wrote you a song*
> *'Bout a funny ol' world that's a-comin' along*
> *Seems sick an' it's hungry, it's tired an' it's torn*
> *It looks like it's a-dyin' an' it's hardly been born*

The last verse represents a sort of religious devotion:

> *I'm a-leavin' tomorrow, but I could leave today*
> *Somewhere down the road someday*
> *The very last thing that I'd want to do*
> *Is to say I've been hittin' some hard travelin' too*

This kind of praise is something important and fundamental to Dylan. He's a genius at it. Nobel Prize–level praise. Nobody praises like Dylan praises. I'm not sure whether it's an inborn talent for eloquence gone wild when it comes to being generous to musicians he loves, or if they've somehow *touched* him more deeply than most human beings who are not flung across the room.

He doesn't have influences, he has demigods he worships in the entire spectrum of American music: Hank Williams first, earliest, he fairly consistently tells us. Little Richard and Chuck Berry's mad midnight Shreveport radio station rock and roll next. Then Odetta. Then, at least according to *Chronicles*, Woody, Woody, Woody, and he's on his way to Greenwich Village to *be* Woody even if he has to fabricate a Woody-like rambling gambling past for all to admire.

But the story doesn't end there, fortunately. When Dylan is introduced or brashly introduces himself into the Greenwich Village coffeehouse scene, his eyes are wide open with precision, observation, and delight in the kind of characters he finds there—and in the unexpectedly copious reading he does in the cold-water flats where he couch surfs while trying to find his footing. These are apartments filled with books by their eccentric but erudite tenants; Dylan devours Greek myths and the memoirs of Civil War generals and finds himself propelled to the grand, capacious New York Public Library, which is his first home in a way, where he became a winter-sheltering autodidact.

Perhaps his greatest act of praise are the two chapters—the first and the last—in *Chronicles*, in which he takes us into the mad melting pot of unique characters that made up the bohemian scene. All the absurdity, surrealism, and crazy characters later to be found in his songs are to be found there, and Dylan's praise for the Village scene has been lost in the stupid controversy over electric versus acoustic music. The Dylan of *Chronicles* in 2004 still loves these characters from 1962, and I have undertaken to praise his praise of that scene so instrumental in making Dylan Dylan.

Those *Chronicles* chapters capture the breathtaking sense of what it was first like to find this nest of bohemians, all deeply serious and some fabulously comic, who offered small-town, suburban-bred Dylan an array of human possibility and eccentricity. They're important, too, because they disclose the source of Dylan's genuine sincerity about one issue (a sincerity that has been debated): civil rights. Before he went down to Mississippi to risk joining in the mortally dangerous activism in the summer of 1963, he had steeped himself in the history of the abolitionist movement and the Civil War by spending hours reading about the antislavery struggle in century-old newspapers he found on microfilm in the New York Public Library. You can see it in the way that one of his chapters is less about Woody than it is about the Civil War.

NOW IT'S BUDDY: DYLAN'S DAWNING

Having established what the mythic view of Woody's influence on Dylan was, we must turn to the astonishing identity switch only disclosed in April 2017—the identity switch in the myth of Dylan's origins, what made Dylan Dylan, at least in Dylan's new account, which might be called Dylan's Dawning. It was not just the sound of his voice but also the tales of his train-hopping hobo life, the mythic communion with America, that Dylan sought to represent in the Woody Guthrie persona he adopted when he first came to New York, according to every single biography of Dylan extant.

He came to sing Woody; he came to seek Woody's people, his disciples, at the center of the Woody cult in Greenwich Village. And to bond with Woody himself, at Woody's bleak bedside quarters in the charity hospital that was doing nothing (nothing was to be done at the time) for his wasting affliction with Huntington's disease.

All this may well be true, but then why Woody's absence (it must have been a conscious erasure) in Dylan's description of his "dawning" in his Nobel Prize lecture?

The Nobel lecture received little attention outside the world of Bobolators, alas. It has some beautiful and revealing moments.

But it was a close call. In April 2017, Dylan had a deadline. One of the requirements of recipients of the Nobel Prize in Literature is that the recipient delivers a lecture of some kind within six months of receiving the prize. By April, nearly six months after the announcement of the prize, one day before the deadline, Dylan hadn't yet delivered the lecture. Oh yes, and he would not be able to collect the million-dollar honorarium from the Swedish Academy if he didn't come through. We know from Dylan's song "Day of the Locusts" (written after what he portrayed as an ordeal in receiving an honorary degree from Princeton) that he was almost allergic to academic occasions. ("You've been with the professors and they've all liked your looks . . . You've been through all of F. Scott Fitzgerald's books," he sneers in "Ballad of a Thin Man.")

On April 17, a day before the deadline, still nothing from Dylan. Would he forego the million dollars to keep himself pure from the need to "lecture"?

Finally, on April 18, he delivered a kind of lecture, his words spoken to the accompaniment of background music. It opened with a description of his "dawning" as a musician.

And at this moment, when every one of the scores and scores of Dylan books offer versions of "it was Woody," Dylan decided to pull a fast one: to erase Woody from his initiation role, from his origins as a singer-songwriter entirely. And to replace him with Buddy Holly.

Here's how he did it, swift as an assassin:

> If I was to go back to the dawning of it all, I guess I'd have to start with Buddy Holly. Buddy died when I was about eighteen and he was twenty-two. From the moment I first heard him, I felt akin. I felt related, like he was an older brother. I even thought I resembled him. Buddy played the music that I loved—the music I grew up on: country western, rock 'n' roll, and rhythm and blues. Three separate strands of music that he intertwined and infused into one genre. One brand. And Buddy wrote songs—songs that had beautiful melodies and imaginative verses. And he sang great—sang in more than a few voices. He was the archetype. Everything I wasn't and wanted to be. I saw him only but once, and that was a few days before he was gone. I had to travel a hundred miles to get to see him play, and I wasn't disappointed.
>
> He was powerful and electrifying and had a commanding presence. I was only six feet away. He was mesmerizing. I watched his face, his hands,

the way he tapped his foot, his big black glasses, the eyes behind the glasses, the way he held his guitar, the way he stood, his neat suit. Everything about him. He looked older than twenty-two. Something about him seemed permanent, and he filled me with conviction. Then, out of the blue, the most uncanny thing happened. He looked me right straight dead in the eye, and he transmitted something. Something I didn't know what. And it gave me the chills.

I think it was a day or two after that that his plane went down.

Wait, Bob, you're talking about the *dawning*. You're talking about a mystical *transmittal* from Buddy. You're saying "he was the archetype." You're speaking of Buddy weaving the three "strands" of American music (country/western, rock, and blues) that he "intertwined" like a magus. His "beautiful melodies and imaginative verse." His kinship. How the two of you looked and played almost alike.

But what about Woody? What about the "million megaton bomb" and the record player flinging you across the room? What about that perfect song, "A Song for Woody"—the first one you wrote and recorded?

Gone, disappeared, erased from the "dawning," and replaced by Buddy Holly. Like the poor apparatchiks Stalin erased from *The Great Soviet Encyclopedia*.

"The land parted," he wrote when he first heard Woody. The song he wrote for Woody still survives, its lapidary perfection intact. But suddenly the real "dawning" was about Buddy Holly.

First of all, let me say that if Dylan was going to rewrite his history, "the dawning of it all," I don't think Buddy Holly was a bad choice (and it may have been more true than Woody, who was his entrée to the inner circle of folkdom). He's been pulling these switcheroos all his life—acoustic/electric, folk/rock, Jew/Jesus—well, they can't all be gems. And this one?

Buddy Holly's songs, beginning with his first hit, "That'll Be the Day"—recorded in some primitive studio on the Texas panhandle near his hometown of Lubbock—were always more intimate and lyrical than Woody's anthemic bombast. It's not well known, but Buddy Holly underwent a conversion that could be called a "dawning" or a transmittal when he first heard Elvis Presley and later opened for Elvis in a concert near Lubbock. Elvis knew—knew who he wanted.

It's interesting that Dylan rarely mentions Elvis as an influence. For one thing, Elvis almost never wrote his own songs, but there's no doubt he had charisma to spare. Probably more quantitatively than Dylan—I say this as someone who once spent Death Week, which is the unofficial Elvis worship gathering (timed by superfans to commemorate the day of his death), in a motel across from Graceland. But the songs Elvis sung were almost never the kind of breakthrough lyrics Dylan wrote.

However, Elvis and Buddy Holly did have something they may have transmitted to Dylan: the intimacy, the sense of speaking softly to the heart of their listeners. Something Woody's brassy banjo anthems lacked.

It's also rarely mentioned that Buddy's first band, the Crickets, which lasted less than a mayfly, had an extraordinary transatlantic influence. When three Liverpool mates were deciding what to call their band, it was no accident that they chose a kind of send-up of Buddy's Crickets, the similarly insectoid Beatles. And many early Beatles songs could easily be Buddy Holly songs and vice versa. It wasn't just word-play, that name. Songs like "Words of Love" and "True Love Ways" offer unashamed personal emotion you rarely find in Woody's work. Can you think of a Woody Guthrie love song, or does he only love "the people"?

I'm not the only one to call attention to the Dylan/Buddy similarity.

When I recently posted a clip on social media of Dylan opening with an electric guitar for the first time at the Newport Folk Festival in 1965—that highly controversial moment when he abandoned acoustic folkie ballads and ripped into "Maggie's Farm"—I got an interesting response. Several people felt motivated to respond saying they thought Dylan was releasing "his inner Buddy Holly" (Buddy always played an electric guitar). They were speaking about something more than an instrumental resemblance: an *attitude*—some common joyful appreciation of rock and roll the folkies never got.

I have, believe me, tried to figure out why it would have been necessary for Dylan to banish Woody from his account of his "dawning of it all" entirely. He could have easily said, "In addition to Woody Guthrie, I want to pay tribute to Buddy Holly."

But no, a stranger reading the Nobel lecture would have no reason to think Woody Guthrie deserved to be in the picture at all. I haven't seen anyone write about this yet, but I believe it will be argued over forever.

I've wondered whether this was Dylan's fabled caustic temper. Perhaps he was sick of being portrayed as a mere acolyte of the Woody Guthrie and popular front culture he found in Greenwich Village. (Popular front, for those late to the party, was the phrase used for the largely Communist Party's attempt to represent itself as twentieth-century Americanism, the vanguard of popular culture most notably represented by Pete Seeger and the Weavers and their comrades, including Charlie Chaplin and Woody, the ones who stopped being anti-fascist as long as the Hitler/Stalin pact lasted.)

I wonder if Dylan got tired of being seen as a satellite of the Communist Party as well as tired of certain strained attempts by biographers to rope him into the popular front. For instance, there's historian Sean Wilentz's tin-eared attempt—in his book *Bob Dylan in America*—to trace Dylan's unique vibe to the tedious, blaring work of popular front composer Aaron Copland. Nothing could be further from Dylan's caustic skepticism than the musical bloviation of Copland's condescending "Fanfare for the Common Man."

I can imagine Dylan thinking, "I've got to put a stop to all these academics trying to include me as a fellow traveler in their cultural Marxist analysis. I'm cutting Woody loose, and maybe they'll get the message." But they seem to be stuck to their fellow-traveler narrative.

The popular front's condescending fetishization of "the common man" portrayed Dylan as little more than an epiphenomenon of popular front culture.

So, I can imagine Dylan waking up on the day the Nobel lecture was due (or a couple days before) and, in a nasty mood, deciding to upend all those Woody worshippers who didn't understand just how radically—theologically—as well as musicologically different Dylan's protest songs were from the anodyne left-wing pabulum Woody was feeding the folkies. They were protesting (justly) against war and for civil rights. He was protesting the moral structure of creation.

And—presto!—Woody was gone, swept away. You could say Woody culture *was* "Maggie's Farm" for Dylan—there's one fewer mystery left to solve; he had to do the work of rousing the proletariat or he was nothing. So he made Woody nothing.

Maybe, just maybe, though, it has something to do with Dylan's obsession with justice. Justice, yes, in the civil rights, Hattie Carroll sense. But also justice when it came to that which Dylan knew best: musical roots.

His radio shows, *Theme Time Radio Hour* (which originally aired from May 2006 to April 2009), were a wonderful treat to hear— Dylan displaying encyclopedic knowledge of obscure music history, rooting around the roots of roots music, telling us that this or that ancient blues guitarist of the Mississippi Delta juke joints was really responsible for *that* semifamous song or for a phrase like "Open the door, Henry."

This was Dylan as Steve Buscemi in *Ghost World*. A connoisseur of old vinyl in brown paper sleeves.

Maybe he felt he could right a karmic wrong by bestowing on Buddy what had been mistakenly given solely to Woody. He had that power. He had the Swedish Academy, and they weren't likely to question him or flunk his lecture.

Granting Buddy a posthumous immortality that the tragic plane crash had stolen.

Yes, Don McLean tried to do it with "American Pie" (and its refrain about Buddy's death, "The day the music died"), which alluded to but never mentioned Buddy Holly by name.

Dylan did. Dylan can be criticized for erasing Woody, but he should also be celebrated for enshrining Buddy. The two sides of Dylan: he giveth and he taketh away. There is reason to be grateful to both.

CHAPTER 12

SINCERITY VERSUS AUTHENTICITY

B ob Dylan has said a number of strange things in the scores of interviews he's given over the years. Often it's diffi- cult to separate out the ones that were merely meant to provoke or further mystify from the others that could be seen to go deeper.

I was struck, for instance, when I came across his re- sponse to a standard interview question with a strange insistence I'd rarely seen him manifest in the past.

This is the quote:

> So when you ask some of your questions about
> songs I've sung in the past you're asking them to
> a person who's long dead. You're asking them to
> a person who doesn't exist. But people make that
> mistake about me all the time. I've lived through
> a lot. Have you ever heard of a book called *No*

Man Knows My History? It's about Joseph Smith, the
Mormon prophet. That title could refer to me.

I found this on an unofficial Mormon website linked to by Mikal
Gilmore. A site that sought to match that quote up with the Mormon
focus on the transfiguration—that moment in the gospels, only a minor feast day now, shortly before Christ's arrest, "trial," crucifixion,
and resurrection. Sean Wilentz, author of *Bob Dylan in America*, has
noted that Dylan once dedicated a concert to Brigham Young (it was
in Utah).

The transfiguration in the New Testament is the moment when
Jesus summons three of his twelve disciples and appears to them bathed
in a kind of supernatural glory, looking semidivine, telling them that
he knows what is to come—and how he will be transfigured to a state
beyond their imaginings. But here is one step in the process of reas-
cension to the right hand of God. (Not your father's Jesus, you might
say.) He wanted—according to the gospel authors—to let these special
three disciples in on what was to come so they could interpret it for
the apparently lesser figures in the flock.

However, I think there's something more to that Dylan quote than
a transfiguration reference. Especially "you're asking [these questions
about songs from the past] to a person who doesn't exist. But people
make that mistake about me all the time."

Well, it's true there's a long line of Dylan quotes such as "I'm not
there," "It ain't me babe," and the like in his work. And the more I
think about it, the more it reminds me of a Jorge Luis Borges essay
that considers the refutation of continuity of consciousness, part of *his*
effort to refute time (as continuity).

The relevance is Dylan's oft-cited *problem* with performance: summoning or miming the emotion he felt while writing the songs after singing them onstage scores of times. Faking sincerity, you might
say. The Dylan website claims he's sung "Tangled Up in Blue" 1,200
times! (Hat tip, Michael Gray.)

But I think the Borgesian thought experiment with time, continuity, and the question of whether consciousness is a continuum helps explains what Dylan might mean by "that person doesn't exist."

It would be easy to take this as one of Dylan's old familiar baffle-the-interviewer tricks. Or something mundane like "that's way in the past." But I think it's worth examining what it might mean if he meant it literally. That he's given away the game here. It's a fascinating one. He doesn't wish to think of himself as a unitary person—of his consciousness as a continuum. He is implicitly making the same argument Borges does, that no one exists as a continuum but only as a record of successive appearances, as discrete snapshots, like the twenty-four frames per second on a filmstrip. Each exists as a separate still photograph, only giving the illusion of continuity of identity. As a continuous self.

I once wrote an essay about Borges and his attempt to refute the continuity of time, and thus the continuity of personhood.

It starts off with my discovery of an obscure essay/review Borges wrote for a now-out-of-print collection called *Other Inquisitions*. The essay was entitled "The Creation and P. H. Gosse." Gosse was a popular Victorian evangelical writer and speaker and an opponent of Darwinism.

Gosse had written in response to pro-evolutionists who were claiming that the discovery of dinosaur bones proved that the universe was older than 4,004 years (as the anti-evolution evangelicals had it) because the bones were fossils of now-extinct creatures that had to evolve and thrive and then die off over a period of many thousands of years.

But Gosse had a nonevolutionary "explanation" for the dinosaur bones being dug up: God had *planted* them in the earth to test the faith of man in His creation story. The imagined dinosaurs had never lived, their bones had never joined. They were a false past.

Borges was fascinated by this argument, in particular by its irrefutability. If you believe in a sky god with superpowers, as all the monotheistic faiths do, then He could easily implant a few suggestive-looking bones to test men's faith.

But Borges took off on another track. If God had created the universe just 4,004 years ago and planted bones to deceive, how do we know that God didn't create the earth *two minutes ago* and implant memories of a nonexistent past in our minds? Like dinosaur bones. A nonexistent past inhabited—as Dylan might put it—by selves that didn't really exist?

Taking this thought experiment one step further, think of the strip of film. Run through an imaginary celestial projector and lights, it gives the *illusion* of continuity, but each image is disconnected from the ones before. And if we wished, we *could* apply the reasoning to our sense of the continuity of time—we each at every moment have a memory of past time frames, but there is no necessary connection between the frames. We *could* say each frame is inhabited by a different person, each implanted with a memory of false past yet with no "real" existence but the present moment. Discontinuous consciousness—I'm not advocating it, but it bears a resemblance to the Humean denial of an intrinsic connection between cause and effect.

What does this have to do with Dylan? I think that's intuitively what he means when he says "you're asking [questions] to a person who doesn't exist." It's not me—it ain't me babe—it's that guy in some previous frame with a resemblance but no continuum connection.

Why does he want to dispute that guy's existence? I believe it's a matter of sincerity and authenticity, or sincerity versus authenticity in performance—a question that preoccupied him at least until the early twenty-first century. It was his disparagement and distrust of the faked sincerity of performance, the inauthenticity of it.

There can be no authenticity of a performance that's not *truly* sincere, or one that knowingly pretends to sincerity. This is why I think Dylan ultimately abandoned folk music, because he saw through its pretense to authenticity—just because it mimicked sincerity. Folkies tried to recreate authenticity with their sincerity, but it wasn't enough.

Folk music was at first a refuge of authenticity, until he got to know the folk musicians. (I'm sorry: Once I learned that Ramblin' Jack Elliott's real name was Elliott Adnopoz, it did make a difference, unlike Dylan's name change; the tidal wave of his talent, such as it was, made his change seem irrelevant. He didn't call himself Ramblin' Bob.) Once he began to see that, for all their devotion to purity and alleged authenticity and rural virtues, they were urban strivers like him for the most part, he turned against authenticity, especially when it came in the guise of obtrusive sincerity.

This concern with authenticity (or the lack of it) is a dynamic that explains a lot of Dylan's later twists and turns.

If he's singing a love song he's sung two dozen—or two hundred—times before, it just can't be fresh to him. But if he believes the guy who sang the song before *doesn't exist anymore*—if ever—it means he is singing the words with the freshness of a first time. He will have reclaimed authenticity from feigned sincerity, which has always been the object of his derision.

Remember again what the great Shakespearean director Peter Brook used to say: in rehearsal, he wanted his actors to get to the point where they weren't *reciting lines* but, onstage in front of an audience, were spontaneously speaking the *only words possible* as if for the first time, every time. Yes, I think Dylan is as mystical as that. You need something like that to understand apparently unintelligible remarks like "that person never existed."

It also—and maybe here's the key—makes painful memories easier to bear. Because they didn't happen to you. That person never existed. Or no longer does.

Consider Dylan's recording practice. He has been many things to many people, but musicians—at least every musician I've heard or read in an interview—are both in awe of him and yet mystified by the way he prefers to record a track. He will almost never tell the band he's assembled to play behind him where he's going musically. "His whole concept of making an album," said one engineer who worked on *Blood on the Tracks*, "seemed to be 'go ahead and play it. It's what happens at the moment.'" And they can never know.

Expert session musician after expert session musician speaks of having to watch Dylan's fingers to guess what chord or key he would be playing in, much less the rhythm and melody, and to simultaneously catch up with him and guess where he's going next. It's a tribute to the sheer craftsmanship of so many of those backup players.

For example, Eric Weissberg played on the New York sessions for *Blood on the Tracks*, and over the years he had been used to intuiting where Dylan wanted to go musically by watching his fingers—no other telltale signs. But this time, he said, "It was weird: you couldn't really watch his fingers 'cause he was playing in a tuning arrangement I had never seen before. If it had been anyone else I would have walked out. If it hadn't been [that] we liked the songs and it was Bob . . . his talent overcomes a lot of stuff."

Some might want to write this off as an unwillingness to practice or rehearse disguised as a fetish for spontaneity, masking sloppiness. And yet his recordings are not sloppy. Or if they are, you still almost always wouldn't want them to be neater.

But I've come to believe Dylan has long had a metaphysical predisposition to believe he was "not there." He was "not him," "It ain't me," in those past recordings.

I can think of two sources for this. There is the Beat aesthetic of "spontaneous bop prosody" in which the poet or singer utters what the totality of the Moment prompts him to. This is often applied to post-bop improvisational jazz artists, to abstract expressionists, and to John Ashbery–like poets. It is not them playing instruments, or plying their art—it is the Universe playing them. Dylan's insistence (for a long time; less now) on no rehearsal, no disclosure of keys and chords, leaves the music more open to be played by the Moment, more open to express the forces at play within and without the music and the musicians.

So there's that. There's the Borgesian refutation of the continuity of Time and consciousness that frees him from mundane determinism and insincere repetition.

But there's more. It must be admitted that Dylan has a deep and wide mystical streak. One that extends to psychics and tarot card readers. His wife Sara was reputed to be both, and many, often-jealous female rivals felt she had him under some spell (something he might agree with). This was something I picked up from the idle gossip of the Ibiza girls I came to know in the years before I interviewed Dylan.

In fact, I was unaware that this reached closer to home—to my own family. This is how I described it in the introduction to my interview with him:

> Late one afternoon, Dylan began telling me about
> Tamara Rand, an L.A. psychic reader he'd been
> seeing, because when the world falls on your head,
> he said, "you need someone who can tell you how
> to crawl out, which way to take." I presumed
> he was referring obliquely to the collapse of his
> 12-year marriage to Sara Dylan. (Since the child-
> custody battle was in progress as we talked, Dylan's
> lawyer refused to permit him to address that subject
> directly.) Dylan seemed concerned that I understand
> that Tamara was no con artist, that she had genuine
> psychic abilities. I assured him I could believe it
> because my sister, in addition to being a talented
> writer, [now a psychology professor], has some
> remarkable psychic abilities and is in great demand
> in New York for her prescient readings. Dylan
> asked her name (it's Ruth) and, when I told him, he
> looked impressed. "I've heard of her," he said.

It could be my imagination, but the mention of psychics seemed to be a turning point in my relationship with Dylan. Almost as if he felt a connection on "a whole other level."

I think anyone who spends time as I have, reading all manner of Dylan lore, will come to the conclusion that he has a mystical streak.

And of course, he believes in astrology. Sara is a "Scorpio sphinx."

"There's a mystic in all of us," he said to a *TV Guide* writer in 1976. "My being a Gemini explains a lot, I think. It forces me to extremes. I'm never really balanced in the middle . . . I'm up in the sky, down in the depths of the earth . . . I can't tell you how Bob Dylan lived his life."

Can't tell you because I'm not him. I'm not there. Who was that masked man? I'm not him. I'm not there. It ain't me. Or "the past doesn't exist," he adds, a Borgesian aphorism against Time's continuity. There are only discrete, successive, "present moments." Not saying I buy it, but *he* may.

This sincerity versus authenticity discourse might help to explain the Never Ending Tour he's been on for nearly three decades. By popping up every generation in places like Ecuador and Croatia, he's never the same old Bob for each new set of geopolitically diverse listeners. He can be "authentically" sincere for them.

It's also important to note how this discourse is occasionally resolved, as it is in the case of the kind of Dylan song I call anthems, such as "Forever Young," "Wedding Song," and especially "Every Grain of Sand."

The anthems are sincere affirmations—and yet simultaneously *accusations*. As in "Every Grain of Sand." If God is responsible, e.g., for every sparrow's fall, then He is responsible for every innocent's slaughter. A simultaneous affirmation and accusation, simultaneous sincerity (you'll stay forever young) and authenticity (but you know you're going to die).

CHAPTER 13

LATE DYLAN— OR, THE DYLAN NOBODY KNOWS

The art critic Marjorie Perloff wrote about certain pencil scratchings on a museum wall. Faint charcoal-colored, irregular loops and casual, almost parallel sheafs of gray pencil on flat white walls—like a bored graffiti artist doodling during study hall. Lines no longer than a couple of inches, none of which added up to a recognizable image. Distracted, abstract afterthoughts. The bitter gray graphite, colorless end of abstract expressionism. But wait:

Cy Twombly's "writing"—the gestural scratching, clotting, and smearing that is this noted postmodern painter's trademark—is, as Roland Barthes put it in a much cited essay of 1979, "decipherable, but not interpretable; the strokes themselves may well be specific, discontinuous; even so, their function is to restore . . . the vague which paradoxically excludes any notion of the enigmatic."[6]

---

6 Marjorie Perloff, "Cy Twombly, the Postmodern Painter," *Times Literary Supplement*, February 10, 2017.

"Restore the vague." Is that a good thing, worth spending one's life on? Many international museums thought so. In this context, yes.

I have little patience for most postmodernist bloviations, but I was struck by the discriminating intelligence of this distinction: the enigmatic versus the vague.

What does this have to do with the apparent inscrutability of Dylan's later songwriting—and its elusive, seductive magic, which I would argue has been utterly missed and misunderstood by those baffled by what I think of as songwriting on a "whole other level"?

It's all in the contrast between the enigmatic and the vague, and I believe there's something important to the distinction, beyond postmodern pettifogging (and a misreading or mistranslation of the vague in this context).

When you think about it, "enigmatic" is not really as *puzzling* as it might sound. Just as the famous Enigma machine was designed and succeeded in decoding otherwise inscrutable German coded messages. An enigma always has a solution. An enigma is simplistic in the sense that it implies this is a puzzle that has an answer—a singular answer. A solution. An enigma that can then be disposed of like a solved crossword puzzle. Once read, then dead.

"Vague," however, is about the denial of reductiveness—a refusal to be solved, a refusal that permits an untamed expansiveness of significance(s). It liberates the polysemous and opens up a peacock's fan of allusiveness. Vague means "wave," in contrast to the enigmatic particle.

This distinction—between the enigmatic and the vague—is analogous to the effect Late Dylan's work has. It's nontranslatable—not reducible to a single meaning. It doesn't make sense; it makes senses. But it somehow *speaks* to you in a luxuriance of linguistic ambiguity. It's the particle/wave distinction where the wave offers a spectrum of possibilities, the particle only one.

Of course, all of this—the metaphysical speculation about the dialectic inside his head, really about how Dylan's mind works—might not have much interest to the casual listener. But I find this question of how Dylan's mind works—indeed, how the mind of any artist of his stature works—to be of paramount interest. With Dylan, it's his songwriting methods that are most mysterious and deserve the most attention—and that provide the salient clue to the mind behind them.

In particular, there's the astonishing shift in his songwriting in the post-Jesus period. A shift that produced some remarkable exemplars that few have paid much attention to, at least in comparison to his pre-Jesus work. Songs that Dylan himself sometimes left off major albums—orphaned—or were just lost amid the dross on albums that were released in the 1980s and after.

These songs ring out as powerfully as any of the earlier works but have been tragically obscured by the drop-off in interest in Dylan, at least in the United States. And by the slush-to-gold ratio of the tracks on many of those albums. Most (not all) rock critics have been too timid to seek out and take note of the jewels within the dross and instead seek to craft generalizing statements about the albums rather than specific assessments of the songs. Few have made the effort to find what lies behind the apparently unrelated words and phrases and brief unrelated scenarios that characterize Dylan's later songwriting.

Almost all the critics have been derelict in making his albums the unit of discourse about his post-Jesus work, to the detriment of the one or two songs on each album—or the one or two left off—that transcend its antiquated ten- or twelve-song context that the industry prefers for ease of advertising and pricing. The one or two songs he left off his post-Jesus albums (for no apparent reason) include the dystopian masterpiece "Blind Willie McTell," the game-changing "Things Have Changed," and the conclusive summation of Dylan's search, "Dignity."

It's the songs that don't seem to make sense—that go beyond the enigmatic to the vague—that fascinate me.

You would be justified in saying they don't make any (conventional, linear, logical) sense. Nor do they "stop making sense," as the Talking Heads enjoined; they never tried. But they often seem to aim for something more than mere sense.

237

Call it a gestalt they achieve, a cumulative babble of voices—not a Tower of Babel but a bower of babble.

They are sensational songs, some of them: emotional, mystical, enigmatic, esoteric, compelling. Superstitiously, I'm reluctant to make this analogy, but Vincent van Gogh died before his stunning major work was known but slenderly ("thou knowst thyself but slenderly Master Falstaff"), if at all. Dylan's later work, if you sift through it carefully, contains gleaming, illuminated jewels that deserve to be singled out by someone. Not to be dismissed because of surface "difficulty."

A MISSION

Someone"? The title of one of the orphaned songs—this one left off *Blood on the Tracks*—is "Up to Me." That song is notable not for a grim hunt for significance but for recapturing the joie de vivre of the *Highway 61* era and combining it with the time and space shifting of "Tangled Up in Blue" and "Simple Twist of Fate." But, sadly, "Up to Me" was one of those orphaned songs dropped for no apparent reason from *Blood on the Tracks*, else it might have been singled out as a classic, signature Dylanesque effort for decades now. (It was only released on a compilation album of orphans and outtakes in 2007.)

But I dwell on it here for its title: "Up to Me." As in "[You Know It Must Be] Up to Me," with its shame-faced confession of unmet *responsibility*: everybody else has abandoned the field, I guess it must be up to me. Every time I hear it now, I hear an injunction of a sort, a wearily good-natured obligation to restore justice—specifically to do justice to all the neglected works of the later phase of Dylan's genius. I used to love Dylan for his antinomian defiance of conventional piety (the only law is love), but in his later work he almost seems to come around to finding a way to affirm . . . virtue? Yes, that thing.

Oh well, everyone else bailed, it must be up to me.

In this case it's my job, it's up to me to do (Yoda: "Do or do not; there is no try"), to take up the task of doing right by Dylan—telling people just how exceedingly fine Late Dylan songs are, though they are so often ignored or rarely even listened to by many because of the Jesus period drop-off.

I get the impression Dylan doesn't care—or doesn't want us to *think* he cares (it would be so uncool). As always, it's as if he knows what he's doing is right for him, if not for us, for God's sake. He can't do anything else but.

He's the last thing, the opposite thing from a self-promoter. He's a throw-it-out-there-and-those-who-get-it-will-get-it type of guy.

There's something about his *modesty*, even in the earlier, more flamboyant years, that is appealing. He flees from the idea of self-promotion in a culture that calls for it, demands it.

There is something about this artist who has meant so much to so many and yet has been misunderstood, misapprehended, not given his just due. Yes, he won the Nobel Prize, but to some people he's still just a joke, a nonsense rhymer, whose old folkie songs are sitting ducks for a parody. It's up to me to set them straight.

LOST GEMS

I used to feel that way about certain novels before they were given the recognition they deserved—such as Thomas Pynchon's *The Crying of Lot 49* and Joseph Heller's *Catch-22* (yes, there was a period when both were almost lost in the shadows). In high school I would write their names (or their symbols—the "muted posthorn," for example) on telephone booths (remember them?). I felt there was an aesthetic injustice in their lack of recognition that needed to be rectified. I wrote three essays when I'd "grown up" praising the brilliant novelist Charles Portis, demanding that publishers put his work (particularly *The Dog of the South*) back in print. They did! All of his work, in fact. Four out of five of his novels were out of print. It was most satisfying. I would dearly love being able to put the lost gems of Late Dylan back into the forefront of American musical culture. Everyone wants a simple explanation. It may not be easy, it might not even be advisable; the work, while easygoing on the surface, has complex depths that might be too sophisticated for the common taste. I will concede I have gone too far on past occasion, perhaps—badgering Vladimir Nabokov's talented opera-singer son Dmitri into publishing the fragmentary remains of VN's last, posthumous novel, *The Original of Laura*. This even after Dmitri's threat to burn the pages, because I felt it might somehow offer a further elaboration of his father's labyrinthine aesthetic. It was not for everyone, even the completists, but what aficionado of VN would not want to know where his final journey was taking him?

Perhaps I was wrong, but I couldn't bear the idea Dmitri floated of burning the manuscript, even if, as he attested, this was his father's wishes. (A reversal of the Abraham/Isaac dilemma.)

But I began to find a kind of secret society, a kinship, coalescing around a shared passion for the deep pleasures offered by restoring these neglected works to life. (Note, for example, Melanie Rehak's writing to restore the memory of novelist Paula Fox.)

This passion had something to do with their unjust obscurity. The fact that "most people" didn't get them only added to their esoteric appeal. The neglected Dylan songs were more than melodies to hum along to, and the more I listened, the more depth I found to these lyrical compositions—an originality, ingenuity, and seductiveness to admire. Often a whole new way of putting words together. And affording one the pleasure of looking down on those who didn't get them.

Late Dylan does all that for me. Late Dylan has something even early Dylan lacks. But one problem: there is a *lot* of Late Dylan, and only a few songs that I believe qualify as masterpieces. Though the ones that earn the name do more than qualify, they *redefine* Dylan at his "best mountain" peak.

The number or the *percentage* of memorable, unforgettable songs is admittedly smaller than the number on the early albums. All too many songs fall into the rootsy choogling backwoods growling that Greil Marcus proclaimed as the True Dylan, and Dylan seemed to agree and remake them in excess. God knows what personal considerations led Dylan after 2000 to begin issuing album after album for what seemed like financial necessity rather than artistic urgency. The Christmas album, the Sinatra covers, the snoozy "American songbook" ballads. (His almost deliberately dull-as-dishwater "American songbook" covers were, I'd contend, his sly way of saying, "This? This moon/June pabulum is what you choose to elevate to artistic heights? Okay, here you are.") I say give the man a break. They can't all be gems. By which I mean his love for replicating the sound of ancient Black blues singers and ancient white hillbilly blues hollerers seemed often to drown out the spark of originality, the transcendence of origins, that made Dylan Dylan. But the exceptions were often revelatory.

Once or twice on every album—or dropped from every album— there was a work of genius reminding us that the real Dylan lived in the compilation albums such as *Biograph* and *Tell Tale Signs* amid his often scintillating performances in the "official bootleg" series. There we got the thrill of hearing him reevaluate the alternate versions of his greatest songs. And if you strung them together with the few indisputable new works of genius—as I intend to do for you—you could savor the pleasures of the Many-Worlds Dylan.

The ratio of slush to genius is a problem, but it carries its own solution. I can limit myself to eleven new Late Dylan songs that deserve the highest accolades among the dozens that don't, and I can offer them to you almost as a finely honed playlist (if not a Greatest Hits, a Latest Hits) that doesn't require book-length comprehensive exegesis.

In any case, I feel it fell to me, it was "up to me" to make sure the ones that deserve it would not go unrecognized amid the often good but not superb lesser elevations.

The more I listened to these Late Dylan gems, the more I felt a sense of mission, a need to recalibrate the disproportion between these neglected songs' brilliance and their lack of attention. I wasn't seeing anyone else doing it—even the Swedish Academy seemed stuck on his early hits, such as "Blowin' in the Wind" and "The Times They Are A-Changin'," as a social justice justification for celebrating Dylan; the Academy was celebrating the political protest songs he'd left behind rather than the deeper, more metaphysically resonant level of protest—the level of theodicy. Protest against God and the flawed moral structure of the universe—I just don't think the Swedish Academy got this at all. I felt it must be "up to me" to shine a light on the unrecognized connections.

In the following pages, I want to single out these eleven singular Late Dylan songs: "Things Have Changed"; "Series of Dreams"; "When the Night Comes Falling from the Sky"; "Blind Willie McTell"; "Most of the Time"; "Dark Eyes"; "Ring Them Bells"; "License to Kill"; "Every Grain of Sand"; "Mississippi"; and, finally, a perfect, devastating (in a good and bad way) love song, one that Dylan has unaccountably never performed or recorded in forty years, "I'll Keep It with Mine."

Eleven songs that need to be saved. "These fragments," T. S. Eliot wrote, in the very last line of *The Waste Land*, "these fragments I shore against my ruin." Eliot offered snatches of classical-era poetry whose memorable integrity were what was left, to his ear, of the shattered beauty of a vanished civilization he cherished. Similarly, for me, these eleven songs (I could have chosen several more but decided to limit it to eleven) are evidence, more so than the "greatest hits" period, that Dylan had a genius that could not be extinguished, despite what you might call a spiritual concussion.

His late work is at once thrilling, exuberant, complex, and sophisticated yet capable of somehow synthesizing these attributes into song, turning lead to gold in an alchemy one would not expect from someone who has gone through—and come out of—the ordeal he had. Discovering them recalls to me the discovery by enlightened medieval monks in ruined monasteries of the literary treasures that ignited the Renaissance.

I devote a long section to "Things Have Changed" and a bit less so to "Series of Dreams." For the other songs, I have tried just to call attention to the mystery at the core of each. I will leave it up to you, dear reader, to further investigate these gems—and I hope this will encourage you to make a mixtape of them.

1. "THINGS HAVE CHANGED"

I've come to think of the song "Things Have Changed" as the pivotal moment of Late Dylan, for want of a better category name. It was when he started using The Box.

You haven't heard of The Box? The story goes: When the movie studio gave Dylan an office on their lot, an array of supplicants—writers, directors, producers, actors—came to him with their pet ideas, hoping Dylan would get behind them. What often happened instead was that Dylan would point to a cigar box on his desk, then turn it upside down, resulting in a snowflake storm of scraps of paper that he'd accumulated by tearing things out of magazines and newspapers, stories that caught his eye, though unrelated to each other. Dylan would say to the supplicant in question, "That's what I want." You can see the similarity in the apparently unrelated lines throughout Late Dylan lyrics, which *are* related in the sense that they all had an attraction to the same consciousness.

It's where he brought his metaphysical distinction between selves into focus and his strange new way of composing—the aleatory product of The Box—finding unexpected unities in chance scraps of lan-

243

guage colliding in what physicists once called cloud chambers. (With electric guitars, you could call them—the sites of collision—Loud Chambers.) The conjunctions of situations somehow has a pleasing feeling of destiny to them; in some strange way these little aperçus, anecdotes, and two-line mini-dramas *belong* together—or at the least *adjacent* to one another, as if they are meant for one another.

Unaccountably, Dylan left "Things Have Changed" off his 1999 *Time Out of Mind* album, but the song may be more widely known because it was on the soundtrack of *Wonder Boys*, the film made from the Michael Chabon novel that came out in 1999. (Dylan won an Oscar for it.)

"Things Have Changed." It's hard to escape the reference to Ovid's *Metamorphoses* (English translation: "The Changes"), an album, one might say, of classical tales featuring identity changes of legendary figures of myth. It includes nymphs such as Daphne (fleeing to escape the erotic attentions of a god) turned into a tree.

There's an intriguing study (by Robert Polito) comparing Dylan's songs of love and regret with Ovid's verses from exile, the *Tristia*, a comparison that has a point regardless of whether Dylan read the work. However, I suspect he did read it during his early years couch surfing in the Village flats of fellow autodidacts. There is also a millennia-long tradition of "dejection odes" that Dylan deserves entry into.

I've spoken of Dylan's fascination with the discontinuity of selves. So let us look at the function of change in the sense of metamorphosis in the lyrics of "Things Have Changed," which features more than a dozen selves if you look at it closely, each emerging from a short stretch of connected words that become raised to "a whole other level":

> *A worried man with a worried mind*
> *No one in front of me and nothing behind*

At first glance, the song doesn't make sense. Connections are missing. But the clues are there.

He all but gives the game away in the first stanza: "No one in front of me and nothing behind." Recall the analogy of the filmstrip with twenty-four frames per second where each appears to be a still photo that can give the illusion of motion when they are rapidly run through a projector *but* when looked at from the perspective of an individual frame it seems as if the person in the preceding frame is dead or stone-cold paralyzed, and the person in the *next* frame exists in a future that has not yet come into being, so does not yet truly exist. The person in the middle may exist, but they have no connection to the one in the frame before and no connection to the frame to come. No future, no past.

Dylan is alone in his frame of the filmstrip, you might say. Only *he* is real—not the Dylan in front or the one behind. Those Dylans "don't exist," as he says in that key interview.

He seems to emphasize the filmstrip metaphor for authenticity of Being by including a filmmaking phrase: "I'm locked in tight / I'm out of range." In film-set jargon, "locked in" means the focus range is set for the camera.

"No one in front of me and nothing behind."

What a perfect (metaphorical) definition of what it is to be a momentary frame in the filmstrip of the universe.

This, then, is the lonely, static position of the first self in the song. I would like to lay out what I think are more than a *dozen* selves in "Things Have Changed." Every new scene is a new dream from which a new self has awakened. (In fact, he had previously written a mesmerizing song called "Series of Dreams," discussed below.)

Most of his songs or ballads are written from a first-person narrative view or a hidden third person. Occasionally the second person, such as "[You] come gather round people wherever you roam" in "The Times They Are A-Changin'."

By the 1980s, when so many rock critics were calling him creativity exhausted, Dylan started writing some mystifying songs in which there are not one or two but *as many as twelve* voices. They speak their one- or two-line pieces together—or not together—each telling a different tale, setting up a different tone possibly utterly unrelated to each other even on a deep, deeper, deepest level. You can hear it in "Things Have Changed."

What's going on here? What is the connection—if any—in the first stanza between the worried man, the woman drinking champagne in his lap, and the fellow who's "well dressed / waiting for the last train"? Is this all the same scenario, the same soul? Is there a narrative being constructed? I don't think so; I believe they are three separate selves in three separate time frames. Three different parallel worlds. All they have in common is Dylan's observational consciousness.

I can't help but think of what's become known in quantum physics as the "many-worlds theory," or sometimes "the multiverse," in which every act of observation generates two slightly different parallel universes. One where Schrödinger's cat lives and one where it dies. And each of those universes may generate two more each time an observation is made. It was a theory first advanced by Princeton's Hugh Everett III and for a long time rejected, until it has gradually become nearly standard quantum speculation.

Everett's story is a sad one, which I learned, strangely enough, from Johnny Cash's daughter, the singer Rosanne Cash, who knew Everett's son. It seems Everett (the father) committed suicide in part because of early ridicule of a theory now widely accepted. His son was the lead singer of a band called the Eels. And who knows if, in the 1980s when the many-worlds theory was being fought over, there was a Cash/Dylan conversation (Rosanne wouldn't have told me) that could well have influenced the kind of many-worlds songwriting Dylan began doing—juxtaposing parallel worlds in a way that wouldn't necessarily seem connected.

So what about the "worried man" in the opening stanza of "Things Have Changed"?

Yes, "worried." But also "drinking champagne." Time is urgent ("the last train"), but then again maybe in one of the many worlds rather than another.

Does Late Dylan's songwriting reflect a belief in parallel lives in slightly differing universes, multiple worlds? It's as slippery as The Eels.

In any case, one can count at least twelve voices, separate selves calling out from separated universes in that one Dylan song.

There's worry on one timeline; there's an assassin babe on another, ensconced on his lap. There's a shocker that returns us to his early lynching songs: "Standing on the gallows with my head in a noose."

Bob, please, what's going on? In the next stanza after the hanging, apparently he's "gonna take dancing lessons, do the jitterbug rag." Where did that come from? Perhaps because the death kicks of the lynched were often referred to as "dancing lessons." Another self, another universe, another scrap from the celestial cigar box?

Are we being put through what poet Arthur Rimbaud called the "systematic derangement of the senses"? Or is it the rearrangement of the selves?

The next stanza concludes with a provocative aphorism: "All the truth in the world adds up to one big lie." Which sounds like something Sun Pie would say ("All the good in the world's been done already").

Look at the successive selves one could separate in the song:

1. The worried man.
2. The guy with the champagne-drinking assassin on his lap.
3. The guy all dressed up, waiting for the last train.
4. The man with the gallows rope around his neck. (The first four guys are heading for a fall, or as the hangman says, "the drop.")
5. The guy who thinks he could be in Hollywood, where the moving filmstrip reigns.
6. The guy who's "gonna dress in drag."
7. The guy who's walking forty miles of bad road on the way to the apocalypse.
8. This is a good one: the guy who's trying to get "as

far away from myself as I can" (not as easy as it sounds). Another Dylan koan. The lie is—the wish is for—that familiar concept: the continuity of self.

9. The guy who feels like "falling in love with the first woman" he meets.
10. The guy who's in love with a woman who doesn't even appeal to him. (What's his problem?)
11. The guy who hurts easy and doesn't show it.
12. The guy who jumps in a lake.

Now look at the same song in its entirety. A rabble, a Babel of situational setups, a snowfall of flakes from the cigar box, opening lines from a dozen dramas by different selves. Each a portal, lifting the curtain to a dark drama we only get a glimpse of.

The point is: it's a mistake to try to unify these twelve selves into a single singing soul. The individual selves *are* unrelated—they're an ecclesiastical chorus awakening with a hangover after a drunken feast in a parallel universe. Or, as Bottom puts it in *A Midsummer Night's Dream*, "I have had a dream, past the wit of man to say what dream it was." He knows not the sense they made or unmade.

Bottom is awakening to the mystery of how and why he's sharing a bed (or bower) with the glorious, glamorous queen of the fairies, awakening to how he's been changed and giving us his wary, worried take on his changed circumstances. Things have definitely changed. And soon will be changed back again. No matter who changed them or why, there's been a strange change; things are changed and then strangely changed back. Things have changed, and they are understandably worried. Not only "the times they are a-changin'," but the selves they are exchanging.

The Age of Anxiety, the era of awakened worry, has the changes jostling together, exchanging their nervous plights, their often-fretful existence. An awakening to an America wherein, for instance, the most prescribed drug—in the tens of millions a year—is Klonopin, the antianxiety remedy. Walt Whitman wrote an exuberant "Song of Myself"; Dylan writes a jittery song of *themselves*.

He's giving them each their voice, their due, their moment in the spotlight, but he's not trying to incorporate them into the single singer of the song.

Cumulatively, the twelve selves are jostling and destabilizing each other; worry shimmers and shivers and trembles through their souls. Worry, that disrespected emotion that provokes the question: Are those who are unworried really just unaware?

Or is he speaking of a Higher Worry such as Kierkegaard's *Fear and Trembling*? Is this Dylan's argument with God reprised?

In the words of that expressive title—*Fear and Trembling*—the state of Being that the great Danish philosopher Kierkegaard obsesses over, he reprises the story of Abraham and Isaac, one that Dylan, with a father named Abraham, riffs cagily upon in "Highway 61"—"God said to Abraham, 'Kill me a son' / Abe says, 'Man, you must be puttin' me on.'"

In Kierkegaard, Abraham's worry—his fear and trembling caught between cruel divine command (kill his son as a "sacrifice" to his ruling deity) and Biblical ethics ("thou shalt not kill")—leads to what has become famous as "the leap of faith," the decision to shut out doubt and denial and obey the bloody injunction to kill as his only escape from the painful, soulful shivers. Sometimes I wonder at the way some philosophical admirers of Kierkegaard tend to valorize the leap of faith, which after all is willingness to commit the ultimate crime—child murder—which is the suicide of the rational soul to prove irrational obedience. Dylan deftly de-valorizes the leap of faith in "Highway 61," but there certainly is a lot of fear and trembling in his later work, this one—"Things Have Changed"—in particular. Who sings songs on Kierkegaardian themes? Late Dylan, that's who. Who has recovered from, awakened from, what his God has demanded of him and, despite the last-second reprieve, nonetheless proceeds to deny the deity, not without fear and trembling?

I think some version of that drama of tragic anxiety is buried in "Things Have Changed." Most of Ovid's metamorphosis tales are initiated by rapacious lust or raging anger. Dylan gives us Everyman fragmented, a fractured Greek chorus of angst and grief, a cumulative crack-up along fearful fault lines.

"Things Have Changed." Things are always changing; we are always going to find ourselves in a place where we don't feel we belong. Or, in a Heraclitean sense, we never step into the same self twice.

And for good measure he throws in what seems to be a reference to the many-worlds quantum physics theory that Roseanne Cash explained to me, theory that involves the universe splitting into two separate worlds every time a subatomic particle splits. And this continuous splitting produces many, *many* noncontiguous worlds every minute.

Or a verse late in "Series of Dreams." In one dream fragment, he has a guy holding "bad cards," or maybe they're "from another world." The day I took note of this in February 2025, the *New York Times* published a piece about what seems to be yet another variation of the many-worlds or multiverse theory—the successive universes theory now advanced by the U.K. physicist Roger Penrose, who is accounted by some as the smartest person on the planet (he discovered black holes long before slowpoke Hawking, just didn't make a big deal and cash in on it). It appears Penrose is going further than discontinuity of selves, beyond discontinuity of worlds, to discontinuity of entire universes. Would Dylan go that far? We need to learn not to underestimate the brain in that curly head.

P.S.: I want to make clear that all *my* talk of many worlds, of quantum cosmology and successive universes, doesn't constitute a claim that this is the language or the thought process Dylan *himself* uses to explain his attitude toward performance. His drive, his ambition to achieve a kind of radical authenticity as opposed to the mere sincerity of replication that seemed to be the rather grim goal of the folkies he tired of, is something more instinctual than a phrase like "discontinuity of the self" might suggest.

As witnessed by the kind of irritated response he'd often snap back at an interviewer who happened to ask him about the emotion he'd expressed in past performances of "The Lonesome Death of Hattie Carroll" or "Masters of War," say. "That person [who sang those songs] doesn't exist" is more than a statement that it was long ago—almost that it never was, at least to him.

I've come to believe that in his quest for radical authenticity it's important to him to feel and express the emotion almost as if it's coursing through him the first time, rather than recited, however sincerely, from rote memory.

And to do that he almost needs to feel it as if never felt before, thus no connection with the existence of a self who has delivered those lines dozens, scores of times before. That person, those persons, may as well have never existed.

This also helps explain something that some Dylan concertgoers had taken note of: how, at times when doing the old favorites from the concert, stage Dylan would almost deliberately, defiantly, go out of his way to drain the songs dry of emotion to make it clear he was flattening them out, mumbling them, denying the concertgoers what they most wanted, as if no use pretending, mimed sincerity could rescue those dry husks of what was once seductive music.

That's one reason I often thought the studio recordings for the LP releases felt more alive with authenticity even at the seventeenth take than the delivery to a roaring crowd was. Although there are exceptions often in live duets. I'm thinking of the profound feeling of authenticity that woke me up listening to his duet with Patti Smith on "Dark Eyes" at New York's Beacon Theatre in the late '90's. It was almost as if it had woken *him* up, too.

2. "SERIES OF DREAMS"

Those people skeptical of the idea that Dylan is writing songs from the point of view of a series of selves might well consider a song in which he even more explicitly discloses his new method. I'm speaking of "Series of Dreams." I think it would help if you went to the YouTube version of this beautiful, mystical song, where you can read the full lyrics along with the performance.

Dylan begins this strangely beautiful song by casually saying he was thinking about a series of dreams. And then proceeds to offer up verses of mostly two-to-four-line fragmented, discontinuous descriptions of dreams, no through line or narrativity.

But here's the great twist or trick. These are most likely not necessarily *his* dreams, as you night first suspect. The song makes sense—sort of—if you think of it as Dylan offering up a series not of his own dreams but the dreams of other people. There are people—I knew one woman—who have the esoteric power of being able to somehow know what other people dream, most often close friends or lovers.

Maybe Dylan has that power or dreams he has that power, but the song makes the most sense—to me, anyway—if it's a series of other people's dreams given a kind of unity by all of them popping up in Dylan's consciousness. But again, not *his* dreams. Most of the time. To return to the filmstrip metaphor, it's as if the guy in the single filmstrip cell is somehow aware of the *dreams* of the occupants of those in other cells, even if he still can't see or know if their existence is more than a dream.

Seem far-fetched? Well, look at the last two lines of this epic song:

> *And there's no exit in any direction*
> *'Cept the one that you can't see with your eyes*

Bingo! Not the Sartrean "no exit" but the Borgesian: there *are* no other selves as far as he can see, but he *can't see*—not with his eyes. Only with his dreams.

He doesn't even know he's one part of a discontinuous self. Or if he only exists at all for a moment perhaps in someone else's dreams. It's dizzying, I'll admit, but that's what's great about it. That's what's Dylan about it. He doesn't even know what direction he might be going or if he's only dreaming anyone else exists. No direction home. Never was a home.

"No exit" again. Not from the final frame, the still photograph he's trapped in.

"A series of dreams" experienced by a series of selves. "No exit in any direction"; trapped in a strange self.

Being enraptured in the moment is something, a mystical thing for many. For Dylan it sometimes sounds like being in a prison cell, a frozen film cell.

So many of his early songs are about being stuck, trapped in conventionality, and the struggle to escape it. "Stuck Inside of Mobile with the Memphis Blues Again" could be heard as "Stuck inside IMMOBILE." And so many of the songs represent revolts against that entrapment—"I Shall Be Released"—and the figurative imprisonment of the mind. They are a revolt against physical and metaphysical imprisonment of the mind. "Revolt" being the characteristic Dylan response. Trapped and fighting to get out.

No exit. No past or future to torment him with regret or desire. Alone in an eternal present with his thoughts and rhymes, his memories of a person who did not exist and would not exist beyond the moment. With only the lonely consciousness to dream up fictional selves to prevent himself from going mad. That's how I see it.

The boundaries of a dream can be fuzzy or razor sharp. As in one's fate, the cards can come from another world. Dreams are the multiverse, exemplars of the many-worlds of quantum physics. In Late Dylan, we get not a revivified absurdism but something entirely new, not fun house mirrors of this world but FedEx deliveries of messages from another world.

This what I want to do: restore Dylan's "series of dreams" to life. Give them the attention they deserve. Offer a tour of these alternate worlds, these multiple universes, that Dylan was now playing with "on a whole other level."

3. "WHEN THE NIGHT COMES FALLING FROM THE SKY"

The first mystery of this song is the title: "Night Comes Falling," says the lyric book. And one instinctively thinks of nightfall.

And yet there is an echo of "night comes *fallen*" as in "fallen man" that is inescapable.

What does it even mean to say the night is falling? Does it mean darkness is disappearing, to be replaced by the Homeric rosy-fingered dawn? Something like a shade drawn up as the night falls down—no longer ruler of half the earth but on its way out?

Or can it connote that the night comes crashing down—staggering in—on all things bright and beautiful, obliterating their allure?

One thing the song is about is letters. Not just any enveloped missives but *burning letters*. The Kabbalah is written, some say, in burning letters. Note the line in the first stanza: "From the fireplace where my letters to you are burning." Who's doing the burning? Is it in his fireplace or hers? It could be either one of them.

And in the last verse—"Well, I sent you my feelings in a letter"—is that the one that's burning in someone's fireplace?

I must say I find this song more of a mystery than I may be able to untangle. Enigmatic *and* vague. Both intimate and mystical, the way the finest Dylan love songs always were, covering up the agony and the ecstasy of love torn apart.

"Smoke is in your eye." Fire reflected in teardrops. The icy wind that's "howling in your eye."

This is an eye-centered song—perhaps an "I" centered song?

Letters and tears. Letters burning, smoke in the eye, flames reflected in teardrops.

And yet for all its enigmatic vagueness, it has the urgency of a racehorse gallop.

4. "BLIND WILLIE MCTELL"

This song is the blues as funeral oration, the kaddish for the entire landscape of Western civilization all the way "from East Texas to Jerusalem."

You might call it a global "Desolation Row" 2.0 in which we return to the original sin of slavery and lynching.

I'm not going to risk comparison with Michael Gray's epic exegesis. Or argue with Clinton Heylin about whether Dylan meant it as an ode to a *different* blind blues singer. Whoever, it's like a monument, so monumental it abolishes those sacrilegious monuments to the Confederacy and blinds their stone-cold eyes.

5. "MOST OF THE TIME"

Not all these songs are scorched-earth ballads. Dylan returns to love—particularly to love's irony—in "Most of the Time." Except he forgoes the blithe pseudo-irony of "Don't Think Twice." This could be called "Don't Think Twice" 2.0.

This is a heart-shattering, cardiac operation of a song of regret. I've said Dylan owns regret, and here he displays his ownership so nakedly that it's almost emotionally unbearable. In "Don't Think Twice," he leaned hard on the pretense of not caring, only letting the wounded emotion sneak out. Here it has become tragically obvious. But I had a strange, conflicted reaction to the song, which caused me to sob with memory and regret.

And, on the other hand, anger. This is a song whose fragile beauty truly causes the night to come falling from the sky. And yet pallid, vapid, insipid songs of romantic loss from the so-called Great American Songbook—a cheap promotional branding that has given a spurious dignity to what is largely superficial fluff—reveal their insubstantiality beyond Greatest Generation nostalgia in the shadow of Dylan's masterpieces.

These masterpieces are apparently too complex for the endless, tedious hosannahs to the "Great American" bores. Nobody knows this song. Everyone should. At least if you want to progress beyond the trivializing level of Great American Songbook pabulum. No one knows.

In short, four-beat lines for the most part (most of the time), for instance, Dylan tries but fails miserably to lie to himself:

> I can survive, I can endure
> And I don't even think about her
> Most of the time.

6. "DARK EYES"

Once upon a time, back in the Warner Bros. Burbank lot, Dylan told me he was working on an album based on Chekhov stories. How perfect an idea. So much of Chekhov depends on random romantic collisions fructifying into heartbreaking fictions. An almost explicit parallel to the evolution of many-worlds complexity from oh-so-simple encounters. Many worlds means that, in some sense, there is no such thing as fiction: in one of the infinite worlds, everything in a work of fiction becomes fact. Dylan declared himself working with the self-proclaimed son of Sholem Aleichem (I'm dubious, but who could really check?), and the two songs in which his influence seems most evident, "Simple Twist of Fate" and "Tangled Up in Blue" (along with "Up to Me"), seem closest to the juggling of time and space in parallel worlds.

Most critics are satisfied with identifying the Chekhovian work Dylan spoke of with *Blood on the Tracks*, whose inspiration he attributed to Chekhov and Aleichem, yet I never felt there was a match. *Blood* is just a bit (a lot) too floridly melodramatic. As heart-shattering as many of the songs are, they aren't the glancing blows of a Chekhov offhand, chance-encounter story.

It took Dylan twenty years to release a song that has the Chekhovian deceptive simplicity baked into it.

"Dark Eyes" was released during my unforgiving period of boycotting Late Dylan because of the Jesus betrayal (yes, I took it personally). I first heard it when he performed it as a duet live onstage with Patti Smith in the threadbare old Beacon Theatre on New York's Upper West Side. As I mentioned, it was indeed a Chekhovian setting: the sprung springs in the seat cushions and the worn velvet curtains were all like one of those once-prosperous Chekhovian estates on the verge of abandonment.

And from the first words of the first stanza, you are transported back to Chekhov's "Lady with a Lapdog" and "A Doctor's Visit":

> Oh the gentlemen are
> talking and the midnight moon is on the riverside
> They're drinking up and walking and it is time for
> me to slide
> I live in another world where life and death are
> memorized

He "lives in another world"—the many-worlds theory once again.

Where the earth is strung with lovers' pearls and all
I see are dark eyes

Do I need to say more?

The gentlemen are talking. So many of Chekhov's plays consist of gentlemen talking. The moon glittering on the snow, romantic entanglements talked to death.

"Earth is strung with lover's pearls"—the sudden intrusion of romance in its thrilling simplicity. An apparent simplicity is heart piercing; it is Chekhov come to life in the candlelit gleam of those dark eyes, the moonlit glow of the illuminated waters.

7. "RING THEM BELLS"

Here, Dylan is in the mode of ecstasy. He reignites a beautiful second-generation reprise of his most unmediated ode to joy, personal and political: "the chimes of freedom" 2.0. Celebration. Cerebration. Or, as Bob Marley sang, "ultimate vibration." Vibration for the sake of vibration. There isn't much out-and-out celebration in Dylan. Here and there, distinguished by its rarity, is an anthem like this. The difference from the earlier odes is that he *names* the bells: St. Peter, St. Catherine. He knows the bells wherever they are. He doesn't just wander into a cacophony of bells; he wanders into a sonic cathedral he feels in his blood.

8. "LICENSE TO KILL"

Most interpretations of this song are, I believe, just plain wrong. They miss the point entirely. They make it seem like it's about ecology, saving the planet, and other worthy things. But I'm afraid not. Yes, man may have a license to kill life on the planet. A license that should be revoked. But there's something less blandly universal, something solitary, something more *personal* about the "license to kill" spoken of here:

> Now, they take him and they teach him and they
> groom him for life
> And they set him on a path where he's bound to get ill

Sounds like "Subterranean Homesick Blues" 2.0. As a result, we're told:

> There's a woman on my block
> Who sits on a hill
> Saying "Who's gonna take away
> His license to kill?"

But whose license? Who was killed? There's something so personal about the lone grieving woman that makes this more than a song about climate change.

It's about something—*someone*—she's already lost: a husband, a child. Someone she's lost through a terrible, unaccountable accident, metaphorically fate's hit-and-run. What the insurance company fine print calls an "Act of God."

And "Who's gonna take away / *His* license to kill?" The song is another plaintive episode in Dylan's ongoing argument with God. A deity everyone is supposed to worship for his goodness and blessedness and yet one who permits the flourishing of cruelty and evil—the torment of the innocent. It's an ode whose title is a question, one that may never have a satisfactory answer. But one that Dylan will not let rest. It's the ultimate protest song.

About a terrible hole in existence with no way to fill it.

9. "EVERY GRAIN OF SAND"

In a way, this is a beautiful hymn, but in another way it's perfectly paired with "License to Kill." A return to theodicy, Dylan's subterranean theme. If God can control the shifting of every grain of sand, God has the power to control the destiny—often horrifically tragic—of those grains. The flip side of God knowing every sparrow's fall is that God is responsible for every sparrow's fall.

And yet this is a mighty hymn, reminding one of the seventeenth-century Anglican hymns of the English Civil War. The devout—and poetic—Cavaliers versus the sterile (artistically) Puritans. The beauty was on the losing side, alas. But as the great Murray Kempton reminded me—citing the earl of Clarendon's beautiful prose in his *History of the Rebellion and Civil Wars in England*—the truth, or the beautiful prose, is often to be found "in the loser's locker room." Not just in sports but in theology and poetry.

So we learn—if we pay attention to "Every Grain of Sand."

10. "MISSISSIPPI"

Here I must throw up my hands and concede that I have no clue how to approach this song. Neither, in fact, does Dylan. I think that's clear from the indecisiveness that led him to insist on *three* different versions of this song on the compilation album *Tell Tale Signs*.

Yes, the state of Mississippi takes us back to other, further reaches of the shaping of Dylan, such as that courageous and (it must be said) likely terrifying trip to assist voter registration efforts in deep lynching country in the summer of 1963, a year before the murder of those heroic civil rights volunteers from New York.

And that refrain: "One thing I know / I did wrong / Stayed in Mississippi / A day too long."

Whatever regret could he be speaking of so recurrently?

And, finally, this dark conspectus: "You can always come back, but you can't come back all the way."

Yes, I think Mississippi—the state of shackles and enslavement—can be allegorized as a terrible *mental* state of enslavement: the period when Dylan was shackled to born again dogma of the most rigorous, self-righteous, and sterile sort. Yet I think there's more to it, more to this song. I don't have it, but I will not give up trying to get it.

11. "I'LL KEEP IT WITH MINE"

I'm breaking the rules here. I did say I wanted to make a playlist of Dylan's best *post-Jesus* songs, but this one, perhaps his greatest love song, was written more than ten years before Jesus appeared to him in his Tucson motel room. And yet there may be a connection. This song, long a secret, long a song he would never perform live or record, must be one of the strings of pearls. It was only released forty years after he'd written it. By that time, it had long become an underground legend.

This is a song of such simple, quiet urgency done in a flat, almost threatening monotone that by the time you get to the refrain . . .

> Come on, give it to me
> I'll keep it with mine

. . . practically breathtakingly, somehow, the song seizes you by the throat, or by the heart. Because that's what the mysterious "it" he wants to keep "with mine" is. The unspoken object of desire, the "it," is your heart.

When I say it was a legend, there were all sorts of stories attached to its conception. Was it written for Edie Sedgwick, invariably called the tragic debutante or doomed socialite, who fell into Andy Warhol's perilous clutches? Or was it written for Nico, "the German chanteuse" who recorded an obscure Germanic-sounding version of it? Or was it written for the widely admired English folk-balladeer Sandy Denny, who also recorded a somewhat dreary version?

And what about the title? For years I sought to come to an understanding of its mystical-sounding refrain. I'll keep *what* with mine? Recently, however, I had a kind of breakthrough (or breakdown, take your pick) and could see it as "I'll keep [your heart] with mine." Try singing it to someone you want to fall in love with. It's strong medicine.

And in the last verse—"the train leaves at half-past ten / but it'll be back tomorrow / same time again"—it suddenly seems obvious that it is also about faithfulness.

I suppose I shouldn't close a string of beautiful songs with one that has a tragic history. But, forgive me, it's beautiful and dangerous, and no book about Dylan would be complete without it.

CHAPTER 14

THE GATES
OF SWEDEN

At times I think there are no words
But these to tell what's true
And there are no truths outside the gates of Eden
—Bob Dylan, "Gates of Eden," 1967

H ow does one end the biography of—or, should I say, bi-ographical meditation on—someone who denies he has a past? "That person doesn't exist." "I'm not there." "It Ain't Me Babe." Or who changes his past radically. It was Woody Guthrie who made Dylan's head explode with the force of a "million megaton bomb." No, Woody who? It was all Buddy Holly who was the agent of revelation and transmittal.

Almost as if Dylan were back in the days when he was telling people he traveled with carnivals for years and lived in Gallup, New Mexico. Then he didn't.

He was born once, then born again, then unborn again.

There are clues—two theories—in the narrative, the drama, of Dylan and the Nobel Prize. There's the embarrassment theory, and (in the next chapter) the Swedish neutrality theory.

The announcement of the award of the Nobel Prize in Literature to Bob Dylan on October 13, 2016, presented problems to many:

some who thought his work wasn't literature, and others who took the position that even if it was literature it wasn't good enough, Nobel-worthy, literature.

For a while, it looked like a literary lynch mob was forming. You might say they were selling hot takes of the hanging. (Ironic, considering the role lynching played in forming Dylan's consciousness.) Poets with pitchforks, critics with tiki torches were on the march, coming after him and the Swedish Academy. True, in some respects, it was hard to argue that, say, Philip Roth didn't deserve the prize more; he certainly had campaigned more strenuously for it. (The interview that Roth just happened to give a Stockholm newspaper in 2014, for example, was a shameless ploy to mitigate the misogyny rap that might be a stumbling block for the Swedish Academy.) Still, by some metrics, Roth's output was more conventionally *literature*. The lines were all the same length, after all.

On the other hand, there was never a worldwide groundswell for Roth's endless, painfully repetitive lucubrations on Jewish identity. He hadn't changed the game so much as made it his own. *Sabbath's Theater* had profoundly moved many graduate students and generated (or degenerated) many Ph.D. theses. Meanwhile, Dylan had become a worldwide multicultural intersectional phenomenon. For more than half a century, his words, his voice, have been a force to be reckoned with, from Beijing to Bolivia, Croatia to Canberra.

The argument that Dylan had demonstrated the power of words worldwide is a strong one for those concerned with the waning authority of literature. It's an argument not entirely dispositive but probably what disposed the Swedish Academy to choose him over favorites of mine such as Don DeLillo. DeLillo's prose is freakishly, relentlessly intelligent, perhaps too intelligent for a worldwide cult. Never the "conscience of a generation" (a phrase Dylan hated to be burdened with but which stuck like glue). Not choosing DeLillo for the Nobel should not diminish DeLillo's accomplishments—or those of any other plausible winners, though try telling them that.

But the choice presented a problem at least as great to Bob Dylan himself as to anyone else, judging by his subsequent peculiar behavior. The problem of embarrassment. The question of authenticity at stake again.

Let it be said that there may be no one on earth more self-assured than Bob Dylan. I cite a perhaps apocryphal but not unbelievable conversation between him and Leonard Cohen, he of the "put a medal on Mount Everest and call it 'Best Mountain'" analogy for Dylan's Nobel.

Cohen supposedly said to Dylan, "I'm the number two best songwriter in America, you're number one," and Dylan replied, "No, you're number one and I'm number zero."

Number zero! One that can't be numbered. Is beyond numbering. As in that enigmatic, esoteric line in Shakespeare's "The Phoenix and the Turtle" about how the perfection of their union has meant "Number there in love was slain."

Death to number when it comes to Dylan. And yet evidence suggests Dylan was thrown off-balance by the prize.

That shouldn't have been a surprise to anyone familiar with his doleful account—in the song "Day of the Locusts"—of receiving an honorary degree from Princeton in 1970. It's an ode to discomfort, to embarrassment. After all, he was long the man who ridiculed those who had "been with the professors" and "been through all of F. Scott Fitzgerald's books." He was the one who ridiculed those who worshipped the false idols and shabby gilt emptiness of the honors the world bestowed.

And here he was, asked if he would accept perhaps the most honored honor of them all. Acceptance of which would leave him open to the great horror threaded throughout his work: the horror of hypocrisy.

Silence for three full weeks. Dylan would not return a call or reply to a letter from the Swedish Academy. Speculation mounted. Sentiment seemed to shift from "Does he deserve it?" to "Will he refuse it?" How dare he? One had to believe he couldn't work out an honorable way out of the authenticity dilemma. The most self-assured fellow in the world was stymied. Perhaps he read Sartre's 1964 rejection of the prize: "If I sign my name 'Jean-Paul Sartre writer' it is one thing. If I sign my name 'Jean-Paul Sartre winner of the Nobel Prize' it is another."

Even if Dylan wasn't familiar with Sartre's exact words, one has to feel he felt the force of them. Or he might have felt secretly justified for the years of condescension he had suffered from self-styled intellectuals. But he would probably die before admitting that he cared. (That's my private conjecture of the balance of forces within; I have no proof except that his behavior seemed inconsistent, if not conflicted.)

As we pause while Dylan dithers, it might be worthwhile to quote the secretary of the Swedish Academy on its rationale: "He is a great poet in the great English tradition stretching from Milton to Blake and onward. And he's a very interesting traditionalist in a highly original way. Not just the written tradition but also the oral one. Not just high literature but also low literature."

This is interesting in that it does *not* give a nod to Dylan's musicality. Indeed, I too have sought to let others argue that this chord or that is what makes it work, or even soar. I have focused on the words, on the literature (high and low), and avoided the fatally crippled subjectivity of such musical analysis, opaque and often obscurantist. I have preferred to stick to the *words*, arguing not that they are what make his lyrics complete but that they are complete enough to stand on their own.

But let's return to Dylan's initial lack of response to the Swedish Academy. I believe he was displaying discomfort, indecision, embarrassment.

He was embarrassed? Funny that he had spent his career embarrassing others. (Look at the film *Don't Look Back*.) And it's an emotion he sneaks into some of his best songs, such as the line in "When the Night Comes Falling from the Sky"—"the sky was embarrassed." Talk about projection.

And "Positively 4th Street," the song that opens with "You got a lot of nerve," is an epic attempt to embarrass a jealous hanger-on. I once felt the sting of the Dylan embarrassment machine from the sharp tongue of acolyte/stooge Bobby Neuwirth, whose supercool attitude is threaded throughout.

I was having a beer at Lucian K. Truscott's Village loft and had made the mistake of characterizing someone not in the room as one who "thinks he's heavy"—that is, important/profound—and, like a whip, Neuwirth lashed out smirkingly at the hubris of that offhand comment by saying something like, "Yeah, I hate people who think they're heavy." I.e., me. I suppose there was a germ of truth in it, but the punishment did not fit the crime as attested to by the fact that I still cringe at the sting of it years later.

Neuwirth had sort of disappeared from the Dylan entourage by the time of the Nobel, but I wonder if Dylan was thinking, "What would Bobby say?" if he embraced his en-Nobelment in an unironic way.

"The sky was embarrassed." The embarrassed sky projected there reminds me of Christopher Ricks—Oxford Professor of Poetry Emeritus, Dylan fan, and superb exegete (he once played me selections from his treasured bootleg collection)—whose wonderful study of Keats he called *Keats and Embarrassment*. Embarrassment is not widely recognized as a poetic trope. Yet both Keats and Dylan sometimes share an ability to infuse such blatant—some might say overripe—richness into their verse that it becomes almost embarrassing.

Then, on November 16, more than a month after the award announcement, Dylan sends a polite letter to the Swedish Academy, thanking them for the award but saying "other commitments" make it impossible for him to come to Stockholm in December to receive the prize at the formal ceremony and dinner. Yet he has no concerts planned for that week. "Other commitments" seems like a shameless dodge. Insulting, almost. But clearly the desperate act of someone frozen in embarrassment.

What has awakened this contrary disposition that takes us back to the rude, crude Dylan of *Don't Look Back*?

The deliberate rudeness to the royal family and the Nobel people seems almost childish. I think it may well be Sweden. The Sweden that proclaimed itself neutral at the outset and the duration of Hitler's war yet sold iron ore for tanks and guns to Hitler's armies while Holocaust slaughter was devouring millions of people just miles away in SS-ruled Denmark and occupied Europe. (Sweden's neutrality—and the way history seems to have given them a pass—I've always wondered about; how should it be judged?)

He nonetheless writes a speech for the December banquet, and the speech is read by the US ambassador to Sweden:

> I'm sorry I can't be with you in person, but
> please know that I am most definitely with you
> in spirit and honored to be receiving such a
> prestigious prize. . . . From an early age, I've been
> familiar with . . . the works of those who were
> deemed worthy of such a distinction: Kipling,
> Shaw, Thomas Mann, Pearl Buck, Albert Camus,
> Hemingway. These giants of literature whose works
> are taught in the schoolroom, housed in libraries
> around the world, and spoken of in reverent tones
> have always made a deep impression. That I now
> join the names on such a list is truly beyond words.
>
> . . . I suppose that anyone writing a book, or a
> poem, or a play anywhere in the world might
> harbor that secret dream deep down inside. It's
> probably buried so deep that they don't even know
> it's there.
>
> . . . I recognize that I am in very rare company, to
> say the least.
>
> I was out on the road when I received this
> surprising news, and it took me more than a few

minutes to properly process it. I began to think about William Shakespeare, the great literary figure . . . I would reckon he thought of himself as a dramatist. The thought that he was writing literature couldn't have entered his head. His words were written for the stage. Meant to be spoken, not read. When he was writing Hamlet, I'm sure he was thinking about a lot of different things: "Who're the right actors for these roles?" "How should this be staged?" . . . "Are there enough good seats for my patrons?" "Where am I going to get a human skull?" I would bet that the farthest thing from Shakespeare's mind was the question "Is this literature?" . . .

Not once have I ever had the time to ask myself, "Are my songs literature?"

My best wishes to you all.

Most important line: "Not once have I ever had the time to ask myself, 'Are my songs literature?'"

It's the one line I might take issue with. Not with Dylan's assertion about himself but with his assertion about Shakespeare. One of the most interesting controversies I examined in my Shakespeare book involved the question of how seriously Shakespeare took his *own* playscripts. Did he consider them literature and involve himself in revising and correct-ing the early printed texts (as seems certain with *Hamlet* and *Lear*) as a "literary" author might? The late-twentieth-century consensus was that they were just blueprints for staging and that quibbling over his apparent revisions was inappropriate to his sense of their secondary status. But around the turn of this century, an influential book by Lukas Erne—*Shakespeare as Literary Dramatist*—as well as polemics by the revisionist school made the case that Shakespeare was indeed very, earnestly concerned with his playscripts as literature, not merely fodder for the stage, and opinion began to swing the other way from the glib assertion that he didn't care how the words made their way from handwritten playscript to printed text. Dylan seems to use this "aw shucks, I wasn't thinkin' literature" line as a way of getting out from under the burden of sounding over-serious about his ambitions.

However, now he is cornered, and the world wants to know what he thinks about that. And he's not sure.

"WHERE AM I GOING TO GET A HUMAN SKULL?"

Perhaps the *best* line of the speech is Dylan channeling Shakespeare thinking about Hamlet: "Where am I going to get a human skull?" It's a question that almost seems like he's asking about himself.

He was, after all, in effect playing Hamlet in regard to how he felt, implying, "I have that within me that passeth show." *Passeth* being impressed or wanting to be impressed by the Swedish Academy's accolade.

And let's face it, there's something more than human about what goes on in—and comes out of—that skull. Which makes the question "Where am I going to get a human skull?" almost touchingly personal.

It makes me think of Peter Brook again, the great Shakespearean contemplating Shakespeare and talking about the way some people are ten percent alive, some one hundred percent alive, but what made Shakespeare Shakespeare was that he was *"a million percent alive."* I'd give Dylan ten thousand percent.

It still troubles him, though, the dialectic of humility and authenticity. He can't be unaware of those who are making a mountain out of a molehill. (Recall how Leonard Cohen put it: they were putting a medal on a mountain that said "best mountain.")

That line about being the "number zero" songwriter in America says it all about whether he felt worthy. About whether he *knew*. Knew just how much more alive he was than his contemporaries. Of course this left open the question of whether he wanted to be seen as knowing—or seeking validation of—his worthiness.

PATTI SMITH FORGETS THE LYRICS

The next development in our saga of Dylan and the Nobel is that of Patti Smith and "A Hard Rain's A-Gonna Fall." Here, also, embarrassment is a key theme.

The two of them were famously friends since the Chelsea Hotel days in the 1970s and 1980s and had done duets together in concert. (I had the good fortune of seeing them do the Chekhovian "Dark Eyes" together. An experience that almost single-handedly brought me back to Dylan after two decades of post-Jesus rejection.)

In the wise and moving piece Smith wrote for *The New Yorker* after her harrowing experience in trying and failing at first to sing a Dylan song in Stockholm, she says she got a mysterious call *in September* out of the blue from the Swedish Academy asking her if she'd sing at the December Nobel Prize banquet. Orchestral backing and luxe hotel on the seaside included. (It's not as if she hadn't been deemed worthy of awards herself—her 2010 memoir, *Just Kids*, about coming of age and becoming a female rock icon, had won the National Book Award for Nonfiction.)

It seems obvious to me that the Swedish Academy must have already made up its mind to give the award to Dylan, and Smith must have known or at least guessed why she was invited, but she doesn't let on or let us know whether she let him know.

And then Dylan got the prize and "previous commitments" prevented him from showing up (sure), so she asked him if she could sing one of his songs at the dinner.

The story of her preparing the Dylan song "Hard Rain," with its seemingly hundreds of verses—and losing her way in the middle of that dark wood of Dantesque words—is something she made into a kind of parable of how the experience of losing one's way (as Dante did) was a way of finding a way into Dylan. It's priceless and deeply moving.

Here is a memorable excerpt from her *New Yorker* essay:

> I thought of my mother, who bought me my first
> Dylan album when I was barely sixteen. She found
> it in the bargain bin at the five-and-dime and
> bought it with her tip money. "He looked like
> someone you'd like," she told me. I played the
> record over and over, my favorite being "A Hard
> Rain's A-Gonna Fall." It occurred to me then
> that, although I did not live in the time of Arthur
> Rimbaud, I existed in the time of Bob Dylan.

And then that moment when she discovered she'd forgotten the lyrics, and learned "there's no success like failure and failure's no success at all":

> As if in a fairy tale, I stood before the Swedish King
> and Queen . . . armed with a song in which every
> line encoded the experience and resilience of the
> poet who penned them.

She concludes this way:

> In the breakfast room, I was greeted by many of
> the Nobel scientists. They showed appreciation
> for my very public struggle. They told me I did
> a good job. I wish I would have done better, I
> said. No, no, they replied, none of us wish that.
> For us, your performance seemed a metaphor for

our own struggles. Words of kindness continued
through the day . . . I had to come to terms with
the truer nature of my duty. Why do we commit
our work? Why do we perform? It is above all for
the entertainment and transformation of the people.
It is all for them. The song asked for nothing. The
creator of the song asked for nothing. So why
should I ask for anything?

And the whole experience of the Nobel Prize becomes integrated into
the emotional life of one of Dylan's acolytes in the way it does, prize
or no prize.

CHAPTER 15

DYLAN'S LAST ALBUM

What was it, then, that made accepting the Nobel Prize with a bit of grace so difficult for Dylan?

We should all have such problems.

It took me a while to come up with a tentative theory. Yes, I'm sure fear of being seen as hypocritical might be part of it: Dylan the icon of anti-commercial purity, the one who disdained commodification of his art and rejected the superficial tokens of material success, such as bowing before a king and the objectification of women. (If you've ever seen the lingerie-clad "angels" swooning around Dylan as he mimes guitar playing in that Victoria's Secret music video ad for the song called "Love Sick," you would set aside the antimaterialist explanation for Dylan's reticence.)

But I think the secret (not Victoria's) of his dilemma might be found in the second half of that Nobel Prize lecture. It's the section that follows Dylan's self-described "dawning"—after Dylan has disposed of Woody Guthrie, got him out one door and invited the shade of Buddy Holly in another.

In this second half of the "lecture," Dylan says he's been asked to tell us—since the prize is for literature—some of his thoughts on that subject, in particular what books have shaped his sensibility. He takes us back to his childhood, where he names the usual middle school suspects, such as *A Tale of Two Cities*, but puts the spotlight on three works in particular. Two are unsurprising—Homer's *Odyssey* and Melville's *Moby-Dick*—and he gives us mainly sixth-grade-level summaries. But the third is not the usual gifted child fare, and it elicits from Dylan one of the most amazing soliloquies one can find in all his works. A Hamlet-like cry for help. His third choice is a German novel from the late 1920s—Erich Maria Remarque's *All Quiet on the Western Front*—the World War I novel of the horrors of trench warfare told from the point of view of a German soldier.

The novel was famous in its time and remained influential for decades, more than anything because it captured the extreme mental and moral degradations inflicted on the enlistees by relentless, murderous trench warfare. In its English translation, it had a powerful antiwar effect that many cultural historians believe responsible for (or at least contributed to) the appeasement mentality of the left and the right in the 1930s that enabled Hitler to rise and conquer a Europe unprepared to stop him.

In Dylan's telling, coming upon Remarque's book turned out to be an epiphany for him, the sort of thing he used to say about his discovery of Woody Guthrie (or, later, Buddy Holly). Or like the uncovering of one of those long-buried unexploded bombs that are still sometimes discovered beneath the blast-scarred fields and forests of Central Europe where the worst, most murderous fighting had left more death behind, waiting in sinister silence. Usually these are World War II explosives, but sometimes even poison gas shells from World War I bombs are found, causing evacuations of entire towns or small cities for fear their time has come.

For Dylan, the time had come to talk about *All Quiet on the Western Front* and what it means about Western civilization.

You might not catch on to what he's doing at first, but you could think of this fierce piece of prose, its burning letters, as Dylan's last album. In which he *impersonates* Remarque's frenzy of degradation, compresses the evil of war, the evil of the world. His lengthy description of Remarque's novel was nothing less than Dylan's account of his visit to Hell, the way epic heroes all do—in the *Odyssey*, in Virgil, in Dante—an extended ode to death and corpse stench. He allows Remarque to inhabit him.

Dylan's description of Remarque's description is a work of ferocious eloquence, perhaps the most impassioned "lyrics" of any in his albums. It is shocking, this lecture, perhaps the most shocking evocation of Hell on Earth in contemporary literature.

Another Dylan-centered way of describing it is to think of it as comparable to Jimi Hendrix's thunder-and-lightning-maddened version of Dylan's original "All Along the Watchtower."

In a book report.

It's a takeoff point for Dylan's vision of the Inferno. It's Hell, somewhere far, far beyond or below "Desolation Row." It made me think—and I wonder if it made Dylan think—of the "Shark Massacre" chapter in *Moby-Dick* in which blood-maddened shark gangs are driven to tear out and eat their own entrails.

Contemplation of Remarque provokes Dylan to a scorching vision of Western civilization as a searing blast furnace of screaming armaments bent on murder. Armies devouring each other. One thinks of the passage in *Macbeth* as well wherein (as an evil omen) horses are seen to literally devour themselves—and maybe Dylan thought of Pynchon's opening line of *Gravity's Rainbow*—"A screaming comes across the sky." The entire piece is written at that pitch. Not that I wish it so, but it might well be the last best thing Dylan writes. It hasn't gotten the attention, the accolades, it deserves. You know it must be up to me.

One way to look at this is as vindication a half century later of Dylan's belief that "Hitler WAS history." Discovery of Remarque's book in his small-town library was evidently a profound shock to the young schoolboy, an unforgettable introduction to a world where insatiable evil ruled this world. The death-camp universe that the rest of the world was trying to ignore or forget. And pretend did not exist.

Deniers! A vision of the submerged absurdist horror almost like the white whale awaiting, invisible, just beneath the surface. Or a buried bomb.

You could think of this apocalyptic prose set to music as Dylan's last album. One epic, maddened dirge.

THE RETURN

And yet there's something familiar about it. It's a return, in a sense, to the lit-by-lightning, raging electric guitar storms that frightened the folkies. It scared me.

And a return in another way. Dylan's inability to respond to the politesse of the Swedish Academy dignitaries, his refusal to grant them a special dignity, was the bad-boy disrespectful mode of "Subterranean Homesick Blues" and "Maggie's Farm." It was a direct frontal attack on authority and propriety as embodied in the Swedish Academy and the Swedish king who were summoning him. He wouldn't go in person. Instead, he gave them this dark, insidious mirror in which they could see what their "civilization" had produced—and tried to bury.

There was no more pretense of acceding to the pious puppet show of courtly propriety. It's like Hamlet's sneering dismissal of the court and family hierarchy in the second scene of *Hamlet*. An attempt that ends in self-subversion. Embarrassing weeks to reply to an invitation, declining and getting someone else to read his speech for the prize banquet, and someone else again (Patti Smith) to sing for his supper on that occasion. Many selves.

Dylan's first line in his demonically pitched essay to the Nobel Academy is about *All Quiet on the Western Front,* which he call "a horror story." Not just a wartime horror story, but a moral horror story. And then he gives us all of Western history as a horror story. He gives us Hitler as history.

It's "[a] book where you lose your childhood, your faith in a meaningful world, your concern for individuals." A book that leaves you "stuck in a nightmare sucked up into a whirlpool of death and pain. You're defending yourself against elimination" in the hell of the trenches. Dylan's summary continues:

> Day after day, the hornets bite you and worms lap
> your blood. You're a cornered animal. You don't fit
> anywhere. The falling rain is monotonous ["Lost
> in Juarez in the rain"]. There's endless assaults,
> poison gas, nerve gas, morphine, burning streams
> of gasoline, scavenging and scabbing for food,
> influenza, typhus, dysentery. Life is breaking down
> all around you, and the shells are whistling. This
> is the lower region of hell. Mud, barbed wire, rat-
> filled trenches, rats eating the intestines of dead
> men, trenches filled with filth and excrement.
> Someone shouts, "Hey, you there. Stand and fight."

This is Dylan, taking Remarque to "a whole other level."

Dylan goes on like this for—trust me—a long, agonized, and agonizing time, rendering more of Remarque's worst, most-painful-to-read patches as if deliberately seeking to inflict injury on the reader as punishment.

What is he trying to accomplish? There is one passage in his "lecture" on Remarque that sums up his view of what he has described—and why. I think of these epic evocations of the underworld as akin

279

to the extremely long song "Sad Eyed Lady of the Lowlands" on his album *Blonde on Blonde.*

Next up on the jukebox from Hell is the song I'd call "All That Culture." And now we're getting to the bottom of it all. Dylan writes:

> All that culture from a thousand years ago, that
> philosophy, that wisdom—Plato, Aristotle,
> Socrates—what happened to it? It should have
> prevented this. Your thoughts turn homeward. And
> once again you're a schoolboy walking through
> the tall poplar trees. It's a pleasant memory. More
> bombs dropping on you from blimps. You got to
> get it together now. You can't even look at anybody
> for fear of some miscalculable thing that might
> happen. The common grave. There are no other
> possibilities.
>
> Then you notice the cherry blossoms, and you see
> that nature is unaffected by all this. Poplar trees,
> the red butterflies, the fragile beauty of flowers, the
> sun—you see how nature is indifferent to it all. All
> the violence and suffering of all mankind. Nature
> doesn't even notice it.

So, don't blame nature unless you're speaking of that odious thing: human nature.

Suddenly you realize he has pulled a Dylan trick here. The passage about human nature is no longer about the demonism of war but about your complicity, the fact that there is no escape, no Sweden of the mind. You're the deserter in the forests. You were unnatural, *Unheimlich*—the German word used to describe Hitler in the 1920s when he was still a mystery. *Unheimlich.* "Unhealthy" (sick). Complicit, the Swedish Academy is out there in the woods with you.

In other words, don't get on my case over some banquet RSVP.

One way to look at it is as vindication a half century later (when he's seventy-two) of a twenty-two-year-old's prescient vision of a submerged, absurdist, terror-filled vision that can be found—like the fearsome, fulsome white whale—in the realm extending from just beneath the surface to the fathomless hellish depths below.

It's an absolutely torrential, lit-by-lightning derecho (a word we've begun to learn more than enough about: those natural firestorms raging uncontrollably though the western half of our continent). An utterly unexpected, deeply frightening vision of the world that he tells us he has gotten from *All Quiet on the Western Front*. He sees this quintessential World War I novel through the eyes of World War II and its Holocaust.

There's nothing like it, nothing so terrifyingly final like this in his latest (twenty-first-century) songs, either his own compositions or those painfully mediocre Sinatra cover albums he does later, the ones that made it seem he was coasting into obscurity or mediocrity, worn out, burned out by genius. It seemed like the person who could complacently put out something like those albums of "standards" had stopped trying, no longer had the creative energy, and was content to coast or drift not far from the shore, no longer daring the deep, just fulfilling a contract. The albums you should get in this period are compilations like *Biograph* and *Tell Tale Signs*.

But no, no no no. His words on the whale and his words on the *Odyssey* ("no direction home" indeed) are really not much more than plot summaries that could have been written by any undergraduate. Yet his words on *All Quiet on the Western Front* could only have been written by Bob Dylan. I would not call them drunken ravings, but they have that terrified-by-the-soul-of-man-and-the-works-of-human-civilization feeling to them.

It took me two times to get through that unrelenting, burn-down-the-mountain, poison-gas-filled ode to the collapse of civilization. "Desolation Row." I almost could not look. That's how scarifying they are, those words that, upon reading them, one feels deeply scarred by, recognizing his vision of the world. He fused Remarque's vision and the dark, Dantesque truth he saw from the time in his twenties when, drunkenly raving, perhaps, he wrote "Hitler WAS History."

He was writing about the experience of the Holocaust he imagined from a close reading of a World War I novel/memoir to tell us it wasn't a fiction. He was, through Remarque, making a radical attack on conventionality with the kind of radical energy that fueled his fire when he was starting out and breaking away from covering sixteenth-century folk-ballad styles.

It's shocking to see the nervy way that Dylan's prose has such wicked, bloody eloquence in its distillation of the horror of *All Quiet on the Western Front*. He slowly makes it about *you* and your experience in those stinking, festering, filthy, rat-ridden trenches. You will not recover from this, he seems to be saying to the monarchs of neutral Sweden. For him, this might well be his last testament about existence itself, and it comes in the form of a book report to a stodgy crew of Nordic dignitaries in a nation that was officially (but only officially) neutral while Hitler slaughtered millions under their nose with the weapons that they helped to provide. It was a take-no-prisoners jeremiad all the more defiant—all the more defiantly shattering—of the facade of dignity they were asking of him but that he would no longer pay obeisance to. All the more defiant and all the more apropos. The old Dylan was back in old age, and he was in no mood to soothe the feelings of Swedish academicians. Especially Swedish academicians.

I could imagine Dylan thinking about the Swedish Academy incarnation of pious propriety and self-satisfied pretension to being the soul of dignity even while they provided the iron ore for Hitler's tanks. When not raging "against the dying of the light" (another Dylan's line), he channels the utmost, bleakest despair in Remarque's novel when he continues his distillation, his channeling, of Remarque:

Who knows how long this mess will go on?
Warfare has no limits. You're being annihilated,
and that leg of yours is bleeding too much. You
killed a man yesterday, and you spoke to his corpse.
You told him after this is over, you'll spend the rest
of your life looking after his family. Who's profiting
here? The leaders and the generals gain fame, and
many others profit financially. But you're doing
the dirty work. . . . You can't see how anybody in
civilian life has any kind of purpose at all. All their
worries, all their desires—you can't comprehend it.

More machine guns rattle, more parts of bodies
hanging from wires, more pieces of arms and legs
and skulls where butterflies perch on teeth, more
hideous wounds, pus coming out of every pore,
lung wounds, wounds too big for the body, gas-
blowing cadavers, and dead bodies making retching
noises. Death is everywhere. Nothing else is
possible. . . .

You wait to hear the news. You don't understand
why the war isn't over . . . Sickness and humiliation
have broken your heart. You were betrayed by your
parents, your schoolmasters, your ministers, and
even your own government . . .

You've come to despise that older generation that
sent you out into this madness . . . comrades are
dying. Dying from abdominal wounds, double
amputations, shattered hip bones, and you think,
"I'm only twenty years old, but I'm capable of
killing anybody. Even my father if he came at me."

I don't think Dylan could have ignored the fact that, in his participation in the Nobel award ceremonies, he was being asked to dignify a nation that was neutral in a war with Hitler. What is neutrality in the face of slaughter across the border, he makes a point of asking in his inflammatory rant.

He offers no escape; he seeks to transport you into the extermination camp of Western consciousness, the death camp of Western civilization. As shrewd students of the past century's history recognize, World War I—its unresolved "settlement" at Versailles—paved the way for World War II, the horror of the first setting the stage for the second.

That he chose the Nobel lecture, the purported apex of civilization's virtues, set in a state too fastidious to offer resistance to Hitler (like Norway did), seems to me no accident.

He is saying, "let us not talk falsely" (from "All Along the Watchtower"), "the hour is getting late." Let us not pretend there is not a pack of howling wolves with bloodstained teeth circling around the watchtower, that faux fortress of rationality.

Indeed, circling within. The Swedish Academy, target of the slings and arrows, the red-hot rocks he hurls—that Swedish Academy is a latter-day "Maggie's Farm" for Dylan, and he seems to be saying "I gave at the office." I ain't gonna work for—preserve the illusion of—decorum of the academy's farm—the vineyards of its proprieties and pieties about the salvific role of high art—anymore. Not going to be complicit in the web of delusion hanging over the pit of Hell.

I began writing this book with what I believe is a neglected mode of discourse about Dylan in mind: theodicy. Dylan's argument with—or against—God. In the passage quoted above referring to Plato and Aristotle, we see his argument against Man. Don't blame it all on God, although He (or She) doesn't escape unscathed. Blame it on the dependence of Man, on the puny defenses philosophy erects to achieve denial of the six million, the white whale beneath the surface of Dylan's work—the shambles of theodicy that Dylan, of all people, of all folk singers, seems most acutely aware of.

Where was God if Hitler WAS history? Not on our side, that's for sure, and only fools—perverse deniers—believed he was. It is there, that huge and awful truth beneath the surface, and I wanted to call attention to it, make it visible, because if Dylan and I share nothing else—you don't want to hear me sing—we share an awareness of the fraudulence of the comforts theodicy offers.

Dylan isn't the place to seek comfort. Not the comfort of disengagement, neutrality. Even the comfort of love is almost always a source of sorrow and regret. But I always thought it was this—theodicy—that made Dylan a serious artist, if not a prophet, a Jeremiah. Even a madcap Job at times. It made his work in that he had a vision of the relation of God and man that deserved more attention. Initially, I had many other notions that I felt deserved more serious attention. But the meaning of "Hitler WAS history" seemed paramount. You know, "it must be up to me" to sight and cite the presence of Hitler and the Holocaust in shaping Dylan's zeitgeist. I had a lot of other things to say in the six years or so I spent in thinking about the man and his work, not all of them about extermination, many about love, loss, regret, and remorse. Well, I guess those are the consequences of a world of extermination, too.

But I can't say I haven't been *pleased* by his indirect affirmation of that observation in this "last album." I can say that this final testament (may he live to one hundred) confirms my intuition that, for Dylan, Hitler was more than history; rather, he is a dark, *contemporary* presence. I felt a chill when I realized that, in this dark final chapter, this demonic book report, Dylan seems to feel the need to affirm that presence.

Hitler's shadow, *his* extermination, merely regularized the disorganized slaughter Remarque was writing about in his novel. I can say I felt that my focus on the shadow of the death camp as a shaper of Dylan's view of the world was not misplaced. Nor the consequent vision of unrelenting slaughter as the underminer of propriety and of conventional, piety-centered civilization.

These maddened riffs, they're like songs from an album from Hell.

The philosophers, especially the ones always wrangling about all the alleged achievements of millennia of philosophy by the cleverest of thinkers—all of them Dylan sees as, in some sense, Holocaust deniers.

Here he gives a name to the enemy: civility. The false rationality of civility, "the mask of the red death" in deed. A mask that attempts to convince us that the world, even the world of the trenches, makes any kind of sense.

The depths of his sorrow at the world can seem unlimited.

> You're so alone. Then a piece of shrapnel hits the
> side of your head and you're dead.

> You've been ruled out, crossed out. You've been
> exterminated. I put this book down and closed it
> up. I never wanted to read another war novel again,
> and I never did.

"Once you loved life and the world," Dylan writes, "and now you're shooting it to pieces."

This suggests, doesn't it, that he's absorbed the fierce injunction of that other Dylan: "Do not go gently into that good night."

ACKNOWLEDGMENTS

My thanks go, in particular, to Dennis Johnson, dedicated publisher and believer in writers.

To Julia Zafferano, wise and open-minded editor.

To everyone in the Kathy Robbins Office, and Kathy.

To agent Paul Bresnick, who gave me valuable guidance.

AND

To all Dylan fans, Bobolators, everywhere. I respect your passion.

Finally, it will likely mean little or nothing to him, but thanks to Bob for a lifetime of music that has enlightened my life.

ABOUT THE AUTHOR

RON ROSENBAUM is a longtime journalist and columnist who has written for the *Village Voice*, the *New York Observer*, the *New York Times Magazine*, *Esquire*, *Vanity Fair*, and *Slate*. He is the author of *The Shakespeare Wars* as well as the *New York Times* bestseller *Explaining Hitler*, which was also a *New York Times* Notable Book of the Year.